MORE
Results-Oriented
J O B
Descriptions

Roger J. Plachy • Sandra J. Plachy

MORE
RESULTS-ORIENTED
JOB
DESCRIPTIONS

226 Models to Use or Adapt—
With Guidelines for Creating Your Own

AMACOM

American Management Association
New York • Atlanta • Boston • Chicago • Kansas City • San Francisco • Washington, D.C.
Brussels • Mexico City • Tokyo • Toronto

*This book is available at a special
discount when ordered in bulk quantities.
For information, contact Special Sales Department,
AMACOM, a division of American Management Association,
1601 Broadway, New York, NY 10019.*

*This publication is designed to provide accurate and authoritative
information in regard to the subject matter covered. It is sold with
the understanding that the publisher is not engaged in rendering
legal, accounting, or other professional service. If legal advice or
other expert assistance is required, the services of a competent professional person should be sought.*

Library of Congress Cataloging-in-Publication Data

Plachy, Roger.
    More results-oriented job descriptions / Roger J. Plachy and
Sandra J. Plachy.
       p.   cm.
    Includes index.
    ISBN 0-8144-7961-8 (comb/pbk.)
    1. Job descriptions. I. Plachy Sandra J. II. Title.
HF5549.5.J613P578   1997
658.3'06—dc21   97-35903
                                        CIP

Printing number

10 9 8 7 6 5

Thanks to
Adele, Joe, John, and **Lila,**
and the Loyal Order of the Moose Teenage Club, Berwyn, Illinois

Contents

Alphabetical List of Job Descriptions, Including Software File Names

Job Descriptions by Occupation

Preface

Managers, employees, human resources professionals, resume writers, career counselors, and others continue to recognize the power of a results-oriented job description to focus attention on the important outcomes of work. Clearly, writers affirm to us, this writing style is more valuable than merely listing duties as is done in traditionally written job descriptions.

Quite simply, as our consulting experience demonstrates, communication between managers and employees is clearer, especially when objectively written job planning and appraisal criteria are based on expected job results instead of behavioral job activities.

Explaining why work is important—the result produced when duties are performed—is a critical factor in an organization's relationship with its employees. Why individual job results are important is directly linked to why the organization exists.

New thinking is revolutionizing organization structure and management. Thinking small and narrowly is out. New opportunities and relationships are being sought constantly. Bold strides are stretching people's minds.

The old-fashioned way of describing work expectations is not supporting the revolution. Managers say one thing—the results they want—while job-management documents demonstrate cramped thinking.

Let's face it, most people work in fairly straightforward jobs. Work comes in, it gets processed, it gets forwarded. However, swirling around employees' heads are consumer, quality, efficiency, value-added, shareholder, stakeholder, and team revolutions. Workers' eyes can no longer be focused down on processes but must be lifted up to new relationships.

Organizations will fully implement the revolution only when managers and employees think first about the results that need to be accomplished before thinking about the way that work is accomplished.

Organizations also continue to struggle with implementing accountability-oriented, pay-for-results programs because the documents that support pay judgments—job descriptions and appraisal criteria—are usually oriented toward behaving well or having the required competencies instead of toward accomplishing job results. A results-oriented job description sets the right tone from the beginning and leads to drastically different appraisal criteria.

Author's Note

In 1993, AMACOM published *Results-Oriented JOB Descriptions* with 225 job descriptions. This volume contains 226 additional job descriptions and can be used on its own or with the earlier book. Two combined listings—alphabetical and by occupation—of all 451 job descriptions appear as an Appendix in this volume.

Introduction
The Why and How of This Book

Writing job descriptions is not a lot of fun for most people, for whom writing can be tedious and time-consuming. This compendium solves this problem by offering models that anyone can simply edit and begin using.

The Results-Oriented Format

There are several compendiums of job descriptions on the market, but only this and its companion volume, *Results-Oriented JOB Descriptions,* presents job descriptions in a results-oriented format.

The results-oriented format makes clear *why* work is important. In addition to stating job duties, as most job descriptions do, a results-oriented job description also explains the purpose of the work, what is accomplished by performing the duty.

Focusing work on results changes the emphasis and enhances the usefulness of job descriptions. In recent years, so-called management gurus have denounced job descriptions because they restrict employee attention. These gurus suggest eliminating job descriptions altogether. When job descriptions are written as a laundry list of little things people are required to do, they are not worthwhile. However, we recommend that you improve your job descriptions instead of eliminating them.

We believe in job descriptions. How else can you communicate your organization's purpose and what must be accomplished by each person for the organization to succeed? At the same time, do job descriptions have to be restrictive? Of course not. Flexibility and resourcefulness are issues of style, not elements of a job description. People who advocate the elimination of job descriptions have forgotten what it means to manage, have misunderstood solid communication techniques, or have never seen a results-oriented job description.

Who Should Use This Book?

This book is for all who need to communicate job expectations. They include:

- *Human resources professionals* who analyze, describe, and evaluate jobs; hire and test job candidates; guide reorganizations; negotiate with unions; monitor disciplinary actions and resolve grievances; develop succession plans and career paths; or design pay structures.
- *Supervisors and managers* who define and organize work; orient and train employees; plan, monitor, and appraise employee job results; or encourage employee growth and development.
- *Executives* who chart the course of their organization and want people to focus their efforts on common purposes.

How to Use This Book

The job descriptions included in this compendium represent a cross-section of industries and occupations. They were selected to include those titles most frequently used. Many of these descriptions will probably meet your needs with few alterations. Still, you will undoubtedly need to edit most of the job descriptions to state your organization's specific job requirements.

Chapter 1 explains the concept of the results-oriented job description and illustrates the new focus and structure.

Chapter 2 demonstrates how to edit the models offered in this compendium so you can start using them quickly.

Chapter 3 gives you standard results-oriented statements to help you assemble new job descriptions or adapt our models.

Chapter 4 teaches you how to write results-oriented job description statements and includes writing tips and sample forms.

Chapter 5 provides legal guidelines pertinent to the use of job descriptions, including discussions of the Americans with Disabilities Act, the Fair Labor Standards Act, the Equal Pay Act, Title VII of the Civil Rights Act of 1964, and the Occupational Safety and Health Act.

If you have already read *Results-Oriented JOB Descriptions,* you can read Part I as a review or skip directly to the job descriptions in Part II.

This book comes with a disk containing a word processing file for every job description in this book. Instructions for using the disk can be found at the back of the book. The alphabetical listing of job descriptions in the Appendix also identifies the file name for each job description.

Here's a tip: Create files with complete job descriptions or lists of job results that best suit your needs. The files on the diskette will certainly save you keying time. A copy here and a paste there and you're on your way.

The Many Uses of Job Descriptions

A job description is the basic understanding or "contract" between an employer and an employee. It discusses what needs to be accomplished to fulfill the organization's purpose and describes the employee's commitment.

Job descriptions are an essential element in managing the work of the organization. They are used to:

- Define or revise the organization structure.
- Plan human resources requirements.
- Advertise jobs and recruit candidates.
- Evaluate relative job value.
- Determine exempt/nonexempt status.
- Establish career progressions.
- Analyze work flow and methods.
- Downsize.
- Adjust work requirements to meet medical and family leave requirements.
- Meet diversity goals.
- Post jobs.
- Interview and select job candidates.
- Orient new employees.
- Identify training requirements.
- Conduct pay surveys.
- Prepare affirmative action plans.
- Comply with employment laws.
- Establish a base for incentive plans.
- Bargain with unions.

The Need for a New Philosophy of Job Descriptions

Job descriptions have been around for a long time. For most of that time, much of what we understood about how people worked concerned desirable traits and behaviors. What people did was put under a microscope.

Not until the middle of the century did managers look up and realize that they were missing the point. What people did made sense only in relation to what they were or were not accomplishing. The philosophy of management-by-objectives taught managers to focus first on the target and then on how they might reach the target.

A results-oriented job description starts the manager-employee relationship off on the right foot. It directs managers and employees to look together at what outcomes are necessary. The first step in this process is to make sure both understand where they are going.

A results-oriented job description is what good management and good communication are all about.

Part I
A New Philosophy of Job Descriptions

1

Why Use Results-Oriented Job Descriptions?

Results and duties are both stated.

A results-oriented job description states two components of work: the result that must be accomplished and the duties that must be performed in order to accomplish the result.

For example: **HELPS CUSTOMERS**
by
answering the telephone.

Effective managers tell their employees not only what they want them to do—in this case, answer the telephone—but what they want them to accomplish—in this case, help customers.

Employees are taught why work is important.

In clarifying results, managers explain *why* work is important, that is, where a particular task, activity, or behavior fits into the overall scheme of a department function and, thus, where the job fits in as the organization moves toward accomplishing its mission and objectives. A results-oriented job description makes the purpose of work clear and keeps the employee focused on what is truly important about job performance.

Not just duties are stated.

Traditional job descriptions state duties, such as "answers the telephone." Yes, it's logical to assume that an employee would know that the reason for answering the telephone is to help customers. However, it is better management to make this expectation very clear. Surely you have been on the receiving end of telephone answerers who have not helped you—who did not understand *why* their jobs existed.

"Here's what I want you to *do*" may typify the way managers have traditionally talked to employees. Telling employees only what to do on a job is not enough anymore. Actually, it never was.

Accomplishing is emphasized over doing.

If they adhere to a job description written in the traditional duties-oriented style, employees can be "doing" the job without understanding the *why* of the job and without accomplishing important results. An employee who answers the telephone is "doing" the job if that is all the job description requires. Psychologically, a supervisor can be caught in a defensive word game by an employee who has not been told explicitly that the job requirement is to help customers. When the supervisor hands a job description to an employee, the employee can rightly expect that what is printed is what is required.

The focus is on results.

With a results-oriented job description, the focus of managing work switches from doing the work to the results accomplished. Results are easier to manage than duties because results are either accomplished or not accomplished, whereas duties, because they are the process of work, go on interminably.

Focusing on duties easily misses the *why* of work. The supervisor who also wants the employee to answer the fax machine may hear the customary "It's not in my job description," while the customer waits on the line trying to place an order. Focused on helping customers, employees can easily learn to understand the different aspects of the job that add up to the desired outcome.

Focusing on results is a different way of thinking about work. Results describe the strategy of work, whereas duties emphasize the tactics of work. The strategy of the job takes into account where the job fits into the overall scheme of the organization and how the job contributes to the organization's mission. Most of the time, managers and employees merely focus on the work right in front of them, because the language of the job description points them in that narrow direction. Emphasizing results elevates their thinking so they understand why the organization exists and why the organization needs their contribution.

Results and duties are contrasted.

To illustrate the difference between results and duties, consider this sample job description, written in two ways, for a Patient Receptionist in a dental clinic. In the right column are the duties, augmented by the results that must be accomplished when the duties are performed. The traditional duties-oriented style is in the left column.

Duties-Oriented	*Results-Oriented*
1. Greets and refers patients and visitors.	1. **PROVIDES INFORMATION** by greeting and referring patients and visitors.
2. Notifies dentist of patient's arrival, reviews adherence to schedule, and reminds provider of delays.	2. **KEEPS PATIENT APPOINTMENTS ON SCHEDULE** by notifying provider of patient's arrival, reviewing adherence to schedule, and reminding provider of delays.

Duties-Oriented	Results-Oriented
3. Anticipates patient anxieties, answers questions, and maintains orderly reception area.	3. **COMFORTS PATIENTS** by anticipating anxieties, answering questions, and maintaining an orderly reception area.
4. Schedules appointments in person or by telephone.	4. **OPTIMIZES PATIENTS' SATISFACTION, PROVIDER TIME, AND TREATMENT ROOM UTILIZATION** by scheduling appointments in person or by telephone.
5. Enters and retrieves patient scheduling data on a computer terminal while maintaining confidentiality.	5. **COMPLETES AND UPDATES PATIENT SCHEDULING FILE** by entering and retrieving data on a computer terminal while maintaining confidentiality.

Most people find that the addition of results clarifies the purpose of the duties, that the duties become more meaningful, that the employee has a much better understanding of why the work is important, and that knowing the results intended actually allows an employee to discover new ways to accomplish results, as long as the results are still accomplished.

Results are not buried.

When you pick up an average job description, you generally find only a list of duties. Your job, you are told, is to "interview candidates." On an occasional job description, you may find a few results buried in the verbiage: "Interviews candidates in order to determine their qualifications." This result—to determine qualifications—is easy to miss.

Describing jobs with a focus on results is not just a method of expression. Spelling out the result of work is important in helping an employee understand the work itself. Unlike writing mystery novels, in which building up to the climax is the whole point, the goal of educating and instructing employees is to start with the answer: "This is where you need to arrive. Now, this is how you get there."

DETERMINES CANDIDATES' QUALIFICATIONS
by
conducting interviews.

Without a focal point for concentration, the employee's mind searches for meaning among the duties and instructions.

The writing style is clear.

The job descriptions in this compendium follow a formula so that each expectation is clearly stated both in terms of the result that must be accomplished and the duty(ies) that must be performed. Both are necessary to understand the expectation.

The formula is: **THE RESULT TO BE ACCOMPLISHED**
by
the duty(ies) to be performed.

Descriptions are easier to read and simpler to understand.

Graphically, the result to be accomplished is printed in capital boldface letters in order to bring obvious emphasis to the statement. Right away the employee knows that something is different here.

Written in this style, job descriptions are easier to read and simpler to understand. The writing style is clear and concise. Most job descriptions are just too wordy, and their meaning is obscured.

Employees quickly see the connection between the work that they will do and the results they will have to accomplish; together, the result to be accomplished and the duty(ies) to be performed make sense. Such a job description offers supervisors two ways to discuss job expectations—what is being accomplished and what is being done.

The presentation formula is strictly followed.

The result to be accomplished and the duty(ies) to be performed are separated by the word "by" and are printed on three separate lines.

HELPS CUSTOMERS
by
answering the telephone.

The expectation could be printed "**HELPS CUSTOMERS** by answering the telephone" to save space, but using three lines brings dramatic attention to each portion of the requirement.

There are nearly as many styles of writing job descriptions as there are job description writers. Some writers merely write one long paragraph. Some writers offer an exhaustive list of items in an attempt to be thorough. Some writers say nearly the same thing over and over trying to make their point clear. Some writers use different categories that seem to say the same thing—expectations, accountabilities, and responsibilities. The formula used in this compendium is simple and straightforward. In this way, supervisors and employees get used to the regular, predictable presentation.

The result and duty are read together.

The result to be accomplished and the duty to be performed must be read as one statement to distinguish between jobs. Some jobs may have the same result but different duties. For example:

SERVES CLIENTS
by
analyzing programming needs.

and

SERVES CLIENTS
by
writing programs.

The highlighted focus gives supervisors help in demonstrating common objectives.

Results make the uses of job descriptions more relevant.

Results-oriented job descriptions serve the traditional uses of job descriptions better than ancestral models. Job descriptions are often used to:

- Recruit candidates.
- Interview candidates.
- Test candidates.
- Orient employees.
- Train employees.
- Plan job results.
- Monitor job results.
- Appraise job results.
- Coach employees.
- Discipline employees.

Because results-oriented job descriptions answer the question, "why is this job important?", management and employee actions become more relevant. Recruiting candidates focuses on job outcomes needed and legitimate requirements, instead of personal characteristics. Interviewing candidates focuses on ability to reason, instead of skill to perform specific tasks. Testing candidates focuses on applicability of skills, instead of skills aptitude. Orienting employees focuses on the reasons that the job exists, instead of things to do and places to go. Training employees focuses on use of learning, instead of classroom performance. Planning, monitoring, and appraising job results focuses on work outcomes, instead of personal attitudes and behaviors. Coaching and disciplining employees focuses on improved outcomes, instead of personal weaknesses or punishment.

Results make job descriptions useful.

Anyone who has seen the often inferior and generally uneven quality that is typical of job descriptions will not be surprised at their poor reputation. Writing and using job descriptions often occurs only when the personnel department requires them.

The job description gives life to the employment relationship between the employer and the employee, just as the charter gives life to the corporation. The job description deserves a quality of writing equal to its role, which is to guide supervisors and employees as they accomplish the work of the organization.

Furthermore, job descriptions must be changed when job requirements change. One reason the lowly job description never achieved much status in the past was that keeping it current meant having it completely retyped whenever requirements changed. Word processing and the attendant ease of editing may be the technological development that allows the job description to be elevated to its proper role.

2
Editing Job Descriptions in This Compendium

Although you may find many of the job descriptions in this book ready to use, chances are you will need to adapt others to fit your organization's particular needs. Here's how to edit a job description to conform to your specifications.

Study the job you need to describe.

Start with an understanding of the responsibilities of the job you are describing. You will need to conduct some form of job analysis to understand these responsibilities, perhaps by interviewing the employee on the job and the supervisor or by asking them to complete a questionnaire. You may also observe the job yourself.

Find the job description you need.

Find the job in the compendium that matches, or most closely matches, the responsibilities of the job you want to describe. Look through related job titles to see whether statements in other jobs might be helpful even though the job titles may appear to describe somewhat different requirements.

Revise the job statement.

To revise the job statement to fit your needs, follow these steps:

1. Eliminate results and duties that do not apply.
2. Add, delete, or substitute words in the results and duties statements to meet your exact requirements.
   a. The precise wording of the result may vary from one organization to another as each organization spells out its special values. Defining the result is a useful tactic for managers and employees to help them develop a common understanding of expectations.
   b. Specific duties will vary according to the size and structure—and thus, the work assignments—of each organization.

3. Add results and duties that need to be included.
   a. Edit standard results and duties statements in Chapter 3.
   b. Write new statements according to the guidelines in Chapter 4.

Revision Example 1

For example, suppose that you are writing the job description of a Client Service Coordinator. The closest job description is Client Service Manager.

For purposes of illustrating the changes made to the Client Service Manager job description, words to be deleted are shown shaded, and words that are to be added are shown in *italics*.

JOB TITLE: CLIENT SERVICE MANAGER *COORDINATOR*

JOB PURPOSE: SERVES CUSTOMERS
by
guiding *supporting* clients to accomplish profit goals.

ESSENTIAL JOB RESULTS:

% of
time

_____ • **IMPLEMENTS CLIENT-SPECIFIC BUSINESS PLANS**
by
establishing and developing *coordinating* plans with sales representatives; managing strategic and *coordinating* action plans with internal resources; analyzing *summarizing* profit and loss statements for trends; coordinating production, sales, and related business activities.

_____ • **PROVIDES CLIENT SERVICES**
by
researching and documenting issues and problems; forwarding necessary actions; leading client service team; providing response to client; guiding *arranging* internal resources; measuring and ensuring *tracking* results.

% of
time

_____ • **SUPPORTS MARKETING OBJECTIVES**
by
developing standard *assembling requirements for* marketing and installation plans for use in sales call packages; obtaining approvals from *coordinating requirements with* functional areas; adhering to time lines.

_____ • FINALIZES *ARRANGES* **CONTRACT APPROVAL**
by
preparing *assembling* business deal recapitulations; drafting *keying* contracts; obtaining approvals; verifying understandings among parties; monitoring status and quality.

% of
time

____ • **RESOLVES AND PREVENTS
CONTRACT PROBLEMS**
by
researching and documenting issues and
problems; forwarding necessary actions;
leading client service team; providing
response to client.

____ • **MAINTAINS CLIENT DATA INTEGRITY**
by
determining marketing and installation
plans; reconciling pricing sheet expenses
to services outlined in contract;
controlling quality of data from sales
through contracting setup process;
communicating data to and obtaining
support and approvals from functional
areas.

% of
time

____ • **MAINTAINS PROFESSIONAL AND
TECHNICAL KNOWLEDGE**
by
attending educational workshops;
reviewing professional publications;
establishing personal networks;
benchmarking state-of-the-art practices;
participating in professional societies.

____ • **CONTRIBUTES TO TEAM EFFORT**
by
accomplishing related results as needed.

Revision Example 2

Suppose your organization has a Diversity Consultant and wants to add a Diversity Trainer. You
can use both the Diversity Consultant and Performance Technologist job descriptions to write the
new description.

JOB TITLE: DIVERSITY CONSULTANT *TRAINER*

JOB PURPOSE: MAXIMIZES HUMAN RESOURCES DIVERSITY
by
supervising staff; identifying diversity issues; providing training and guidance;
measuring program impact.

ESSENTIAL JOB RESULTS:

% of
time

(from the Diversity Consultant description)

_____ • MAINTAINS DIVERSITY STAFF by
recruiting, selecting, orienting, and training employees; maintaining a safe, secure, and legal work environment; developing personal growth opportunities.

_____ • ACCOMPLISHES STAFF RESULTS by
communicating job expectations; planning, monitoring, and appraising job results; coaching, counseling, and disciplining employees; developing, coordinating, and enforcing systems, policies, procedures, and productivity standards.

_____ • EXPLORES DIVERSITY ISSUES by
reviewing publications; benchmarking state-of-the-art thinking; forming focus groups; conducting surveys; requesting internal and external input from those in a position to contribute; measuring diversity tension.

_____ • RECOMMENDS DIVERSITY STRATEGIC GOALS by
gathering pertinent business, financial, service, and operations information; identifying and evaluating trends and options; choosing a course of action; defining objectives; evaluating outcomes; conducting cost/benefit analyses.

_____ • DEVELOPS DIVERSITY AWARENESS TRAINING by
preparing content, training media, and intervention techniques.

(from the Performance Technologist description)

% of
time

_____ • IMPROVES PERFORMANCE by
providing or conducting training.

_____ • PROMOTES *DIVERSITY* GROWTH AND DEVELOPMENT by
offering educational opportunities; encouraging participation in educational opportunities; reviewing and recommending development policies and practices.

_____ • EVALUATES *DIVERSITY* TRAINING AND DEVELOPMENT EFFECTIVENESS by
studying organization performance data, individual performance appraisals, disciplinary and counseling actions, job postings, promotions, and hiring requests; interviewing managers and employees.

(from the Diversity Consultant description)

_____ • BALANCES DIVERSITY AND WORKFORCE QUALIFICATION GOALS by
studying essential work requirements; identifying potential opportunities to provide supplemental training to diverse candidates who nearly meet those requirements; identifying possible facilities and equipment modifications.

_____ • MAINTAINS INTEGRATED TEAMS by
developing communication, problem solving, and appreciation of differences programs; evaluating attitudinal, behavioral, and work-result outcomes.

% of
time

_____ • **AVOIDS EMPLOYMENT DISCRIMINATION LITIGATION** by
identifying units within the organization where minorities or women are significantly underrepresented as compared to the availability of qualified candidates; determining whether there is a reasonable explanation; exploring whether active or passive discrimination occurs.

_____ • **PROVIDES TOOLS FOR MANAGING DIVERSITY** by
gathering information on the availability and hiring levels of minorities and women by organization unit or department; identifying working relationships on recruitment and promotion.

_____ • **ATTRACTS A WIDENING CUSTOMER BASE** by
retaining a diverse workforce mirroring the diversity of potential domestic and foreign markets; conducting business recognizing the diversity of the market.

% of
time

_____ • **MAINTAINS QUALITY SERVICE** by
enforcing quality, diversity, and customer service standards; analyzing and resolving quality, diversity, and customer service problems; identifying trends; recommending system improvements.

_____ • **MAINTAINS PROFESSIONAL AND TECHNICAL KNOWLEDGE** by
attending educational workshops; establishing personal networks; participating in professional societies; creating *coordinating* mentoring programs for minority employees.

_____ • **CONTRIBUTES TO TEAM EFFORT** by
accomplishing related results as needed.

3
Standard Job Results and Duties

Many jobs are more similar than they at first appear. Thus, many job results and duties statements can be standardized and then easily used or adapted in cases where you need to write your own job descriptions. Standard job results and duties are included here to help you in this task. For guidance on writing unique job descriptions, refer to Chapter 4.

When you begin to write a job description, search through the following standard statements to find those that describe or nearly describe your situation. Edit them to fit your organizational requirements.

Standard Statements

The standard results and duties are organized into the following categories:

- Confidentiality and legal requirements
- Education
- Equipment and supplies
- Information
- Management
- Operations
- Problem solving
- Quality
- Safety
- Service
- Standards and procedures
- Universal

Confidentiality and Legal Requirements

These statements cover safeguarding customer, product, and operational information while complying with legal requirements.

MAINTAINS CUSTOMER CONFIDENCE AND PROTECTS OPERATIONS
by
keeping information confidential.

MAINTAINS ORGANIZATION'S STABILITY AND REPUTATION
by
complying with legal requirements.

MAINTAINS PRODUCT AND COMPANY REPUTATION
by
complying with federal and state regulations.

COMPLIES WITH FEDERAL, STATE, AND LOCAL LEGAL REQUIREMENTS
by
studying existing and new legislation; anticipating legislation; enforcing adherence to requirements; advising management on needed actions.

Education

These statements concern updating professional and technical knowledge and providing information and learning opportunities to others. In view of the emphasis on learning in many organizations, we now routinely include a result in each job description that reminds the employee of the importance of growth and development.

DEVELOPS STAFF
by
providing information, educational opportunities, and experiential growth opportunities.

MAINTAINS PROFESSIONAL AND TECHNICAL KNOWLEDGE
by
attending educational workshops; reviewing professional publications; establishing personal networks; benchmarking state-of-the-art practices; participating in professional societies.

MAINTAINS TECHNICAL KNOWLEDGE
by
attending educational workshops; reading technical publications.

Equipment and Supplies

Here are statements for completing maintenance and operational requirements, maintaining supplies inventories, and conserving resources.

ENSURES OPERATION OF EQUIPMENT
by
completing preventive maintenance requirements; following manufacturer's instructions; troubleshooting malfunctions; calling for repairs; maintaining equipment inventories; evaluating new equipment and techniques.

KEEPS EQUIPMENT OPERATIONAL
by
following manufacturer's instructions and established procedures.

MAINTAINS SUPPLIES INVENTORY
by
checking stock; anticipating needs; placing and expediting orders; verifying receipt.

CONSERVES RESOURCES
by
using equipment and supplies as needed to accomplish job results.

Information

These statements are for obtaining, providing, maintaining, and securing information and for preparing reports.

MAINTAINS DATABASE
by
entering, verifying, and backing up data.

MAINTAINS DATABASE
by
writing computer programs; entering and backing up data.

MAINTAINS DATABASE
by
developing information requirements; designing an information system.

SECURES INFORMATION
by
completing database backups.

MAINTAINS HISTORICAL RECORDS
by
filing and retrieving documents.

PROVIDES INFORMATION
by
answering questions and requests.

PREPARES REPORTS
by
collecting, analyzing, and summarizing information and trends.

COMPLETES REPORTS
by
entering required information.

REPRESENTS THE ORGANIZATION
by
preparing a strategy; collecting data; presenting information at hearings.

Management

These statements deal with hiring, scheduling, training, and counseling employees and achieving financial objectives.

COMPLETES WORK
by
scheduling and assigning employees; following up on work results; conducting training.

MAINTAINS (DEPARTMENT) STAFF
by
recruiting, selecting, orienting, and training employees; maintaining a safe, secure, and legal work environment; developing personal growth opportunities.

ACCOMPLISHES (DEPARTMENT) STAFF RESULTS
by
communicating job expectations; planning, monitoring, and appraising job results; coaching, counseling, and disciplining employees; initiating, coordinating, and enforcing systems, policies, and procedures.

ESTABLISHES (DEPARTMENT) STRATEGIC GOALS
by
gathering pertinent business, financial, service, and operations information; identifying and evaluating trends and options; choosing a course of action; defining objectives; evaluating outcomes.

ACHIEVES FINANCIAL OBJECTIVES
by
forecasting requirements; preparing an annual budget; scheduling expenditures; analyzing variances; initiating corrective actions.

CONTROLS EXPENSES
by
gathering and submitting information; scheduling expenditures; monitoring variances; implementing corrective actions.

Operations

The following statements are for identifying, scheduling, maintaining, and coordinating work flow.

PREPARES WORK TO BE ACCOMPLISHED
by
gathering and sorting documents.

COMPLETES OPERATIONS
by
developing schedules; assigning and monitoring work; gathering resources; implementing productivity standards; resolving operations problems; maintaining reference manuals; implementing new procedures.

MAINTAINS WORK FLOW
by
sorting and delivering information.

CONTRIBUTES TO PROGRAM EFFECTIVENESS
by
identifying short-term and long-range issues that must be addressed; providing information and commentary pertinent to deliberations; recommending options and courses of action; implementing directives.

MAINTAINS INTER- AND INTRADEPARTMENTAL WORK FLOW
by
fostering a spirit of cooperation.

MAINTAINS CONTINUITY AMONG CORPORATE, AREA, AND LOCAL WORK TEAMS
by
documenting and communicating actions, irregularities, and continuing needs.

COMPLETES PROJECTS
by
training and guiding technicians.

Problem Solving

These statements concern collecting and analyzing information, evaluating optional courses of action, and resolving problems.

RESOLVES DISCREPANCIES
by
collecting and analyzing information.

ACHIEVES WORK OBJECTIVES
by
gathering pertinent data; identifying and evaluating options; choosing a course of action.

RESOLVES ASSEMBLY PROBLEMS
by
altering dimensions to meet specifications; notifying supervisor to obtain additional resources.

Quality

MAINTAINS QUALITY SERVICE/PRODUCT
by
establishing, following, and enforcing organization standards.

If your organization places a strong emphasis on quality service, you may want to routinely include a statement like the above in each of your job descriptions.

Safety

These statements concern complying with and promoting safety requirements and protecting others.

> **MAINTAINS SAFE AND HEALTHY WORK ENVIRONMENT**
> by
> establishing, following, and enforcing organization standards; adhering to legal requirements.

> **MAINTAINS SAFE AND HEALTHY WORK ENVIRONMENT**
> by
> following organization standards and legal regulations.

If your organization is under strong scrutiny for safe and healthy operations, or simply wishes safety and health to be constant concerns, you may want to routinely include a statement like the above in each of your job descriptions. As an alternative for managers, you could include "maintaining a safe and healthy work environment" as a duty under "Maintains Staff."

> **PROTECTS PATIENTS AND EMPLOYEES**
> by
> adhering to infection-control policies and protocols.

> **PROMOTES HEALTHY WORK ENVIRONMENT**
> by
> coordinating and cooperating with federal, state, and local agencies.

Service

These statements cover identifying service requirements and documenting actions.

> **IDENTIFIES PATIENT SERVICE REQUIREMENTS**
> by
> establishing personal rapport with potential and actual patients and with other persons in a position to understand service requirements.

> **IDENTIFIES CONCERNS**
> by
> surveying conditions and recommending actions.

> **DOCUMENTS PATIENT CARE SERVICES**
> by
> completing charting in patient and department records.

> **IDENTIFIES CURRENT AND FUTURE CUSTOMER SERVICE REQUIREMENTS**
> by
> establishing personal rapport with potential and actual customers and with other persons in a position to understand service requirements.

DOCUMENTS ACTIONS
by
completing production and quality logs.

Standards and Procedures

These statements cover writing, updating, and following procedures, as well as verifying output.

MAINTAINS OPERATIONS
by
following policies and procedures; reporting needed changes.

MAINTAINS GUIDELINES
by
writing and updating policies and procedures.

PRODUCES PRODUCT/SERVICE
by
establishing standards and procedures; measuring results against standards; making necessary adjustments.

MAINTAINS OPERATIONS
by
initiating, coordinating, and enforcing program, operational, and personnel policies and procedures.

VERIFIES SETTINGS
by
measuring positions, first-run parts, and sample workpieces.

MAINTAINS PRODUCTION AND QUALITY
by
observing machine operation; detecting malfunctions; adjusting settings.

Universal

This statement is for a position that requires flexibility in accepting job assignments.

CONTRIBUTES TO TEAM EFFORT
by
welcoming new and different work requirements; exploring new opportunities to add value to the organization; helping others accomplish related job results as and where needed.

BUILDS AND STRENGTHENS CORPORATE/DEPARTMENT REPUTATION
by
taking ownership for completing new and different requests; exploring new opportunities to add value to job accomplishments; enhancing job knowledge; fulfilling corporate customer

service mission; protecting corporate assets; keeping information confidential; complying with legal requirements and corporate policy; accomplishing related results as needed.

These standard statements replace the traditional "Performs related duties as may be needed," in order to explain why extra demands may be made from time to time.

Another possible *why* is "Completes department projects." Sometimes teamwork and individual contributions to the group effort are not the *why* of work. Thus, the result for a Meeting Planner might be changed to "Maintains client satisfaction."

The purpose of the universal statement is to communicate to employees that job descriptions are not designed to identify each and every expectation that may be required of an incumbent. This statement makes it clear that there may be times when some result or duty may be required that cannot be anticipated. When those times occur, results or duties will be temporarily added to the job description so that the organization's purposes can be accomplished. Said another way, this is the organization's flexibility statement.

Edited Examples

Here are some examples of how the standard results and duties statements can be edited. Deletions are shown shaded, and additions are shown in *italics*.

PREPARES *ACCOUNTING* REPORTS
by
collecting, analyzing, and summarizing information and trends.

MAINTAINS CUSTOMER ***PATIENT* CONFIDENCE AND PROTECTS *HOSPITAL* OPERATIONS**
by
keeping information confidential.

MAINTAINS ORGANIZATION'S STABILITY AND ***SERVICE* REPUTATION**
by
complying with legal *government* requirements.

DOCUMENTS ACTIONS ***FINANCIAL TRANSACTIONS***
by
completing production and quality logs *entering account information.*

RESOLVES *RECONCILES FINANCIAL* DISCREPANCIES
by
collecting and analyzing *account* information.

PROVIDES *ENGINEERING* INFORMATION
by
answering questions and requests.

MAINTAINS *CONSUMER LOAN OPERATIONS* STAFF
by
recruiting, selecting, orienting, and training employees; maintaining a safe, secure, and legal work environment; developing personal growth opportunities.

4
Writing Results-Oriented Job Descriptions

In many cases you will be able to either use the job descriptions in this compendium just as they are or edit them here and there to match your unique requirements. In some cases, you will need to write new results and duties. Here is the architecture of the statement for you to follow.

The result to be accomplished is stated first, for example:

MAINTAINS COMPANY TELEPHONE DIRECTORY
[Start with an action verb, then write the object of the action.]

Job results are succinct statements, generally two or three words (occasionally four or five words). More words than that and you should review what you are trying to express to ensure clarity.

Then write the connector word:

by

Then write the duty performed in order to accomplish the result (it's possible to have several duties for one result):

updating files with additions, deletions, and changes.
[What the employee is do"ing"—the verb in the second part of the sentence always ends in "ing."]

Distinguishing Between Results and Duties

To distinguish between a result and a duty, try placing the job element both before and after the "by." Then complete the sentence to see which order makes more sense. Remember, a result answers the question, *Why* are we doing this? A duty, on the other hand, answers the question, *What* must be done to produce the result?

Here's an example.

(as a result)   =   **UPDATES FILES WITH ADDITIONS, DELETIONS, AND CHANGES**
                    by . . .
(as a duty)   =   by
                    updating files with additions, deletions, and changes.

When you complete the statement as:

UPDATES FILES WITH ADDITIONS, DELETIONS, AND CHANGES
by
entering data noted on personnel status change forms; retrieving the employee's data file; deleting information as noted in file; entering new data.

the duties turn out to be job procedures that belong in an operations manual. Procedures are more specific than necessary for a job description.
     When you complete the statement as:

MAINTAINS COMPANY TELEPHONE DIRECTORY
by
updating files with additions, deletions, and changes.

the result describes what's really important about the job. The telephone directory is the outcome produced by updating files, the product of the work. Updating files is *how* the directory is maintained.

Are Results Always Results and Duties Always Duties?

One job's duty can be another job's result. Therefore, whether a statement is a result or a duty depends on the job.

For a Materials Manager

SUPPORTS OPERATIONS
by
maintaining an inventory.

For a Purchasing Assistant

MAINTAINS INVENTORY
by
purchasing supplies.

For a Purchasing Clerk

PURCHASES SUPPLIES
by
preparing requisitions.

Studying the jobs in the organizational or career-path hierarchy above and below the job you are writing will help you understand the results and duties.

Recognizing Results and Duties

Here are two statements. Which is the result, and which is the duty?

1. *Inspects work.*
2. *Meets quality standards.*

Remember, a result answers the question, *Why* are we doing this? A duty answers the question, *What* must be done to produce the result?

The result is: **MEETS QUALITY STANDARDS**
               by
The duty is: inspecting work.

Here are some more statements for you to compare. Which is the result? Which is the duty? Remember, the duty verb becomes an "ing" word, so try the verbs with "ing" endings to understand which is the result and which is the duty.

Directs operations
by
Provides services.

Maintains staff job results
by
Conducts planning and appraisal conferences.

Serves customers
by
Delivers packages.

Maintains staff of employees
by
Recruits, screens, and tests candidates.

Here are the answers:

PROVIDES SERVICES = result
by
directing operations = duty

MAINTAINS STAFF JOB RESULTS = result
by
conducting planning and appraisal conferences = duty

SERVES CUSTOMERS = result
by
delivering packages = duty

MAINTAINS STAFF OF EMPLOYEES = result
by
recruiting, screening, and testing candidates = duties

Some Examples of Duties and Related Results

This is the duty	*This is the result*
Orienting new employees	Prepares employees for assignments
Typing	Prepares reports
Analyzing data	Recommends action
Counseling employees	Improves job results
Inspecting equipment	Completes preventive maintenance
Participating in meetings	Contributes information and opinions
Assessing a situation	Identifies problem
Supervising employees	Accomplishes job results
Verifying work	Completes assignments
Expediting work	Ensures delivery
Processing orders	Fills customer requests
Making appointments	Organizes time
Recording time	Documents actions
Evaluating action	Determines effect
Delivering supplies	Maintains schedule
Interviewing candidates	Determines eligibility

Identifying Results

One way to identify results is by listing the duties of a job. For example, Column A lists typical duties of a Secretary. Then, ask yourself what result (see Column B) each duty accomplishes.

Column A	*Column B*
Answering letters	Serves customers
Using electronic calendaring	Maintains appointment schedule
Filing	Provides historical reference
Formatting text	Provides info-management support
Inputting text	Provides info-management support
Editing text	Provides info-management support
Drafting letters and documents	Conserves manager's time
Formatting graphics	Provides info-management support
Planning and scheduling meetings	Maintains appointment schedule
Answering inquiries	Serves customers
Ordering and receiving supplies	Maintains office inventory
Developing/maintaining filing system	Provides historical reference
Establishing teleconferences	Maintains appointment schedule

Next, group the duties that produce the same result, and arrange the statements according to the "result-by-duty" formula.

PROVIDES INFO-MANAGEMENT SUPPORT
by
formatting text; inputting text; editing text; formatting graphics.

SERVES CUSTOMERS
by
answering letters and inquiries.

MAINTAINS APPOINTMENT SCHEDULE
by
using electronic calendaring; planning and scheduling meetings; establishing teleconferences.

CONSERVES MANAGER'S TIME
by
drafting letters and documents.

PROVIDES HISTORICAL REFERENCE
by
developing/maintaining filing system.

MAINTAINS OFFICE INVENTORY
by
ordering and receiving supplies.

Ensuring That the Result Is Correctly Identified

Identifying the result is the toughest part of writing a job description. Duties are more easily recognized than results because that is the way managers and workers have been taught to think about work. Understanding why a duty must be performed is not always so clear. Here's a tip: Generally speaking, what you can see people doing is the duty.

Remember the story about the three bricklayers?

The first said the job was:	laying brick
The second said the job was:	raising a wall
The third said the job was:	building a cathedral

The first saw:	a job duty
The second saw:	a job result
The third saw:	a job purpose

To identify the result, ask yourself:

1. *What* is the outcome of this duty?
2. *Why* is this duty important?
3. *What* does this duty accomplish?

Keep asking these questions until you understand what is really important about the duty, but don't define a result that is beyond the scope of the duty. Building a cathedral is a worthwhile vision of the job, but not the immediate result of laying bricks. The bricklayer will be held account-able for the wall, not for the cathedral.

In the example of the Purchasing Clerk's job, saying that the result is "Supports operations" is too broad; certainly that is beyond the control of the clerk. The immediate outcome of preparing requisitions is "Purchases supplies."

Arranging Results and Duties

The results and duties statements are arranged in the job description to communicate expectations logically, in one of these three sequences:

1. Most important to least important
2. Most time spent to least time spent
3. In the order accomplished

Choosing the Correct Words for Job Results and Duties

Each word in a job description is important to help people understand and clarify job expectations. The correct verb differentiates responsibilities and authorities among jobs. Each of the following verbs defines a different level of job responsibility.

Prepares	purchasing contracts by . . .
Reviews	purchasing contracts by . . .
Audits	purchasing contracts by . . .
Interprets	purchasing contracts by . . .
Enforces	purchasing contracts by . . .

Here is a quick reference to help you select the verb that most accurately describes the job requirements and authority.

Controls	obtains	calculates	manages	carries
adopts	orders	compiles	oversees	clears
anticipates	pays	computes	represents	collates
approves	releases	extends	schedules	disassembles
closes	remits	figures	supervises	enters
collects	requires	inventories		feeds
consolidates	routes	invoices	*Distributes*	handles
contracts	secures	reconciles	circulates	opens
deletes	selects	totals	disseminates	processes
disburses	signs		furnishes	stacks
ensures	traces	*Directs*	issues	types
expedites		administers	renders	
finds		assigns		

follows up
locates
maintains
defines
designs
develops
establishes
executes
formulates
implements
initiates
institutes
organizes
plans
prepares

Records

attaches
catalogues

Counts

adds
balances
bills
charts
classifies
codes
copies
enters
files
indexes
itemizes
lays out
lists
places
posts
receives
registers
tabulates
transfers

authorizes
delegates
determines

Studies

analyzes
appraises
ascertains
audits
estimates
evaluates
examines
inspects
investigates
observes
rates
reviews
scans
screens
searches

Operates

aligns
assembles
surveys
tests

Teaches

guides
instructs
interprets
trains

Verifies

affirms
amends
checks
compares
corrects

Originates

arranges
conducts
creates
edits
proofreads
revises

Writes

composes
describes
drafts
outlines
summarizes

Should Job Standards Be Included in the Results and Duties Statements?

It is not necessary to use evaluative terms in results and duties statements. Do not add words that attempt to define how well the result is to be accomplished or how well the duty is to be performed, as in these examples:

Completes studies *efficiently and competently.*

Designs systems *effectively and appropriately.*

Makes recommendations *that are novel.*

Completes reports *promptly and properly.*

Greets customers *in a courteous manner.*

Qualifying words not only lengthen the statement but blur its meaning. Vague words only make the mind stop and spin as it wonders how to interpret words such as "efficiently" and "appropriately." The goal when writing job standards is to be concise and clear.

Results and duties, as well as planning and appraisal criteria, are more easily understood when they are stated separately but linked in format. When you define planning and appraisal criteria for your organization, here is a useful way to present them:

Job Results Management Profile ©			
MAINTAINS COMPANY TELEPHONE DIRECTORY by updating files with additions, deletions, and changes.			
☐ **Result Required**	☐ **Problem**	☐ **Learning Required**	☐ **Performance Option**
Outcomes management wants.	*Outcomes management doesn't want—the things that can go wrong.*	*What an employee needs to learn to accomplish the Result Required.*	*More than is expected—true innovation; a role model for others.*
Additions, deletions, and changes are entered within four hours of receipt. Data entered are verified against personnel status change forms. Discrepancies are questioned.	Information is misdirected. Time is wasted. People are unaware of requests. Customers are unhappy with service.	☐ Managing time. ☐ Collecting required information. ☐ Verifying information. ☐ Referring questions to supervisor.	Recommends improved reference system.

© 1995 Job Results Management Institute, Winston-Salem, N.C.

Stated in this manner, the job description and appraisal criteria produce clearer communication between managers and employees when managing work.

Improving Your Writing

Here's a writing tip: *Fewer words are usually better!*

Change this:	*To this:*
Makes sure that shipments are complete.	Completes shipments.
Keeps customers informed.	Informs customers.
Keeps customer accounts up-to-date.	Maintains customer accounts.
Ensures that automobile fleet is in good condition.	Maintains automobile fleet.
Ensures quality and timeliness of administrative services.	Provides administrative services.
Ensures accuracy of data.	Verifies data.
Makes sure that each manifest is balanced and that product codes agree with customer's order.	Balances manifests and correlates product codes with customer's order.

Writing the Job Purpose

The job purpose is a one-sentence synthesis that tells why a job exists. The job purpose statement follows the result-by-duty formula.

There are several styles of job purpose statements from which you can choose. The first and briefest style, used in this book, highlights the results and duties that differentiate the job from other jobs.

Job Purpose Style 1

For example, the job purpose of a Data Center Analyst is:

SERVES CUSTOMERS
by
maintaining system performance.

The job purpose of a Sales Administrator is:

SUPPORTS CUSTOMERS, BROKERS, AND SALES MANAGERS
by
processing orders, invoices, samples requests, and trade promotions.

Job Purpose Style 2

A second style of job purpose statement, slightly longer, simply repeats the essential results (but not duties) in the body of the description.

For example, the job purpose of the Budget Accounting Clerk is:

SUPPORTS FORECAST, BUDGET, AND PLANNING OPERATIONS
by
preparing forecasting, budget, and planning worksheets; providing financial data to planning process users; maintaining budget and forecasting models; supporting cost analysis; providing historical information; maintaining database; providing information; protecting operations; maintaining technical knowledge.

This style highlights the results expected in order to emphasize two levels of job accountability:

1. Why the job exists (the result portion of the job purpose)
2. The key results to be accomplished

Job Purpose Style 3

A third style, a somewhat shorter variation of the second, repeats only the most pertinent results expected, excluding results common to many jobs, such as providing historical information, maintaining database, or maintaining technical knowledge.

In this style, the Budget Accounting Clerk job purpose would be:

SUPPORTS FORECAST, BUDGET, AND PLANNING OPERATIONS
by
preparing forecasting, budget, and planning worksheets; providing financial data to planning process users; maintaining budget and forecasting models; supporting cost analysis.

The style you choose depends on the use you make of the job purpose. For example, style 1 might be useful in employee orientation, style 2 for advertising vacant positions, and style 3 for job postings.

Some people find it easier to write the duties first and then synthesize them in the result portion of the job purpose. Others write the result portion of the job purpose first to set the tone of the job. Write in the sequence that is easier for you.

Where and How Does the Job Fit in the Organization?

The job purpose offers an opportunity to explain where and how the job fits in the mission of the organization.

Why the job exists is the differentiating feature of the job purpose. The "results" portion of the job purpose links the job to a larger organization unit or enterprise mission.

Job Purpose Style 4

Highlighting this overall mission of the job offers you a fourth style of job purpose statement that only presents the result portion of the job purpose. Thus, for the Budget Accounting Clerk, the job purpose would be:

SUPPORTS FORECAST, BUDGET, AND PLANNING OPERATIONS

UNIT MISSION: **SUPPORTS FINANCIAL DECISION MAKING**

Is the purpose realistic?

The job purpose should not be inflated or out of reach for the job described. If, for example, you are describing a Housekeeper in a hospital and the mission of the hospital is to treat patients, you may be tempted to describe the Housekeeper's job purpose as "Treats patients by maintaining facilities."

While you want the Housekeeper to understand his or her role in the unified effort to treat patients, treating patients is beyond the immediate control of the Housekeeper. If, however, the job description states only "Maintains facilities by providing cleaning services," the necessary participation of the Housekeeper in the delivery system is not recognized.

More accurately, the Housekeeper's job purpose is:

MAINTAINS FACILITIES FOR PATIENTS, VISITORS, AND CO-WORKERS
by
providing cleaning services.

Is the purpose meaningful?

You can use the job purpose to elevate a job to its true meaning and value. Sometimes just a slight change of words will do. In the case of an Aircraft Mechanic, the purpose of the organization is to transport people and cargo. You could say that the job of the Aircraft Mechanic is: "Transports people and cargo by maintaining aircraft." Yet the Aircraft Mechanic does not transport people.

One option is to identify the job purpose as: "Maintains aircraft by completing preventive maintenance schedules; installing and repairing parts and systems." Still, you want to tie the Aircraft Mechanic's job to the real purpose of the airline because the work is such an integral and obvious part of the business.

Trying different words, you might conclude that the Aircraft Mechanic:

PROVIDES TRANSPORT FOR PEOPLE AND CARGO
by
maintaining, repairing, and overhauling aircraft and aircraft engines.

Gathering Data for a Job Description

There are a number of sources for the information you need to write a job description. These include:

- Job analyses
- Personnel requisitions and job opportunity bulletins
- Goals set in performance planning
- Corporate and department studies and projects
- Job competencies
- Old job descriptions
- Job descriptions for similar jobs
- Sample job descriptions from books or organizations
- Job procedure lists
- Corporate philosophy and mission statements
- Department mission statements
- Organization charts
- Performance criteria
- Regulatory requirements

Converting Statements to the Result-by-Duty Formula

When you read job descriptions, you may find that they follow a different format than those in this compendium. The expectations may be stated in this manner: The duty is performed *"in order to," "to," "so that," "so,"* or *"for"* the result accomplished.

Consider this example: "Completes analyses to provide management with cost information." The duty and the result are here, but not in the order we use. You can convert the statement into the result-by-duty formula by rearranging its elements in this way:

PROVIDES MANAGEMENT WITH INFORMATION
by
completing cost analyses.

Some Rules for Writing

Write in any way that is comfortable for you. You can begin by listing all of the duties or by specifying the job results.

Remember that good writing comes from good editing; don't try to write perfectly the first time. Write for a while, and, when you get tired, put the work away. Pick up the work later, and edit your previous work.

Set aside some time to write without interruption so you can concentrate better.

Worksheets

Here are some worksheets you can use to organize and guide your work.

WORKSHEET: Job Description Cover Sheet

JOB TITLE: _____

SECTION: _____

WRITTEN BY: _____

REPORTS TO (JOB TITLE): _____

JOB TITLES SUPERVISED: _____

_____

_____

_____

DATE WRITTEN: _____

REVIEWED BY: _____

APPROVED BY: _____

DATE APPROVED: _____

WORKSHEET: Job Purpose

JOB PURPOSE:

_____

by

_____

WORKSHEET: Job Description Results and Duties

Write either the result or the duty first, whichever is easier for you. Jobs typically have about a dozen specific result and duty statements. Fill in the following:

___ **Result**   =   Why is the duty important? What is accomplished by performing the duty?

    by

    Duty   =   What is the activity being performed?

___ **Result**
_____
[*Start with an active verb, such as "completes" or "maintains."*]

    by

    Duty
_____
[*Start with an "ing" verb, such as "recording" or "evaluating."*]

    Duty
_____

___ **Result**
_____
[*Start with an active verb, such as "completes" or "maintains."*]

    by

    Duty
_____
[*Start with an "ing" verb, such as "recording" or "evaluating."*]

    Duty
_____

___ **Result**
_____
[*Start with an active verb, such as "completes" or "maintains."*]

    by

    Duty
_____
[*Start with an "ing" verb, such as "recording" or "evaluating."*]

    Duty
_____

WORKSHEET: Job Qualifications and Job Evaluation Documentation

---

Job qualifications define the knowledge, skill, and ability an incumbent must have in order to accomplish the job results and to perform the job duties.

Job evaluation documentation defines the job demands made on the job incumbent. These job demands are compared with the demands of other jobs to determine which jobs are worth more to the organization and therefore should carry higher salaries. This process is called job evaluation.

The information that identifies job qualifications and job demands can easily be combined into one document. Although this book is not intended to teach you how to define job qualifications or gauge differing job demands, a worksheet that will help you to assemble that information is included. Be sure to use job-specific examples when completing the worksheet!

KNOWLEDGE
What does the incumbent need to know to perform the job at the entry level, regardless of whether the information is acquired through formal education, experience, or self-learning?

_____

_____

_____

INFORMATION PROCESSING
In what way does the incumbent use information mentally?

_____

_____

_____

SCOPE OF RESPONSIBILITY
What decisions are made by the incumbent?

_____

_____

_____

INTERPERSONAL COMMUNICATION
What is the reason for contacts with others?

_____

_____

_____

IMPACT ON RESULTS
What typically might go wrong as a result of an error by the incumbent?

_____

_____

_____

DESCRIBE CONTROLS
What controls exist to prevent errors?

_____

_____

_____

CONFIDENTIAL AND SENSITIVE INFORMATION
What confidential and sensitive information is available to the incumbent?

_____

_____

_____

SCOPE OF FINANCIAL RESPONSIBILITY
What is the incumbent's responsibility for expenditures and funding/revenue?

_____

_____

_____

ENVIRONMENT
What are the physical and mental strains, stresses, or exposures of the job?

PHYSICAL DEMANDS

☐ Balancing	☐ Crouching	☐ Hearing	☐ Seeing	☐ Sitting
☐ Carrying	☐ Feeling	☐ Kneeling	○ Close	☐ Standing
☐ Climbing	☐ Fingering	☐ Lifting	○ Far	☐ Stooping
☐ Crawling	☐ Grasping	☐ Pulling	○ Color	☐ Talking
			○ Depth	☐ Walking

EXPOSURES

☐ Airborne particles	☐ Explosives	☐ Muscular strain	☐ Temperature
☐ Caustics	☐ Fumes	☐ Noise	☐ Toxicants
☐ Chemicals	☐ High places	☐ Odors	☐ Vibration
☐ Electrical current	☐ Moving parts	☐ Physical abuse	☐ Vision strain
			☐ Weather

SUPERVISORY-MANAGEMENT RESPONSIBILITY

In what ways does the incumbent direct the work of others?

☐ Assign and check work	☐ Plan/appraise job results	☐ Train
☐ Hire/discipline/terminate	☐ Recommend pay increases	

Number of employees supervised: _____

How many employees are supervised (including those supervised indirectly, namely, those employees supervised by subordinate supervisors)? _____

> **SAMPLE:** Job Description, Job Qualifications, and Job Evaluation
> Documentation

I. JOB DESCRIPTION

TITLE: Employee Benefits Assistant

DEPARTMENT: Personnel   **FLSA:** N

REPORTS TO: Compensation Manager   **GRADE:** 8

JOBS SUPERVISED: None

CAREER PROGRESSION: Employee Benefits Specialist;
Compensation Analyst

JOB PURPOSE: **PROVIDES EMPLOYEE BENEFITS**
by
answering questions; initiating and continuing membership.

ESSENTIAL JOB RESULTS:

% of
time

__35%__ 1. **RESOLVES EMPLOYEE QUESTIONS AND PROBLEMS**
by
researching policies and procedures; providing answers.

__20%__ 2. **INITIATES NEW-HIRE BENEFITS**
by
obtaining and recording benefit information; informing insurance carriers.

__10%__ 3. **COMPLETES BILLING**
by
organizing carrier reports; requesting disbursements; reconciling accounts.

__15%__ 4. **PRESERVES HISTORICAL REFERENCE**
by
establishing and maintaining record-keeping system; filing and retrieving department information.

% of
time

__10%__ 5. **CONTINUES ELECTIVE RETIREE INSURANCE COVERAGE**
by
tracking payments and depository funds.

__5%__ 6. **MAINTAINS DEPARTMENT SUPPLIES INVENTORY**
by
anticipating needs; placing orders; verifying delivery.

__5%__ 7. **COMPLETES DEPARTMENTAL OPERATIONS**
by
accomplishing related results as needed.

II. JOB QUALIFICATIONS AND JOB EVALUATION DOCUMENTATION

KNOWLEDGE

EDUCATION:	One year of business school preferred.
EXPERIENCE:	Accounts receivable/payable process.
SKILLS AND ABILITIES:	Basic calculator operation. Data entry, 40 wpm. Proven accuracy. Demonstrated telephone operation and courtesy.

INFORMATION PROCESSING
Identifies and answers employee questions and concerns, using defined sources of information.

DECISION MAKING
Identifies correct answer. Transfers and verifies information. Orders supplies.

INTERPERSONAL COMMUNICATION
Clarifies benefits policies and procedures for employees at individual levels of

understanding.

IMPACT OF RESULTS
Errors increase expense to the organization. Incorrect information is an inconvenience to the employee or the employee's family. Incomplete or inaccurate work causes a negative perception of the department.

DESCRIBE CONTROLS
Insurance company verification. Billing errors can be corrected.

CONFIDENTIAL AND SENSITIVE INFORMATION
All personnel files and salary information.

SCOPE OF FINANCIAL RESPONSIBILITY
Orders supplies. Reconciles benefits accounts.

ENVIRONMENT

PHYSICAL DEMANDS

☐ Balancing	☐ Crouching	☒ Hearing	☒ Seeing	☒ Sitting
☒ Carrying	☐ Feeling	☐ Kneeling	⊗ Close	☐ Standing
☐ Climbing	☒ Fingering	☐ Lifting	○ Far	☒ Stooping
☐ Crawling	☒ Grasping	☐ Pulling	○ Color	☒ Talking
			○ Depth	☒ Walking

EXPOSURES

☐ Airborne particles	☐ Explosives	☐ Muscular strain	☐ Temperature
☐ Caustics	☐ Fumes	☐ Noise	☐ Toxicants
☐ Chemicals	☐ High places	☐ Odors	☐ Vibration
☐ Electrical current	☐ Moving parts	☐ Physical abuse	☐ Vision strain
			☐ Weather

SUPERVISORY RESPONSIBILITY
Number of employees supervised: ___
___ Assign and check work   ___ Recommend pay increases

___ Hire/discipline/terminate   ___ Train

___ Plan/appraise job results

5
Legal Considerations

Federal law is remarkably silent about job descriptions. What federal law is not silent about, however, is the protection of employee rights. A judge's decision about the abuse of employee rights may well rest on the job results and duties that are (or are not) stated in a job description. If a job description exists but the actual conditions on the job are different from those stated in the job description, the actual conditions take precedence in determining liability. What this means, of course, is that job descriptions must be maintained and audited.

The following federal laws contain a variety of provisions that are not discussed in this book. The guidelines that follow are derived from provisions to which a job description might be relevant.

State laws are not addressed here because of their diversity.

Americans With Disabilities Act

The Americans with Disabilities Act (ADA), which went into effect in 1990, protects people from discrimination based on physical or mental disabilities. A key factor in this protection is the determination of whether a person with a disability can "perform the essential functions" of the job, with or without reasonable accommodation.

Essential Functions

Essential functions can be defined by answering the following questions:

1. Why does the job exist?
2. Would removing the function fundamentally change the job?
3. Is the function marginal or incidental to the job purpose?
4. Is the job specialized, so that the person in the job is hired for his or her expertise to accomplish the function?
5. Is the function actually accomplished by all current incumbents?
6. Was the function required of past incumbents?
7. Does the incumbent spend a substantial amount of time accomplishing the function? [Time spent is only a rough indicator of a function's importance, because some functions require only a little time to accomplish but are crucial to the outcome of the job. To help

with this consideration, we have included a "% of time" space alongside each result and duty statement.]

8. Would the consequences be serious if the function were not accomplished?
9. Is there a limited number of employees available among whom the function can be distributed?
10. Does a collective bargaining agreement identify the function as part of the job?

Determining What Is Essential

A results-oriented job description can help you define essential functions and carry out the intent of the ADA, but you may have to adjust your language a bit. In the language of the ADA, the issue is whether a person can "perform the essential functions of the job."

Since most descriptions list only job duties, the question becomes, Which of the duties are essential? Interestingly, some of the examples used in the *ADA Handbook,* published by the Equal Employment Opportunity Commission and the U.S. Department of Justice, recognize that defining what is "essential" may not be as easy as you might think.

For example, the handbook notes that "the ability to access, input, and retrieve information from a computer" may not mean that the person has to "enter information manually, or visually read the information on the computer screen. Adaptive devices or computer software can enable a person without arms or a person with impaired vision to perform the essential functions of the job."

Focusing on Results to Clarify What Is Essential

The results-oriented job description helps clarify the issue.

MAINTAINS DATABASE
by
accessing, inputting, and retrieving information from a computer.

Here the emphasis is on the database rather than on accessing, inputting, and retrieving. The implication is that as long as the database is maintained, how it is maintained is not as significant. Focusing on the result, instead of on the duties, helps open the door to new ways of accomplishing the same outcome.

Focusing on results broadens our perspective. As an example, suppose a child daycare center manager is concerned about hiring a person in a wheelchair who he or she anticipates would not be able to "restrain" unruly children. When the result-versus-duty thinking is applied, "restraining children" is understood as a duty that produces the result, "Maintains order."

What might prevent a person from restraining a child? Slow movement; limited strength. Some people in wheelchairs race or play basketball and are quite quick and agile. Others have developed strong upper-torso strength. In other words, a person in a wheelchair might even have an advantage over a person who is ambulatory in accomplishing the desired result.

The result is not necessarily the same as the essential function, because some duties may be essential. Focusing on the result helps clarify what is essential. A close examination of the job description is required.

The Job Description as Evidence

The ADA does not require you to develop and maintain job descriptions, but a written job description prepared before advertising, or interviewing applicants for, a job can serve as evidence in documenting functions.

The ADA does not require that you limit your job descriptions to a definition of essential functions or even that essential functions be identified. However, if you wish to use a job description to document what functions are essential, you should identify those functions as important in accomplishing the purpose of the job.

Do you have to rewrite all of your job descriptions? That depends on the state of your current job descriptions. If your descriptions list only job duties, then your explanation of job expectations is incomplete, by the reasoning employed in this book. Applicants and employees who are disabled can teach managers new ways to accomplish traditional job results.

What Constitutes Reasonable Accommodation?

Debates regarding the ADA will probably center not on the definition of essential functions but on whether a qualified individual with a known physical or mental disability can be reasonably accommodated without undue hardship to the employer.

"Reasonable accommodation" is a modification or adjustment to a job, the work environment, or the way things are usually done that enables a qualified individual with a disability to enjoy an equal employment opportunity. An equal employment opportunity is defined as the opportunity to attain the same level of performance or to enjoy the same benefits and privileges of employment that are available to an average, similarly situated employee without a disability.

Reasonable accommodations may include:

- Making facilities readily accessible and usable
- Restructuring the job by reallocating or redistributing nonessential job functions
- Offering part-time or modified work schedules
- Obtaining or modifying equipment or devices
- Providing qualified readers and interpreters
- Providing reserved parking for a person with a mobility impairment

Legal challenges to the law will probably address the questions of what constitutes an "undue hardship" and how to define "the way things are usually done."

Given two candidates with different disabilities, both requesting that job requirements be reallocated, employers may find they can accommodate one candidate but not the other. Therefore, what is deemed essential at first may not be essential in the final analysis.

While not a consideration of the ADA, accommodation thinking and practices naturally extend to diversity issues including adjustments for older workers, such as brighter lighting, louder signals, larger keyboards, and desk chairs with arms; modifications for races of typically shorter stature; and adaptations for family concerns.

What Is Written Is Essential

We suggest that you start with the position that anything you write in a job description is essential. To label some job expectations as unessential or marginal sends an awkward, if not demotivating, message to employees. Whether a particular function is in fact essential can be determined when you decide whether it can be modified to accommodate an employee or applicant with a disability.

Fair Labor Standards Act

Generally speaking, under the Fair Labor Standards Act (FLSA), employees must be paid overtime for hours worked in excess of forty per workweek, although there is a variety of requirements, exclusions, exceptions, and exemptions, all of which you must thoroughly research to determine their applicability to your organization. The reference is the United States Code, Title 29, Chapter 8, as well as related laws such as the Portal-to-Portal Act, the Service Contract Act, the Contract Work Hours and Safety Act, the Davis-Bacon Act, the Walsh-Healey Act, and the Railway Labor Act.

Whether an employee is exempt from the law is determined by the employee's actual work requirements, typically defined in a job description. Exemptions from overtime pay are defined in four categories: executives, administrators, professionals, and outside salespersons. Here are the exemptions for your easy reference.

Executive Exemption

An executive employee must:

- Earn at least $250 per week.
- Have the primary duty of management of the enterprise in which employed or of a customarily recognized department or subdivision of that enterprise.
- Customarily and regularly direct the work of two or more other employees in that enterprise.

If the executive earns at least $155 per week but less than $250 per week, in addition to the above requirements, he or she must:

- Have the authority to hire or fire other employees or make particularly influential suggestions and recommendations regarding hiring, firing, advancement, promotion, or other change of status of other employees.
- Customarily and regularly exercise discretionary powers.
- Devote no more than 20 percent (40 percent in the case of an employee in a retail or service establishment) of hours of work in the workweek to activities that are not directly and closely related to the performance of the work described above, unless the person is an owner or operator of an independent establishment or branch establishment.

Administrative Exemption

An administrative employee must:

- Earn at least $250 per week.
- Have the primary duty to exercise discretion and independent judgment.
- Perform office or nonmanual work directly related to management policies or the general business operations of the employer or employer's customers or perform administrative functions in an educational setting in work directly related to the academic instruction or training carried on there.

If the administrative employee earns at least $155 per week but less than $250 per week or is a school administrator whose compensation is on a salary basis, in addition to the above requirements, he or she must:

- Customarily and regularly exercise discretion and independent judgment.
- Regularly and directly assist a business owner or another bona fide executive or administrator; work only under general supervision on tasks that are specialized or technical and require special training, experience, or knowledge; or work only under general supervision on special assignments and tasks.
- Devote no more than 20 percent (40 percent in the case of an employee in a retail or service establishment) of time to activities that are not directly and closely related to the work described above.

Professional Exemption

A professional employee must:

- Earn at least $250 per week (there are some specific exceptions).
- Have primary duties in the performance of a learned or an educational profession entailing work that requires the exercise of discretion and judgment or have primary duties in the performance of work requiring invention, imagination, or talent in a recognized field of artistic endeavor.

If the professional earns at least $155 per week but less than $250 per week, he or she must:

- Have primary duties in the performance of a learned, artistic, or educational profession.
- Consistently exercise discretion and judgment in the performance of the primary duties.
- Accomplish work that is predominantly intellectual and varied in character and that cannot be standardized in relation to time.
- Devote no more than 20 percent of work hours in the workweek to activities that are not an essential part of, and necessarily incident to, the work described above.

Outside Salesperson Exemption

An outside salesperson must:

- Customarily and regularly work away from the employer's place of business while making sales or obtaining orders or contracts for services or for the use of facilities for which a consideration will be paid by the client or customer.
- Not engage in work of any other nature for more than 20 percent of the hours worked in the workweek by the employer's nonexempt employees.

These exemptions are explained in detail, with specific examples, in the interpretive bulletin issued by the Department of Labor. Additionally, court cases have clarified specific applications. Note that job titles are not important when determining whether an employee is exempt or whether the company is in compliance with a law. What counts are the job requirements stated under the job title.

Equal Pay Act

Employees may not be discriminated against in pay on the basis of sex when they perform equal work on jobs in the same establishment requiring equal skill, effort, and responsibility and performed under similar working conditions.

The job description of the job accomplished by men is compared to the job description of the job accomplished by women to determine whether they are equal in requirements. Regardless of what is stated in the job description, however, what actually happens on the job is decisive.

Civil Rights Act, Title VII, and Other Antidiscrimination Measures

The Civil Rights Act provides that employees may not be discriminated against because of race, color, sex, pregnancy, religion, or national origin in regard to hiring, discharge, compensation, terms conditions, or privileges of employment. Executive orders extend the protection to cover age, handicap, and status as a Vietnam-era veteran. Other laws protecting employees' rights disallow discrimination based on age (Age Discrimination in Employment Act), handicap (Rehabilitation Act), or veteran status (Vietnam Era Veteran's Readjustment Act).

The qualifications listed in job descriptions are often the basis for hiring decisions, so qualifications that discriminate, or that appear to discriminate, against certain groups of people must be supported by legitimate job results and duties. Be sure that there are no artificial barriers in your job descriptions.

Job Titles

Job titles should not refer to the sex of the incumbent. Use "waitperson" instead of "waiter" or "waitress."

It is important to remember that the issue is discrimination, not the job title. If the title Janitor is defined to mean men's work and Housekeeper to mean women's work, you have a problem.

Masseur or Masseuse is certainly appropriate because a health club would want its members to know in advance the gender of the person giving them a massage. Or a club, secure in its nondiscriminatory practices, may wish to refer to a male Host and a female Hostess because it sounds better (and is obvious) to club members. You'll notice that we included both the male and female forms in the job description list.

Job Evaluations

Job evaluation plans are used to determine the pay associated with different jobs on the basis of the demands of the job. Job descriptions describe the different job demands.

Appraisals

Appraisals of an employee's accomplishments, which may lead to promotions and pay adjustments, must be substantiated with reference to the description of the employee's job. An appraisal of accomplishments, regardless of the form used, ultimately rests on the job requirements and whether the employee has been able to accomplish them.

Occupational Safety and Health Act

Employers must furnish employees with working conditions free from recognized hazards. Job descriptions are used to warn employees about any possible hazards and to inform employees of requirements regarding safety regulations and procedures.

Part II
Job Descriptions

JOB PURPOSE: MAINTAINS RELATIONSHIP WITH CLIENTS
by
completing audits; suggesting improvements.

ESSENTIAL JOB RESULTS:

% of
time

_____ 1. **SERVES CLIENTS**
by
identifying requirements; anticipating
and resolving problems.

_____ 2. **MAINTAINS WORKFLOW**
by
assigning work and monitoring
accounting staff; guiding clerical staff;
meeting deadlines.

_____ 3. **COMPLETES AUDITS**
by
assessing and recommending
accounting controls; reconciling
discrepancies; preparing reports;
resolving procedural problems.

_____ 4. **SUGGESTS CONTROL
IMPROVEMENTS**
by
researching and interpreting accounting
policies and legal regulations.

_____ 5. **MAINTAINS QUALITY SERVICE**
by
establishing and enforcing organization
standards.

% of
time

_____ 6. **MAINTAINS CLIENT CONFIDENCE**
by
keeping information confidential.

_____ 7. **GENERATES REVENUES**
by
attracting new clients; defining new and
expanded services.

_____ 8. **MAINTAINS FIRM'S REPUTATION**
by
complying with regulations and
professional ethics of the American
Institute of Certified Public Accountants
and state accounting society.

_____ 9. **MAINTAINS PROFESSIONAL AND
TECHNICAL KNOWLEDGE**
by
attending educational workshops;
reviewing professional publications;
establishing personal networks;
benchmarking state-of-the-art practices;
participating in professional societies.

_____10. **CONTRIBUTES TO TEAM EFFORT**
by
accomplishing related results as
needed.

JOB PURPOSE: **FOCUSES STAFF ON CLIENT REQUIREMENTS**
by
supervising staff; completing project requirements and reporting project outcomes.

ESSENTIAL JOB RESULTS:

% of
time

% of
time

____ 1. **ACCOMPLISHES ACCOUNTING FIRM STAFF RESULTS**
by
communicating job expectations; planning, monitoring, and appraising job results; coaching, counseling, and disciplining employees; initiating, coordinating, and enforcing systems, policies, and procedures.

____ 2. **MAINTAINS STAFF**
by
recruiting, selecting, orienting, and training employees; maintaining a safe and secure work environment; developing personal growth opportunities.

____ 3. **MENTORS ACCOUNTING STAFF**
by
providing individual guidance and technical expertise.

____ 4. **COMPLETES PROJECT REQUIREMENTS**
by
approving staff work; conducting pre- and postchecks.

____ 5. **MAINTAINS OPERATIONS**
by
initiating, recommending, coordinating, and enforcing program, operational, and personnel policies and procedures.

____ 6. **RECORDS ACTIONS**
by
completing required documentation.

____ 7. **MAINTAINS CLIENT CONFIDENCE**
by
keeping information confidential; cautioning others about potential breaches of confidence.

____ 8. **KEEPS CLIENTS, STAFF, AND PARTNERS INFORMED**
by
analyzing and reporting project status.

____ 9. **ACHIEVES FINANCIAL OBJECTIVES**
by
preparing project budgets; analyzing expense variances; initiating corrective action; monitoring project staffing levels.

____10. **GENERATES REVENUES**
by
recommending new services to clients; developing new clients; participating in civic and business organizations; presenting seminars.

____11. **MAINTAINS PROFESSIONAL AND TECHNICAL KNOWLEDGE**
by
attending educational workshops; reviewing professional publications; establishing personal networks; benchmarking state-of-the-art practices; participating in professional societies.

____12. **CONTRIBUTES TO TEAM EFFORT**
by
accomplishing related results as needed.

JOB PURPOSE: PROVIDES STATE INSURANCE COMPLIANCE STRATEGIES
by
analyzing experience and recommending actions.

ESSENTIAL JOB RESULTS:

% of
time

% of
time

____ 1. **RECOMMENDS RATE ACTION**
by
analyzing loss experience by state
and/or product.

____ 2. **FILES FOR AND NEGOTIATES RATE INCREASES**
by
gathering supporting documentation.

____ 3. **MAINTAINS QUALITY OF SUBMISSIONS TO STATE INSURANCE DEPARTMENTS**
by
reviewing and correcting statistical
data.

____ 4. **MAINTAINS LEGAL COMPLIANCE**
by
coordinating information with
government affairs, client
administration, and/or financial
processing; recommending solutions to
noncompliance.

____ 5. **MAINTAINS DATABASE FOR RATE FILINGS**
by
monitoring data processing systems;
developing update instructions required
by changing regulations; backing up
data.

____ 6. **RECOMMENDS OPTIONS FOR FILING AND IMPLEMENTING NEW RATES**
by
analyzing experience and premium
rates.

____ 7. **RECOMMENDS RESPONSE TO CREDIT INSURANCE ISSUES**
by
furnishing the government affairs
department with information.

____ 8. **REVIEWS QUARTERLY AND ANNUAL STATEMENTS**
by
analyzing inbound and outbound
assumptions; providing pricing support
for transactions.

____ 9. **MAINTAINS TECHNICAL KNOWLEDGE**
by
attending educational workshops;
reviewing publications.

____10. **CONTRIBUTES TO TEAM EFFORT**
by
accomplishing related results as
needed.

┌───┐
| **JOB TITLE:**   **ADMINISTRATIVE MANAGER**   **A008_M** |
└───┘

JOB PURPOSE: **SUPPORTS OPERATIONS**
by
supervising staff; planning, organizing, and implementing administrative
systems.

ESSENTIAL JOB RESULTS:

% of
time

_____ 1. **MAINTAINS ADMINISTRATIVE STAFF**
by
recruiting, selecting, orienting, and training employees; maintaining a safe and secure work environment; developing personal growth opportunities.

_____ 2. **ACCOMPLISHES STAFF RESULTS**
by
communicating job expectations; planning, monitoring, and appraising job results; coaching, counseling, and disciplining employees; initiating, coordinating, and enforcing systems, policies, and procedures.

_____ 3. **PROVIDES RECEPTION, SWITCHBOARD, MAILROOM, AND KITCHEN SERVICES AND SUPPLIES**
by
identifying needs; establishing policies, procedures, and work schedules.

_____ 4. **PROVIDES COMMUNICATION SYSTEMS**
by
identifying needs; evaluating options; maintaining equipment; approving invoices.

_____ 5. **PURCHASES SPECIALTY ITEMS, PRINTED MATERIALS, AND FORMS**
by
obtaining requirements; negotiating price, quality, and delivery; approving invoices.

% of
time

_____ 6. **COMPLETES SPECIAL PROJECTS**
by
organizing and coordinating information and requirements, planning, arranging, and meeting schedules; monitoring results.

_____ 7. **PROVIDES HISTORICAL REFERENCE**
by
developing and utilizing filing and retrieval systems.

_____ 8. **IMPROVES PROGRAM AND SERVICE QUALITY**
by
devising new applications; updating procedures; evaluating system results with users.

_____ 9. **ACHIEVES FINANCIAL OBJECTIVES**
by
anticipating requirements; submitting information for budget preparation; scheduling expenditures; monitoring costs; analyzing variances.

_____10. **MAINTAINS CONTINUITY AMONG CORPORATE, DIVISION, AND LOCAL WORK TEAMS**
by
documenting and communicating actions, irregularities, and continuing needs.

ESSENTIAL JOB RESULTS:

% of
time

____**11. MAINTAINS PROFESSIONAL AND TECHNICAL KNOWLEDGE**
by
attending educational workshops;
benchmarking professional standards;
reviewing professional publications;
establishing personal networks.

% of
time

____**12. CONTRIBUTES TO TEAM EFFORT**
by
accomplishing related results as
needed.

JOB PURPOSE: **TRANSPORTS PASSENGERS AND FREIGHT**
by
flying aircraft to scheduled destinations and maintaining safe operations.

ESSENTIAL JOB RESULTS:

% of
time

% of
time

_____ 1. **ORGANIZES FLIGHT**
by
studying load and fuel requirements;
ordering requirements; verifying crew
availability; preparing and filing flight
plan.

_____ 2. **PREPARES FOR SAFE FLIGHT**
by
completing external and internal
preflight inspections; correcting
deficiencies.

_____ 3. **OBTAINS TAKEOFF, FLIGHT, AND
LANDING INSTRUCTIONS**
by
maintaining contact with flight
controllers.

_____ 4. **FLIES TO DESTINATION**
by
following flight plan; monitoring flight
operations; managing flight deck and
cabin; resolving emergencies.

_____ 5. **MAINTAINS SAFE OPERATIONS**
by
complying with and enforcing Federal
Aviation Administration, company, and
airport regulations; reporting
maintenance requirements.

_____ 6. **COMPLETES REPORTS**
by
entering required information.

_____ 7. **MAINTAINS PROFESSIONAL AND
TECHNICAL KNOWLEDGE**
by
completing proficiency tests; reviewing
professional publications.

_____ 8. **CONTRIBUTES TO TEAM EFFORT**
by
accomplishing related results as
needed.

JOB PURPOSE: SERVES AIRLINE CUSTOMERS
by
managing staff; planning, implementing, and securing operations.

ESSENTIAL JOB RESULTS:

% of
time

% of
time

____ 1. **MAINTAINS AIRPORT STAFF**
by
recruiting, selecting, orienting, and
training employees.

____ 2. **ACCOMPLISHES STAFF RESULTS**
by
communicating job expectations;
planning, monitoring, and appraising
job results; coaching, counseling, and
disciplining employees; initiating,
coordinating, and enforcing systems,
policies, and procedures.

____ 3. **MAINTAINS AIRPORT
DEVELOPMENT PLAN**
by
studying consumer base; estimating air
traffic; calculating ground traffic and
parking requirements; conferring and
negotiating with airlines; consulting with
commission members.

____ 4. **MAINTAINS OPERATIONS PLAN**
by
establishing policies, procedures,
regulations, and landing, taxiing, and
takeoff rules; studying potential
improvements.

____ 5. **SECURES AIRPORT**
by
enforcing Federal Aviation
Administration regulations; contracting
with security force; establishing security
policies and procedures; maintaining
disaster and evacuation plans;
investigating violations.

____ 6. **MAINTAINS FACILITIES**
by
establishing preventive and repair
practices; conducting inspections;
contracting with maintenance and
cleaning services.

____ 7. **ENSURES OPERATION OF
EQUIPMENT**
by
establishing preventive maintenance
requirements; contracting for
maintenance services; maintaining
equipment inventories; evaluating new
equipment and techniques.

____ 8. **ACCOMPLISHES FINANCIAL
OBJECTIVES**
by
forecasting requirements; preparing an
annual budget; scheduling
expenditures; analyzing variances;
initiating corrective action.

____ 9. **PREPARES REPORTS**
by
collecting, analyzing, and summarizing
information.

____10. **REPRESENTS THE AIRPORT
AUTHORITY**
by
providing information and opinions to
local, state, and federal governments
and to civic organizations; participating
in studies.

ESSENTIAL JOB RESULTS:

% of
time

____11. **MAINTAINS PROFESSIONAL AND TECHNICAL KNOWLEDGE**
    by
    attending educational workshops;
    reviewing professional publications;
    establishing personal networks;
    benchmarking state-of-the-art practices;
    participating in professional societies.

% of
time

____12. **CONTRIBUTES TO TEAM EFFORT**
    by
    accomplishing related results as
    needed.

JOB PURPOSE: **PROTECTS CITIZENS AND ANIMALS**
by
taking animals into custody; explaining and enforcing regulations.

ESSENTIAL JOB RESULTS:

% of
time

_____ **1. TAKES ANIMALS INTO CUSTODY**
by
capturing, transporting, or receiving
them.

_____ **2. PROTECTS ANIMALS**
by
removing them from inhumane or
distressing conditions; arranging for
treatment; feeding and housing them.

_____ **3. MAINTAINS COMPLIANCE WITH
REGULATIONS**
by
inspecting animal display and housing
establishments; explaining laws to
animal owners; answering inquiries;
presenting public information talks.

_____ **4. INVESTIGATES COMPLAINTS**
by
interviewing witnesses and owners;
observing conditions; documenting
observations.

_____ **5. ENFORCES REGULATIONS**
by
issuing warnings and citations;
reporting violators to police.

% of
time

_____ **6. COMPLETES REPORTS**
by
entering required information.

_____ **7. PREPARES REPORTS**
by
collecting, analyzing, and summarizing
information.

_____ **8. MAINTAINS VEHICLES**
by
conducting inspections; completing
operator maintenance; adhering to
traffic regulations.

_____ **9. MAINTAINS TECHNICAL
KNOWLEDGE**
by
attending educational workshops;
reviewing publications.

_____**10. CONTRIBUTES TO TEAM EFFORT**
by
accomplishing related results as
needed.

JOB TITLE: APARTMENT HOUSE MANAGER   A016_M

JOB PURPOSE: **MAINTAINS RENTALS**
by
maintaining premises and filling vacancies.

ESSENTIAL JOB RESULTS:

% of
time

% of
time

_____ 1. **ESTABLISHES RENTAL RATE**
by
surveying local rental rates; calculating
overhead costs, depreciation, taxes,
and profit goals.

_____ 2. **ATTRACTS TENANTS**
by
advertising vacancies; obtaining
referrals from current renters;
explaining advantages of location and
services; showing apartments.

_____ 3. **CONTRACTS WITH TENANTS**
by
explaining contract terms and rules of
occupancy; collecting security deposit.

_____ 4. **ACCOMPLISHES FINANCIAL
OBJECTIVES**
by
collecting rents; paying bills; forecasting
requirements; preparing an annual
budget; scheduling expenditures;
analyzing variances; initiating corrective
action.

_____ 5. **MAINTAINS APARTMENT BUILDING**
by
investigating and resolving tenant
complaints; enforcing rules of
occupancy; inspecting vacant
apartments and completing repairs;
planning renovations; contracting with
landscaping and snow removal
services.

_____ 6. **MAINTAINS BUILDING SYSTEMS**
by
contracting for maintenance services;
supervising repairs.

_____ 7. **SECURES APARTMENT COMPLEX**
by
contracting with security patrol service;
installing and maintaining security
devices; establishing and enforcing
precautionary policies and procedures;
responding to emergencies.

_____ 8. **ENFORCES OCCUPANCY POLICIES
AND PROCEDURES**
by
meeting with tenants' association;
providing information and direction;
confronting violators.

_____ 9. **PREPARES REPORTS**
by
collecting, analyzing, and summarizing
information.

_____ 10. **MAINTAINS TECHNICAL
KNOWLEDGE**
by
attending educational workshops;
reviewing publications.

_____ 11. **CONTRIBUTES TO TEAM EFFORT**
by
accomplishing related results as
needed.

JOB TITLE:	AQUARIST	A017_M

JOB PURPOSE: MAINTAINS AQUARIUM EXHIBITS
by
maintaining tank, water conditions, and fish; educating visitors.

ESSENTIAL JOB RESULTS:

% of
time

_____ 1. **PREPARES WORK TO BE ACCOMPLISHED**
by
determining requirements; organizing schedule; setting priorities.

_____ 2. **MAINTAINS WATER CONDITIONS**
by
collecting and testing water samples; adjusting chemicals and temperature.

_____ 3. **MAINTAINS FISH**
by
preparing food; feeding and treating fish.

_____ 4. **DETECTS DISEASE AND INJURIES**
by
observing fish; reporting condition.

_____ 5. **MAINTAINS TANKS**
by
cleaning; inspecting; reporting condition.

_____ 6. **MAINTAINS PLANTS**
by
planting, feeding, and removing them.

% of
time

_____ 7. **MAINTAINS DECORATIONS**
by
constructing, installing, repairing, and removing them.

_____ 8. **COMPLETES REPORTS**
by
entering required information.

_____ 9. **EDUCATES VISITORS**
by
answering questions; providing information; caring for fish in children's petting area.

_____ 10. **MAINTAINS TECHNICAL KNOWLEDGE**
by
attending educational workshops; reviewing publications.

_____ 11. **CONTRIBUTES TO TEAM EFFORT**
by
accomplishing related results as needed.

JOB PURPOSE: SERVES CUSTOMERS
by
developing and illustrating concepts.

ESSENTIAL JOB RESULTS:

% of
time

____ **1. ESTABLISHES ART CONCEPT**
by
researching marketing needs.

____ **2. ILLUSTRATES CONCEPT**
by
designing layout of art and copy
regarding arrangement, size, type size
and style, and related aesthetic
concepts.

____ **3. MAINTAINS CORPORATE IMAGE**
by
monitoring materials and production
quality.

____ **4. MAINTAINS ART PRODUCTION EFFICIENCY**
by
coordinating press operations.

____ **5. COMPLETES ART PRODUCTION**
by
scheduling and organizing jobs;
monitoring production.

% of
time

____ **6. SATISFIES ACCOUNTS**
by
providing information; resolving
problems.

____ **7. MAINTAINS QUALITY SERVICE**
by
following organization standards.

____ **8. MAINTAINS TECHNICAL KNOWLEDGE**
by
attending educational workshops;
reviewing publications.

____ **9. CONTRIBUTES TO TEAM EFFORT**
by
accomplishing related results as
needed.

JOB TITLE: ATTORNEY   A022_M

JOB PURPOSE: **RESOLVES LEGAL ISSUES**
by
researching references; initiating and responding to legal actions.

ESSENTIAL JOB RESULTS:

% of
time

_____ **1. DRAFTS CONTRACTS**
by
reviewing, negotiating, and writing initial
conditions.

_____ **2. PREPARES LEGAL POSITIONS**
by
researching transactional matters.

_____ **3. SUPPORTS BUSINESS UNITS**
by
researching and analyzing contractual
matters; identifying potential issues.

_____ **4. SUPPORTS GOVERNMENTAL
AFFAIRS DEPARTMENT**
by
researching regulatory matters.

_____ **5. PRODUCES WRITE-UPS**
by
researching and analyzing laws;
drafting opinions.

_____ **6. RESOLVES LEGAL ISSUES**
by
responding to regulatory and other
inquiries, complaints, and disputes;
negotiating conclusions.

% of
time

_____ **7. MAINTAINS ORGANIZATION'S
STABILITY AND REPUTATION**
by
complying with legal requirements.

_____ **8. MAINTAINS PROFESSIONAL AND
TECHNICAL KNOWLEDGE**
by
attending educational workshops;
reviewing professional publications;
establishing personal networks;
benchmarking state-of-the-art practices;
participating in professional socletles.

_____ **9. CONTRIBUTES TO TEAM EFFORT**
by
accomplishing related results as
needed.

JOB PURPOSE: **TRANSMITS PROGRAMMING**
by
maintaining equipment and controlling broadcasts.

ESSENTIAL JOB RESULTS:

% of
time

____ 1. **ENSURES OPERATION OF EQUIPMENT**
by
completing preventive maintenance requirements; troubleshooting malfunctions; calling for repairs; maintaining equipment inventories; evaluating new equipment; completing tests.

____ 2. **IMPROVES OPERATIONS**
by
developing modifications; recommending new equipment.

____ 3. **OBTAINS UNIFORM AUDIO AND VISUAL SIGNALS**
by
monitoring broadcasts; recording and interpreting readings; making adjustments.

____ 4. **CONTROLS EMISSIONS**
by
tuning transmitter.

____ 5. **MAINTAINS BROADCAST**
by
diagnosing and correcting malfunctions.

% of
time

____ 6. **MAINTAINS QUALITY SERVICE**
by
following station and Federal Communications Commission standards.

____ 7. **COMPLETES REPORTS**
by
entering required information.

____ 8. **MAINTAINS PROFESSIONAL AND TECHNICAL KNOWLEDGE**
by
attending educational workshops; reviewing professional publications; establishing personal networks; benchmarking state-of-the-art practices; participating in professional societies.

____ 9. **CONTRIBUTES TO TEAM EFFORT**
by
accomplishing related results as needed.

JOB TITLE: BUDGET ACCOUNTING CLERK   B035_M

JOB PURPOSE: **SUPPORTS FORECAST, BUDGET, AND PLANNING OPERATIONS**
by
preparing worksheets; maintaining data and models.

ESSENTIAL JOB RESULTS:

% of
time

_____ 1. **PREPARES FORECASTING, BUDGET, AND PLANNING WORKSHEETS**
by
downloading and verifying general ledger account data.

_____ 2. **PROVIDES FINANCIAL DATA TO PLANNING PROCESS USERS**
by
researching general ledger account information.

_____ 3. **MAINTAINS BUDGET AND FORECASTING MODELS**
by
entering and updating data; providing results.

_____ 4. **SUPPORTS COST ANALYSIS**
by
maintaining resource files and financial models.

_____ 5. **PROVIDES HISTORICAL INFORMATION**
by
assembling general ledger account data; documenting processes.

% of
time

_____ 6. **MAINTAINS DATABASE**
by
entering, verifying, and backing up data.

_____ 7. **PROVIDES INFORMATION**
by
answering questions and requests.

_____ 8. **PROTECTS OPERATIONS**
by
keeping financial information confidential.

_____ 9. **MAINTAINS TECHNICAL KNOWLEDGE**
by
attending educational workshops; reviewing publications.

_____ 10. **CONTRIBUTES TO TEAM EFFORT**
by
accomplishing related results as needed.

JOB TITLE: BUDGET ANALYST

B036_M

JOB PURPOSE: **SUPPORTS FINANCIAL DECISION MAKING**
by
assembling, interpreting, analyzing, and reconciling data.

ESSENTIAL JOB RESULTS:

% of
time

____ 1. **IMPLEMENTS FINANCIAL PROJECTION PLANNING AND CONTROL PROCESSES**
by
following time schedules; monitoring deadlines; adhering to policies and procedures.

____ 2. **ASSEMBLES FINANCIAL PROJECTION PLANNING AND CONTROL DATA**
by
collecting, summarizing, and consolidating data; allocating variances.

____ 3. **ASSEMBLES AND INTERPRETS ECONOMIC AND COMPETITIVE DATA**
by
analyzing and interpreting data; making comparative analyses.

____ 4. **RECONCILES FINANCIAL DISCREPANCIES**
by
researching and correcting variance problems.

____ 5. **PROVIDES PLANNING AND CONTROL INFORMATION**
by
assembling and analyzing historical financial data; identifying trends; providing forecasts; explaining processes and techniques; recommending actions.

____ 6. **PRESENTS FINANCIAL PROJECTIONS**
by
explaining data and assumptions.

% of
time

____ 7. **PREPARES SPECIAL REPORTS AND COMPLETES SPECIAL PROJECTS**
by
collecting, analyzing, and summarizing Information and trends.

____ 8. **COMPLIES WITH FEDERAL AND STATE FINANCIAL AND LEGAL REQUIREMENTS**
by
preparing tax returns.

____ 9. **MAINTAINS SYSTEM PERFORMANCE**
by
developing budgeting and reporting systems applications.

____10. **MAINTAINS HISTORICAL RECORDS**
by
entering and verifying data; maintaining and backing up system.

____11. **PROTECTS OPERATIONS**
by
keeping financial information confidential.

____12. **MAINTAINS TECHNICAL KNOWLEDGE**
by
attending educational workshops; reviewing publications.

____13. **CONTRIBUTES TO TEAM EFFORT**
by
accomplishing related results as needed.

JOB TITLE: BUS DRIVER   B041_M

JOB PURPOSE: **TRANSPORTS PASSENGERS**
by
inspecting and driving bus along designated route; helping passengers;
collecting revenue; maintaining safe operations.

ESSENTIAL JOB RESULTS:

% of
time

_____ 1. **ORGANIZES WORK**
by
obtaining route assignment; completing
paperwork; obtaining fare box.

_____ 2. **PREPARES VEHICLE**
by
completing operator inspections;
reporting required repairs.

_____ 3. **PICKS UP AND DISCHARGES
PASSENGERS**
by
following designated route; stopping at
designated locations; announcing
locations; calling in delays; requesting
emergency maintenance; making
operator repairs.

_____ 4. **COLLECTS REVENUE**
by
monitoring and enforcing fares.

_____ 5. **PROVIDES FOR PASSENGER
COMFORT**
by
regulating heating, ventilation, and
lighting systems; enforcing passenger
conduct rules.

% of
time

_____ 6. **HELPS PASSENGERS**
by
providing directions and route
information; providing assistance to
people with disabilities; reporting
accidents; calling for assistance.

_____ 7. **MAINTAINS SAFE CONDITIONS**
by
complying with traffic regulations;
observing traffic conditions; avoiding
dangerous situations; enforcing
passenger safety rules.

_____ 8. **COMPLETES REPORTS**
by
entering required information.

_____ 9. **MAINTAINS TECHNICAL
KNOWLEDGE**
by
attending educational workshops;
reviewing publications.

_____10. **CONTRIBUTES TO TEAM EFFORT**
by
accomplishing related results as
needed.

JOB PURPOSE: **ACCOMPLISHES SALES AND MARKETING OBJECTIVES**
by
determining process requirements; training customers to use processes.

ESSENTIAL JOB RESULTS:

% of
time

% of
time

_____ 1. **IDENTIFIES PROJECT REQUIREMENTS**
by
interviewing customers; analyzing processes; determining process objectives; documenting results.

_____ 2. **DEVELOPS PROJECT ESTIMATES**
by
determining project phases, hardware, software, and personnel requirements.

_____ 3. **SOLVES PROBLEMS**
by
developing detailed problem definition; describing requirements in process maps; analyzing alternative solutions; recommending plan of action.

_____ 4. **VERIFIES RESULTS**
by
developing pilots and tests.

_____ 5. **PREPARES CUSTOMERS TO USE PROCESSES**
by
conducting orientation workshops and seminars; coordinating development, training needs, and communication requirements for sales and marketing staff; coordinating hardware and software requirements, training services, and information systems.

_____ 6. **PROVIDES REFERENCES FOR CUSTOMERS**
by
writing documentation; ensuring use of consistent messages and terminology in internal communications and promotional campaigns, publications, and presentations; providing support and help.

_____ 7. **MAINTAINS PROCESSES**
by
researching and resolving problems.

_____ 8. **PREPARES REPORTS**
by
collecting, analyzing, and summarizing information.

_____ 9. **MAINTAINS QUALITY SERVICE**
by
following organization standards.

_____ 10. **MAINTAINS PROFESSIONAL AND TECHNICAL KNOWLEDGE**
by
attending educational workshops; reviewing professional publications; establishing personal networks; benchmarking state-of-the-art practices; participating in professional societies.

_____ 11. **CONTRIBUTES TO TEAM EFFORT**
by
accomplishing related results as needed.

JOB PURPOSE: SOLVES ORGANIZATIONAL INFORMATION PROBLEMS AND REQUIREMENTS
by
analyzing requirements; designing computer programs; recommending system controls and protocols.

ESSENTIAL JOB RESULTS:

% of
time

% of
time

____ 1. **DETERMINES OPERATIONAL OBJECTIVES**
by
studying business functions; gathering information; evaluating output requirements and formats.

____ 2. **DESIGNS NEW COMPUTER PROGRAMS**
by
analyzing requirements; constructing workflow charts and diagrams; studying system capabilities; writing specifications.

____ 3. **IMPROVES SYSTEMS**
by
studying current practices; designing modifications.

____ 4. **RECOMMENDS CONTROLS**
by
identifying problems; writing improved procedures.

____ 5. **DEFINES PROJECT REQUIREMENTS**
by
identifying project milestones, phases, and elements; forming project team; establishing project budget.

____ 6. **MONITORS PROJECT PROGRESS**
by
tracking activity; resolving problems; publishing progress reports; recommending actions.

____ 7. **MAINTAINS SYSTEM PROTOCOLS**
by
writing and updating procedures.

____ 8. **PROVIDES REFERENCES FOR USERS**
by
writing and maintaining user documentation; providing help desk support; training users.

____ 9. **MAINTAINS USER CONFIDENCE AND PROTECTS OPERATIONS**
by
keeping information confidential.

____ 10. **PREPARES TECHNICAL REPORTS**
by
collecting, analyzing, and summarizing information and trends.

____ 11. **MAINTAINS PROFESSIONAL AND TECHNICAL KNOWLEDGE**
by
attending educational workshops; reviewing professional publications; establishing personal networks; benchmarking state-of-the-art practices; participating in professional societies.

____ 12. **CONTRIBUTES TO TEAM EFFORT**
by
accomplishing related results as needed.

JOB TITLE:	CABLE SUPERVISOR	C046_M

JOB PURPOSE: **MAINTAINS SERVICE**
by
supervising staff; installing and maintaining cable.

ESSENTIAL JOB RESULTS:

% of
time

% of
time

_____ 1. **MAINTAINS CABLE STAFF**
by
selecting, orienting, and training
employees; developing personal growth
opportunities.

_____ 2. **ACCOMPLISHES STAFF RESULTS**
by
communicating job expectations;
planning, monitoring, and appraising
job results; coaching, counseling, and
disciplining employees.

_____ 3. **PREPARES FOR INSTALLATION**
by
studying construction plans and
drawings; verifying compatibility with
existing equipment; assembling
materials, supplies, and crew.

_____ 4. **LOCATES CONSTRUCTION SITE**
by
studying maps and surveys.

_____ 5. **PREPARES CONSTRUCTION SITE**
by
excavating location.

_____ 6. **MAINTAINS SAFE AND HEALTHY
WORKING ENVIRONMENT**
by
following organization standards and
legal regulations.

_____ 7. **COMPLETES INSTALLATION**
by
supervising work; enforcing adherence
to standards; documenting actions.

_____ 8. **COMPLETES MAINTENANCE**
by
locating and solving problems.

_____ 9. **ENSURES OPERATION OF
EQUIPMENT**
by
completing preventive maintenance
requirements; following manufacturer's
instructions; troubleshooting
malfunctions; calling for repairs;
maintaining equipment inventories;
evaluating new equipment and
techniques.

_____10. **MAINTAINS SUPPLIES INVENTORY**
by
checking stock; anticipating needs;
placing and expediting orders; verifying
receipt.

_____11. **COMPLETES REPORTS**
by
entering required information.

_____12. **ACCOMPLISHES FINANCIAL
OBJECTIVES**
by
forecasting requirements; monitoring
costs.

_____13. **MAINTAINS TECHNICAL
KNOWLEDGE**
by
attending educational workshops;
reviewing publications.

_____14. **CONTRIBUTES TO TEAM EFFORT**
by
accomplishing related results as
needed.

JOB PURPOSE: **PRODUCES PROGRAMS**
by
supervising staff; producing and directing programs.

ESSENTIAL JOB RESULTS:

% of
time

____ 1. **MAINTAINS PROGRAM STAFF**
by
recruiting, selecting, orienting, and
training employees.

____ 2. **ACCOMPLISHES STAFF RESULTS**
by
communicating job expectations;
planning, monitoring, and appraising
job results; coaching, counseling, and
disciplining employees.

____ 3. **PREPARES BROADCAST PLAN**
by
identifying programming, set, and talent
requirements.

____ 4. **HIRES TALENT**
by
contacting agencies; interviewing
applicants; assessing skills.

____ 5. **PRODUCES PROGRAM**
by
developing script; conducting
rehearsals; directing talent; directing
use of recording and mixing equipment;
editing tapes.

____ 6. **ACCOMPLISHES FINANCIAL
OBJECTIVES**
by
forecasting requirements; preparing a
program budget; scheduling
expenditures; analyzing variances;
initiating corrective action.

% of
time

____ 7. **BROADCASTS PROGRAM**
by
operating transmitting equipment.

____ 8. **PREPARES REPORTS**
by
collecting, analyzing, and summarizing
information.

____ 9. **BUILDS COMMUNITY RAPPORT**
by
surveying interests; providing
information.

____10. **MAINTAINS PROFESSIONAL AND
TECHNICAL KNOWLEDGE**
by
attending educational workshops;
reviewing professional publications;
establishing personal networks;
benchmarking state-of-the-art practices;
participating in professional societies.

____11. **CONTRIBUTES TO TEAM EFFORT**
by
accomplishing related results as
needed.

JOB TITLE: CASH MANAGER   C052_M

JOB PURPOSE: **CONTROLS CASH**
by
analyzing requirements; investing surplus cash; developing loan strategies.

ESSENTIAL JOB RESULTS:

% of
time

____ 1. **FORECASTS CASH POSITION AND CASH REQUIREMENTS**
by
analyzing financial records and budget requirements.

____ 2. **DEVELOPS INVESTMENT AND LOAN STRATEGIES**
by
evaluating need for procurement of funds and investment of surplus.

____ 3. **INVESTS SURPLUS CASH**
by
understanding company risk parameters; analyzing risks of alternative investments; placing investments.

____ 4. **CONVERTS SURPLUS REAL ESTATE TO CASH**
by
monitoring changing property requirements and market conditions.

____ 5. **ACCELERATES INFLOW OF CASH FROM OPERATIONS**
by
defining new systems and procedures.

____ 6. **LIMITS CREDIT LOSSES**
by
developing credit policies and procedures; approving credit; setting credit guidelines; monitoring and analyzing customer creditworthiness.

% of
time

____ 7. **MAINTAINS DATABASE**
by
entering, verifying, and backing up data.

____ 8. **PREPARES SPECIAL REPORTS AND COMPLETES SPECIAL PROJECTS**
by
collecting, analyzing, and summarizing information.

____ 9. **PROTECTS OPERATIONS**
by
keeping financial information confidential.

____10. **MAINTAINS PROFESSIONAL AND TECHNICAL KNOWLEDGE**
by
attending educational workshops; reviewing professional publications; establishing personal networks; benchmarking state-of-the-art practices; participating in professional societies.

____11. **CONTRIBUTES TO TEAM EFFORT**
by
accomplishing related results as needed.

JOB TITLE:	CHAPLAIN	C055_M

JOB PURPOSE: PROVIDES SPIRITUAL GUIDANCE
by
conducting religious ceremonies; counseling and comforting clients.

ESSENTIAL JOB RESULTS:

% of
time

% of
time

____ 1. **PREPARES RELIGIOUS MESSAGES AND LESSONS**
by
studying church teachings and pronouncements; writing sermons.

____ 2. **CONDUCTS RELIGIOUS CEREMONIES**
by
leading participants; performing rites.

____ 3. **EDUCATES MEMBERS AND CONVERTS**
by
presenting and explaining doctrine; evaluating learning and application.

____ 4. **COUNSELS CLIENTS**
by
identifying concerns; identifying and evaluating moral and ethical options; explaining doctrine; guiding clients' decision making; recommending a course of action.

____ 5. **COMFORTS CLIENTS**
by
offering condolences and support; building and arranging for support.

____ 6. **PROSELYTIZES POTENTIAL CONVERTS**
by
explaining religious values; overcoming objections.

____ 7. **MAINTAINS DOCTRINAL KNOWLEDGE**
by
attending educational workshops; reading the writings of spiritual leaders; establishing religious community networks; exploring the religious beliefs of others.

____ 8. **RENEWS SPIRITUALITY**
by
attending retreats; examining inner peace and strength.

| JOB TITLE: | CHIEF EXECUTIVE OFFICER | C058_M |

JOB PURPOSE: **MAXIMIZES PROFIT AND RETURN ON INVESTED CAPITAL**
by
accomplishing objectives; serving customers; maintaining the company's
stability; ensuring growth.

ESSENTIAL JOB RESULTS:

% of
time

% of
time

____ 1. **ESTABLISHES AND ACCOMPLISHES ENTERPRISE OBJECTIVES**
by
researching opportunities and problems; recommending strategies to the board of directors; inaugurating programs and processes; meeting financial requirements; evaluating and reporting results.

____ 2. **ORGANIZES THE BUSINESS**
by
selecting and developing key executives and successors; assigning accountabilities; setting objectives and establishing priorities; integrating corporate efforts; monitoring and evaluating results; providing resources; developing strategic partnerships.

____ 3. **SERVES CUSTOMERS**
by
establishing critical service, operations, and productivity criteria; maintaining state-of-the-art technology; benchmarking leading-edge practices; exploiting market channels; leading commitment to quality service; evaluating service results; representing the company to major customers.

____ 4. **CREATES UNDERSTANDING AND POSITIVE IMAGE OF THE COMPANY**
by
building relationships with, and providing information to, the financial community, media, government, and the public; building credibility with shareholders; building employee commitment to the company communities.

____ 5. **MAINTAINS COMPANY STABILITY AND REPUTATION**
by
establishing and communicating a corporate value system; enforcing ethical business practices; complying with, or influencing the development of, laws and regulations.

____ 6. **MAINTAINS PROFESSIONAL KNOWLEDGE**
by
attending educational workshops; reviewing professional publications; establishing personal networks; benchmarking state-of-the-art practices.

____ 7. **CONTRIBUTES TO CORPORATE EFFORT**
by
accomplishing related results as needed.

JOB TITLE:	CHILD CARE AIDE	C059_M

JOB PURPOSE: **NURTURES CHILDREN**
by
providing child care development opportunities.

ESSENTIAL JOB RESULTS:

% of
time

% of
time

____ 1. **ENCOURAGES CHILDREN'S PARTICIPATION**
by
initiating and demonstrating interactive activities.

____ 2. **PROVIDES CHILD CARE**
by
changing diapers; serving snacks and meals; cleaning classroom.

____ 3. **ENCOURAGES DEVELOPMENT OF CHILDREN'S SELF-CONTROL**
by
utilizing classroom management and modeling techniques.

____ 4. **PROVIDES INFORMATION**
by
relaying messages from parents; reporting observed behavioral, health, or developmental changes in children to teacher.

____ 5. **ACHIEVES WORK OBJECTIVES**
by
following child care schedules and procedures.

____ 6. **ENSURES CONTINUOUS CARE OF CHILDREN**
by
assuming responsibility when supervisor is absent.

____ 7. **PROTECTS FAMILIES**
by
keeping personal information confidential.

____ 8. **MAINTAINS TECHNICAL KNOWLEDGE**
by
attending educational workshops; reviewing publications.

____ 9. **CONTRIBUTES TO TEAM EFFORT**
by
accomplishing related results as needed.

JOB TITLE:	CHILD CARE TEACHER	C060_M

JOB PURPOSE: **NURTURES CHILDREN**
by
developing and providing educational programs; keeping parents informed.

ESSENTIAL JOB RESULTS:

% of
time

% of
time

_____ 1. **STIMULATES EMOTIONAL, INTELLECTUAL, AND SOCIAL GROWTH OF CHILDREN**
by
developing and directing educational programs and activities tailored to assigned class.

_____ 2. **PROVIDES SAFE ENVIRONMENT**
by
maintaining orderly, clean, and appealing facilities; removing known safety hazards.

_____ 3. **ENCOURAGES CHILDREN'S PARTICIPATION**
by
providing interactive activities.

_____ 4. **INFORMS STAFF AND PARENTS OF CURRICULUM**
by
preparing and submitting lesson plans; posting schedules and curriculum outlines.

_____ 5. **KEEPS PARENTS INFORMED**
by
posting parent information in the classroom; maintaining and sharing records of child's progress, attendance, and behavior.

_____ 6. **ENCOURAGES DEVELOPMENT OF CHILDREN'S SELF-CONTROL**
by
utilizing classroom management and modeling techniques.

_____ 7. **MAINTAINS CENTER'S PROFESSIONAL STATUS**
by
supervising, training, and evaluating staff and/or field experience students.

_____ 8. **ENCOURAGES CONSISTENCY OF SERVICE**
by
maintaining communications with parents and staff.

_____ 9. **PROTECTS FAMILIES**
by
keeping personal information confidential.

_____10. **MAINTAINS PROFESSIONAL AND TECHNICAL KNOWLEDGE**
by
attending educational workshops; reviewing professional publications; establishing personal networks; benchmarking state-of-the-art practices; participating in professional societies.

_____11. **CONTRIBUTES TO TEAM EFFORT**
by
accomplishing related results as needed.

JOB PURPOSE: **OPTIMIZES CHILD DEVELOPMENT**
by
providing information and coping methods to minimize the stress of
hospitalization.

ESSENTIAL JOB RESULTS:

% of
time

% of
time

____ 1. **DEVELOPS INDIVIDUAL TREATMENT PLANS**
by
assessing children's development, temperament, coping style, medical plan, and available support services.

____ 2. **PREPARES CHILDREN AND FAMILIES FOR THE HEALTH CARE EXPERIENCE**
by
providing preparation and coping methods for diagnostic and treatment procedures; providing information regarding the impact of the health care experience; minimizing psychological trauma; helping children and families maintain normal routines; minimizing the stress of hospitalization.

____ 3. **INTEGRATES THE CHILD LIFE PROGRAM INTO THE HEALTH CARE TEAM ACTIONS**
by
consulting with the health care team regarding individual needs of children.

____ 4. **PROVIDES INTERDISCIPLINARY TRAINING**
by
identifying training requirements; presenting information on the impact of illness, injury, and hospitalization on children and families; coaching students.

____ 5. **PROMOTES APPEALING AND HELPFUL ENVIRONMENT**
by
identifying and explaining the impact of environmental designs and layouts on child behavior.

____ 6. **MAINTAINS PROFESSIONALISM OF CHILD LIFE**
by
practicing according to the Code of Ethical Responsibility and the Child Life Competencies.

____ 7. **MAINTAINS PROFESSIONAL AND TECHNICAL KNOWLEDGE**
by
attending educational workshops; reviewing professional publications; establishing personal networks; benchmarking state-of-the-art practices; participating in professional societies.

____ 8. **CONTRIBUTES TO TEAM EFFORT**
by
accomplishing related results as needed.

JOB PURPOSE: **PROVIDES FOR THE COMMON GOOD**
by
resolving community issues; determining legal requirements.

ESSENTIAL JOB RESULTS:

% of
time

% of
time

_____ 1. **IDENTIFIES ISSUES**
by
meeting with citizens and special
interest groups; studying opinions and
background information.

_____ 2. **CLARIFIES ISSUES**
by
serving on committees; conducting
hearings; examining opposing
positions; investigating inconsistencies.

_____ 3. **DEVELOPS ORDINANCES, RULES,
AND REGULATIONS**
by
conferring with other trustees;
researching precedents and solutions
from other legislative bodies; drafting
proposals.

_____ 4. **ARGUES POSITIONS**
by
describing advantages of proposal;
warning of implications.

_____ 5. **VOTES ON ISSUES**
by
considering arguments; attending
committee hearings and board
sessions.

_____ 6. **SUPPORTS CITIZENS**
by
intervening on their behalf; expediting
actions; arranging contacts; speaking to
groups.

_____ 7. **PROVIDES COMMUNITY SERVICES**
by
determining service objectives,
priorities, and strategies to achieve
objectives and priorities; approving
policies; allocating funds; evaluating
results.

_____ 8. **MAINTAINS FINANCIAL STABILITY**
by
funding programs and projects;
analyzing expenditures; initiating
corrective action; levying taxes and
fees.

_____ 9. **NOMINATES CANDIDATES FOR
APPOINTMENT**
by
studying qualifications.

_____10. **MAINTAINS STAFF**
by
recruiting, selecting, orienting, training,
coaching, counseling, and disciplining a
city/county manager and a board
attorney; communicating manager's
and attorney's job expectations;
planning, monitoring, and appraising
manager's and attorney's job results;
approving systems, policies, and
procedures.

_____11. **MAINTAINS PROFESSIONAL
KNOWLEDGE**
by
attending educational workshops;
reviewing professional publications;
establishing personal networks.

_____12. **CONTRIBUTES TO TEAM EFFORT**
by
accomplishing related results as
needed.

JOB PURPOSE: **SERVES CITIZENS**
by
enforcing requirements; providing professional engineering services.

ESSENTIAL JOB RESULTS:

% of
time

_____ 1. **ENFORCES CODES AND REGULATIONS**
by
approving construction plans, site development, storm drainage, and parking; inspecting projects; conferring with construction managers; stopping illegal and nonconforming work.

_____ 2. **TREATS SOLID WASTES**
by
maintaining and modifying treatment equipment and processes; establishing and reviewing testing procedures.

_____ 3. **CONTROLS TRAFFIC FLOW**
by
analyzing and improving traffic patterns; anticipating changes in traffic flow; approving new housing and office developments.

_____ 4. **SUPPORTS PLANNING COMMISSION DECISION MAKING**
by
providing information and recommendations; conferring with contractors, architects, and engineers; reviewing cost estimates.

% of
time

_____ 5. **PREPARES REPORTS**
by
collecting, analyzing, interpreting, and presenting information.

_____ 6. **MAINTAINS QUALITY SERVICE**
by
establishing and enforcing organization standards.

_____ 7. **MAINTAINS PROFESSIONAL AND TECHNICAL KNOWLEDGE**
by
attending educational workshops; reviewing professional publications; establishing personal networks; benchmarking state-of-the-art practices; participating in professional societies.

_____ 8. **CONTRIBUTES TO TEAM EFFORT**
by
accomplishing related results as needed.

JOB TITLE: CLAIMS EXAMINER	C067_M

JOB PURPOSE: **SERVES CUSTOMERS**
by
resolving claims; ensuring legal compliance.

ESSENTIAL JOB RESULTS:

% of
time

% of
time

____ 1. **DETERMINES COVERED LOSS**
by
studying provisions of policy or
certificate.

____ 2. **ESTABLISHES PROOF OF LOSS**
by
studying documentation submitted;
assembling additional information as
required from outside sources such as
account, claimant, physician, employer,
hospital, and other insurance
companies; initiating or conducting
investigation of questionable claims.

____ 3. **RESOLVES CLAIM UP TO
SPECIFIED LIMIT**
by
approving or denying documentation;
calculating benefit due; initiating
payment or composing denial letter.

____ 4. **ENSURES LEGAL COMPLIANCE**
by
following guidelines, account contract,
business plan, and state and federal
insurance regulations.

____ 5. **MAINTAINS QUALITY FINANCIAL
CLAIMS SERVICE**
by
following corporate customer service
practices.

____ 6. **PROVIDES LEGAL SUPPORT**
by
assembling documentation for
determining settlement action.

____ 7. **SUPPORTS CUSTOMER SERVICE**
by
responding to inquiries.

____ 8. **MAINTAINS QUALITY SERVICE**
by
following organization standards.

____ 9. **PROTECTS OPERATIONS**
by
keeping claims information confidential.

____10. **PREPARES REPORTS**
by
collecting, analyzing, and summarizing
information.

____11. **MAINTAINS TECHNICAL
KNOWLEDGE**
by
attending educational workshops;
reviewing publications.

____12. **CONTRIBUTES TO TEAM EFFORT**
by
accomplishing related results as
needed.

JOB TITLE: CLAIMS INVESTIGATOR

C068_M

JOB PURPOSE: PROTECTS ASSETS
by
investigating claims; preventing losses.

ESSENTIAL JOB RESULTS:

% of
time

% of
time

____ **1. EVALUATES DOCUMENTS**
by
reviewing documents provided;
highlighting items pertinent to claim or
underwriting decision.

____ **2. VERIFIES CLAIMANT INFORMATION**
by
conducting telephone interviews.

____ **3. GATHERS RECORDS AND EXPERT INFORMATION**
by
contacting and interviewing medical
providers, employers, law
enforcement agencies, and medical
examiners.

____ **4. COMPLETES INVESTIGATION**
by
following up on leads; updating claim
system regarding status of
investigations; completing random
activity checks on disability claimants
by telephone.

____ **5. PROTECTS OPERATIONS**
by
complying with legal requirements;
keeping investigative information
confidential.

____ **6. MAINTAINS QUALITY SERVICE**
by
following organization standards.

____ **7. PREPARES REPORTS**
by
collecting, analyzing, and summarizing
information.

____ **8. MAINTAINS TECHNICAL KNOWLEDGE**
by
attending educational workshops;
reviewing publications.

____ **9. CONTRIBUTES TO TEAM EFFORT**
by
accomplishing related results as
needed.

JOB TITLE: CLAIMS MANAGER	C069_M

JOB PURPOSE: ACCOMPLISHES CLAIMS SUPPORT OBJECTIVES
by
managing staff; providing claims processing and administrative support.

ESSENTIAL JOB RESULTS:

% of
time

% of
time

____ 1. **MAINTAINS CLAIMS SUPPORT OPERATIONS STAFF**
by
recruiting, selecting, orienting, and training employees.

____ 2. **ACCOMPLISHES STAFF JOB RESULTS**
by
coaching, counseling, and disciplining employees; planning, monitoring, and appraising job results.

____ 3. **ACCOMPLISHES BUSINESS OBJECTIVES**
by
gathering information and making recommendations for the business plan; preparing for and conducting quarterly reviews; completing action plans and assignments.

____ 4. **ACHIEVES FINANCIAL OBJECTIVES**
by
forecasting functional requirements; preparing annual budgets; scheduling expenditures; analyzing variances; initiating corrective actions; providing information for profit control meetings.

____ 5. **PROVIDES QUALITY SERVICE**
by
enforcing claims support quality and customer service standards; analyzing quality and customer service problems; initiating audits; identifying trends; recommending system improvements.

____ 6. **COMPLETES CLAIMS SUPPORT OPERATIONS**
by
managing claims support process; evaluating work results; enforcing claims support productivity standards; analyzing production problems; initiating audits; identifying trends; identifying new technology; maintaining confidentiality systems and controls.

____ 7. **MAINTAINS ACCOUNTS**
by
managing the transfer of money between agency codes, product, and company.

____ 8. **COMPLIES WITH INTERNAL REVENUE SERVICE REGULATIONS**
by
managing completion of 1099s.

____ 9. **SUPPORTS MARKETS/SALES CENTERS**
by
developing new accounts; maintaining relationships with existing accounts.

____ 10. **SUPPORTS SUBSIDIARIES AND ACCOUNTS**
by
providing reconciliation and claim processing resources.

ESSENTIAL JOB RESULTS:

% of
time

% of
time

____11. **MAINTAINS PROFESSIONAL AND TECHNICAL KNOWLEDGE**
by
attending educational workshops;
reviewing professional publications;
establishing personal networks;
benchmarking state-of-the-art practices;
participating in professional societies.

____12. **CONTRIBUTES TO TEAM EFFORT**
by
accomplishing related results as
needed.

JOB TITLE:	CLAIMS SPECIALIST	C070_M

JOB PURPOSE: **SUPPORTS CLAIMS OPERATIONS AND SERVICE**
by
training staff; auditing and improving processes.

ESSENTIAL JOB RESULTS:

% of
time

____ 1. **PREPARES STAFF TO COMPLETE CLAIMS PROCESSING**
by
designing and conducting financial claims adjudication training programs.

____ 2. **ENSURES CONFORMANCE TO GUIDELINES**
by
conducting off-site and home office audits.

____ 3. **IMPROVES OPERATIONS**
by
conducting process engineering studies; analyzing results of training and audits; recommending changes.

____ 4. **KEEPS MANAGEMENT INFORMED**
by
preparing and presenting reports.

% of
time

____ 5. **MAINTAINS QUALITY SERVICE**
by
establishing and enforcing organization standards.

____ 6. **PROTECTS OPERATIONS**
by
keeping claims information confidential.

____ 7. **MAINTAINS PROFESSIONAL AND TECHNICAL KNOWLEDGE**
by
attending educational workshops; reviewing professional publications; establishing personal networks; benchmarking state-of-the-art practices; participating in professional societies.

____ 8. **CONTRIBUTES TO TEAM EFFORT**
by
accomplishing related results as needed.

JOB TITLE:	CLAIMS SUPPORT SPECIALIST	C071_M

JOB PURPOSE: **MAINTAINS FINANCIAL CLAIMS SYSTEM**
by
designing systems; training processors.

ESSENTIAL JOB RESULTS:

% of
time

% of
time

_____ 1. **IDENTIFIES SYSTEM REQUIREMENTS**
by
interviewing users regarding setup, processing, and payment of claims; analyzing operations; preparing problem definition.

_____ 2. **DEVELOPS PROBLEM SOLUTION**
by
describing requirements in a workflow chart and diagram; studying system capabilities; analyzing alternative solutions; implementing special system needs.

_____ 3. **VERIFIES RESULTS**
by
completing tests; monitoring security.

_____ 4. **PREPARES USERS TO USE SYSTEM**
by
conducting training.

_____ 5. **MAINTAINS WORK FLOW**
by
providing system support including call center applications, sign-ons, and coordination of work requests.

_____ 6. **COMPLETES SYSTEM RESTRUCTURES**
by
coordinating information and requirements with information systems department.

_____ 7. **KEEPS MANAGEMENT INFORMED**
by
analyzing information; preparing reports.

_____ 8. **MAINTAINS QUALITY SERVICE**
by
following organization standards.

_____ 9. **MAINTAINS PROFESSIONAL AND TECHNICAL KNOWLEDGE**
by
attending educational workshops; reviewing professional publications; establishing personal networks; benchmarking state-of-the-art practices; participating in professional societies.

_____10. **CONTRIBUTES TO TEAM EFFORT**
by
accomplishing related results as needed.

JOB PURPOSE: **SERVES CUSTOMERS**
by
guiding clients to accomplish profit goals.

ESSENTIAL JOB RESULTS:

% of
time

____ 1. **IMPLEMENTS CLIENT-SPECIFIC BUSINESS PLANS**
by
establishing and developing plans with sales representatives; managing strategic and action plans with internal resources; analyzing profit and loss statements for trends; coordinating production, sales, and related business activities.

____ 2. **PROVIDES CLIENT SERVICES**
by
researching and documenting issues and problems; forwarding necessary actions; leading client service team; providing response to client; guiding internal resources; measuring and ensuring results.

____ 3. **SUPPORTS MARKETING OBJECTIVES**
by
developing standard marketing and installation plans for use in sales call packages; obtaining approvals from functional areas; adhering to timelines.

____ 4. **FINALIZES CONTRACT APPROVAL**
by
preparing business deal recapitulations; drafting contracts; obtaining approvals; verifying understandings among parties; monitoring status and quality.

% of
time

____ 5. **RESOLVES AND PREVENTS CONTRACT PROBLEMS**
by
researching and documenting issues and problems; forwarding necessary actions; leading client service team; providing response to client.

____ 6. **MAINTAINS CLIENT DATA INTEGRITY**
by
determining marketing and installation plans; reconciling pricing sheet expenses to services outlined in contract; controlling quality of data from sales through contracting set-up process; communicating data to and obtaining support and approvals from functional areas.

____ 7. **MAINTAINS PROFESSIONAL AND TECHNICAL KNOWLEDGE**
by
attending educational workshops; reviewing professional publications; establishing personal networks; benchmarking state-of-the-art practices; participating in professional societies.

____ 8. **CONTRIBUTES TO TEAM EFFORT**
by
accomplishing related results as needed.

JOB TITLE:	CLUB HOST/HOSTESS	C077_M

JOB PURPOSE: **SERVES MEMBERS AND GUESTS**
by
providing welcome, information, entertainment, and activities.

ESSENTIAL JOB RESULTS:

% of
time

% of
time

____ 1. **WELCOMES MEMBERS AND GUESTS**
by
greeting them; verifying membership; making introductions.

____ 2. **PROVIDES INFORMATION**
by
answering questions; providing directions.

____ 3. **PROVIDES FOR MEMBERS' AND GUESTS' PLEASURE**
by
suggesting entertainment and activities; obtaining refreshments.

____ 4. **FULFILLS SPECIAL REQUESTS**
by
securing accommodations; establishing itineraries; obtaining tickets; storing luggage; renting vehicles; running errands; placing communications; fulfilling similar requirements.

____ 5. **MAINTAINS QUALITY SERVICE**
by
following club standards.

____ 6. **MAINTAINS SAFE AND HEALTHY CLUB ENVIRONMENT**
by
enforcing club standards and legal regulations.

____ 7. **OBTAINS REVENUES**
by
recording fees and charges.

____ 8. **SELLS MEMBERSHIPS**
by
explaining advantages and requirements; providing applications; accepting fees.

____ 9. **MAINTAINS TECHNICAL KNOWLEDGE**
by
attending educational workshops; reviewing publications.

____10. **CONTRIBUTES TO TEAM EFFORT**
by
accomplishing related results as needed.

JOB TITLE: COMPLIANCE ANALYST   C086_M

JOB PURPOSE: **MAINTAINS LEGAL AND REGULATORY COMPLIANCE**
by
researching and communicating requirements; obtaining approvals.

ESSENTIAL JOB RESULTS:

% of
time

_____ **1. RESEARCHES REGULATIONS**
by
reviewing regulatory bulletins and other
sources of information.

_____ **2. COMPILES INFORMATION**
by
coordinating rate deviation filings;
maintaining updated rate matrices;
providing overviews of product
disclosures.

_____ **3. KEEPS OTHER DEPARTMENTS
ABREAST OF REQUIREMENTS**
by
researching regulatory and filing
information; writing and communicating
guidelines.

_____ **4. OBTAINS APPROVALS**
by
revising forms and rates.

_____ **5. PREPARES REPORTS**
by
collecting, analyzing, and summarizing
information.

% of
time

_____ **6. MAINTAINS RAPPORT WITH
REGULATORY PERSONNEL**
by
arranging continuing contacts; resolving
concerns.

_____ **7. MAINTAINS QUALITY SERVICE**
by
establishing and enforcing organization
standards.

_____ **8. MAINTAINS PROFESSIONAL AND
TECHNICAL KNOWLEDGE**
by
attending educational workshops;
reviewing professional publications;
establishing personal networks;
benchmarking state-of-the-art practices;
participating in professional societies.

_____ **9. CONTRIBUTES TO TEAM EFFORT**
by
accomplishing related results as
needed.

<table>
<tr><td colspan="2">JOB TITLE: COMPUTER-AIDED DESIGN (CAD) ASSISTANT</td><td>C090_M</td></tr>
</table>

JOB PURPOSE: **MAINTAINS PLANT RECORDS**
by
operating software; updating information.

ESSENTIAL JOB RESULTS:

% of
time

% of
time

____ 1. **MAINTAINS GRAPHICS**
by
analyzing field engineering sketches, specifications, and supporting documents; updating and creating drawings upon completion of projects; maintaining a layout of the graphics system, components, and parts; ensuring accuracy, legibility, uniformity, and quality standards of graphics system information.

____ 2. **UPDATES DATABASE**
by
entering new and modifying old data in microcomputer.

____ 3. **PREPARES AND DISTRIBUTES PROPERTY RECORDS REPORTS**
by
running property records programs on microcomputer; creating hard copies of reports; verifying and reviewing information in conjunction with field engineers and accountants; meeting deadlines; distributing reports to personnel and departments.

____ 4. **VERIFIES PROPERTY RECORDS REPORTS**
by
analyzing and summarizing information in conjunction with field engineers and construction supervisor.

____ 5. **DISTRIBUTES HARD COPIES OF MAP INFORMATION**
by
operating plotter and engineering copier to generate paper copies; furnishing paper copies to field personnel.

____ 6. **RESOLVES DISCREPANCIES IN PLANT RECORDS**
by
collecting and analyzing information; conferring with field engineers and construction supervisor.

____ 7. **CONTRIBUTES TO RECORD KEEPING EFFECTIVENESS**
by
identifying issues that must be addressed; providing information and commentary relevant to operations; recommending options and courses of action.

____ 8. **PROTECTS GRAPHICS AND DATABASE**
by
running backups on microcomputer; storing backups.

____ 9. **MAINTAINS PLOTTER SUPPLIES INVENTORY**
by
checking plotter stock to determine inventory level; anticipating needed supplies; placing and expediting orders for supplies; verifying receipt of supplies.

____ 10. **PROVIDES INFORMATION**
by
answering questions and requests.

ESSENTIAL JOB RESULTS:

% of
time

____11. **MAINTAINS TECHNICAL KNOWLEDGE**
by
attending educational workshops;
reviewing publications.

% of
time

____12. **CONTRIBUTES TO TEAM EFFORT**
by
accomplishing related results as
needed.

JOB TITLE: CONSTRUCTION MANAGER   C092_M

JOB PURPOSE: **SATISFIES HOMEOWNERS**
by
managing staff; building quality homes; pleasing customers; generating profits.

ESSENTIAL JOB RESULTS:

% of
time

% of
time

____ 1. MAINTAINS CONSTRUCTION STAFF
by
recruiting, selecting, orienting, and training employees; maintaining a safe and secure work environment; developing personal growth opportunities.

____ 2. ACCOMPLISHES STAFF RESULTS
by
organizing and coordinating staff; communicating job expectations; planning, monitoring, and appraising job results; coaching, counseling, and disciplining employees; initiating, coordinating, and enforcing systems, policies, and procedures.

____ 3. PLANS CONSTRUCTION REQUIREMENTS
by
deploying company resources; resolving land development issues; planning, monitoring, and appraising critical path results; coordinating information and requirements with the sales manager.

____ 4. MEETS CONSTRUCTION SCHEDULE
by
hiring, orienting, and coaching subcontractors; verifying work in progress; resolving problems; reporting progress.

____ 5. ACHIEVES FINANCIAL OBJECTIVES
by
negotiating subcontractor rates; meeting profit projections; anticipating requirements, submitting information for budget preparation; scheduling expenditures; monitoring costs; analyzing variances; reviewing and approving invoices; recommending revision of estimates.

____ 6. FULFILLS CONTRACT REQUIREMENTS
by
completing pre-construction, pre-drywall, and pre-closing inspections; completing adjustments and corrections.

____ 7. COMPLIES WITH LEGAL AND COMPANY REQUIREMENTS
by
enforcing building codes; following company systems, policies, and procedures; maintaining safe and healthy work practices; monitoring inspections.

____ 8. IMPROVES SERVICE RESULTS
by
evaluating system results; recommending new systems, policies, and procedures; recommending revisions in home plans.

ESSENTIAL JOB RESULTS:

% of
time

% of
time

_____ 9. **MAINTAINS CONTINUITY AMONG CORPORATE, DIVISION, AND LOCAL WORK TEAMS**
by
documenting and communicating actions, irregularities, and continuing needs.

_____10. **MAINTAINS PROFESSIONAL AND TECHNICAL KNOWLEDGE**
by
attending educational workshops; benchmarking professional standards; reviewing professional publications; establishing personal networks.

_____11. **CONTRIBUTES TO TEAM EFFORT**
by
accomplishing related results as needed.

JOB PURPOSE: **SUPPORTS CONSTRUCTION OPERATIONS**
by
assembling, tracking, producing, and forwarding information.

ESSENTIAL JOB RESULTS:

% of
time

% of
time

_____ 1. **PREPARES WORK TO BE ACCOMPLISHED**
by
gathering information and requirements; setting priorities.

_____ 2. **OBTAINS BUILDING PERMITS**
by
completing applications; assembling required plans and information; monitoring critical path of issuance; reporting status; requesting fee checks.

_____ 3. **INITIATES TRACKING OF JOBS**
by
assigning purchase order numbers.

_____ 4. **MAINTAINS PERMIT RECORDS**
by
filing and updating information.

_____ 5. **COMPLETES CRITICAL PATH PROJECTION REPORT**
by
entering and updating data; obtaining approvals; printing and distributing.

_____ 6. **COMPLETES PLAN AND SUBCONTRACTOR PACKAGES**
by
assembling requirements; obtaining approvals; distributing packages; setting up and updating files.

_____ 7. **FORWARDS INFORMATION**
by
answering the telephone; recording and delivering messages; assembling plans and specification packages; maintaining logs.

_____ 8. **PRODUCES INFORMATION**
by
preparing letters; transcribing, formatting, inputting, editing, retrieving, copying, and transmitting text, data, and graphics.

_____ 9. **SECURES INFORMATION**
by
completing database backups.

_____10. **MAINTAINS HISTORICAL REFERENCE**
by
utilizing filing and retrieval systems.

_____11. **MAINTAINS CONTINUITY AMONG CORPORATE, DIVISION, AND LOCAL WORK TEAMS**
by
documenting and communicating actions, irregularities, and continuing needs.

_____12. **MAINTAINS TECHNICAL KNOWLEDGE**
by
attending educational workshops; reviewing publications.

_____13. **CONTRIBUTES TO TEAM EFFORT**
by
accomplishing related results as needed.

JOB TITLE: CONSUMER AFFAIRS ADMINISTRATOR   C094_M

JOB PURPOSE: **SERVES CONSUMERS**
by
resolving product and/or service problems; maintaining records.

ESSENTIAL JOB RESULTS:

% of
time

____ 1. **RESOLVES PRODUCT AND/OR SERVICE PROBLEMS**
by
answering product complaints and inquirles; clarifying the consumer's complaint; determining the cause of the problem; following up to ensure resolution.

____ 2. **MAINTAINS INTER- AND INTRA-DEPARTMENTAL WORK FLOW**
by
providing complaint information.

____ 3. **MAINTAINS CONSUMER RECORDS**
by
updating consumer complaint database.

____ 4. **SECURES RECORDS**
by
backing up data.

% of
time

____ 5. **PREPARES PRODUCT COMPLAINT REPORTS**
by
collecting, analyzing, and summarizing consumer complaint information.

____ 6. **MAINTAINS QUALITY SERVICE**
by
following organization standards.

____ 7. **MAINTAINS TECHNICAL AND PROFESSIONAL KNOWLEDGE**
by
attending educational workshops; reviewing professional publications; establishing personal and professional networks.

____ 8. **CONTRIBUTES TO TEAM EFFORT**
by
accomplishing related results as needed.

```
┌─────────────────────────────────────────────────────────────────────┐
│  JOB TITLE:    CONTRACT DEVELOPMENT ANALYST      C097_M                │
└─────────────────────────────────────────────────────────────────────┘
```

JOB PURPOSE: **DEVELOPS INSURANCE PRODUCTS**
by
researching information; negotiating contracts.

ESSENTIAL JOB RESULTS:

% of
time

% of
time

_____ 1. **ACHIEVES OBJECTIVES**
by
gathering pertinent information;
identifying and evaluating options;
choosing a course of action.

_____ 2. **DETERMINES PRODUCT AND
MARKET FILING AND RESEARCH
NEEDS**
by
researching legislative information,
competitor information, and pre-existing
products.

_____ 3. **NEGOTIATES PRODUCTS**
by
drafting, revising, and consolidating
policy forms; submitting to state
insurance departments; reviewing
insurance department interrogatories
and research statutes, regulations, and
insurance codes.

_____ 4. **MAINTAINS RAPPORT WITH
INSURANCE DEPARTMENTS,
MARKETING, AND OPERATIONS
PERSONNEL**
by
arranging continuing contacts; resolving
concerns.

_____ 5. **INFORMS OPERATING AREAS**
by
issuing product bulletins and policy
issuance Instructions for use of
products in various states.

_____ 6. **MONITORS WORK FLOW**
by
preparing backlog and person-days
reports.

_____ 7. **MAINTAINS QUALITY SERVICE**
by
establishing and enforcing organization
standards.

_____ 8. **PREPARES REPORTS**
by
collecting, analyzing, and summarizing
information.

_____ 9. **MAINTAINS PROFESSIONAL AND
TECHNICAL KNOWLEDGE**
by
attending educational workshops;
reviewing professional publications;
establishing personal networks;
benchmarking state-of-the-art practices;
participating in professional societies.

_____10. **CONTRIBUTES TO TEAM EFFORT**
by
accomplishing related results as
needed.

JOB TITLE:	CONTROL DESK COORDINATOR	C099_M

JOB PURPOSE: **MAINTAINS WORK FLOW**
by
sorting and distributing incoming documents.

ESSENTIAL JOB RESULTS:

% of
time

_____ 1. **PROVIDES INFORMATION**
by
answering questions and requests.

_____ 2. **VERIFIES DOCUMENT IDENTIFICATION**
by
reviewing supporting documentation.

_____ 3. **FORWARDS INFORMATION**
by
sorting and distributing incoming
documents; collecting and mailing
outgoing documents.

_____ 4. **MAINTAINS QUALITY SERVICES**
by
maintaining and following procedures
and manuals; resolving processing
problems; recording time
measurements.

_____ 5. **SUPPORTS OPERATIONS**
by
cross-training on related jobs.

_____ 6. **MAINTAINS SUPPLIES INVENTORY**
by
checking stock; anticipating needs;
placing and expediting orders; verifying
receipt.

% of
time

_____ 7. **MAINTAINS DATABASE**
by
entering, verifying, and backing up
data.

_____ 8. **PREPARES REPORTS**
by
collecting, analyzing, and summarizing
information.

_____ 9. **MAINTAINS HISTORICAL RECORDS**
by
filing and retrieving documents.

_____10. **MAINTAINS TECHNICAL KNOWLEDGE**
by
attending educational workshops;
reviewing publications.

_____11. **CONTRIBUTES TO TEAM EFFORT**
by
accomplishing related results as
needed.

JOB TITLE: COPYWRITER–DIRECT MAIL   C101_M

JOB PURPOSE: **SERVES CLIENTS**
by
preparing direct mail copy.

ESSENTIAL JOB RESULTS:

% of
time

____ 1. **DEVELOPS DIRECT MAIL PACKAGE POSITIONING, STRATEGY, AND EXECUTION FOR NEW PRODUCTS**
by
researching product, marketing objectives, past product performance, and competitors' products and marketing campaigns.

____ 2. **IMPROVES MARKET PENETRATION OF EXISTING PRODUCT MARKETING**
by
researching results; exploring options; anticipating competitors' strategies.

____ 3. **WRITES DIRECT MAIL PIECES**
by
developing formats; creating content; contracting for artwork.

____ 4. **ESTABLISHES MAILING STANDARDS**
by
positioning and customizing control pieces.

% of
time

____ 5. **ATTRACTS PROSPECTIVE CLIENTS**
by
developing and executing marketing presentations.

____ 6. **BUILDS CLIENT RELATIONSHIPS**
by
providing information; resolving problems.

____ 7. **MAINTAINS QUALITY SERVICE**
by
following organization standards.

____ 8. **MAINTAINS TECHNICAL KNOWLEDGE**
by
attending educational workshops; reviewing publications.

____ 9. **CONTRIBUTES TO TEAM EFFORT**
by
accomplishing related results as needed.

JOB TITLE: CORPORATE INTELLIGENCE DIRECTOR C102_M

JOB PURPOSE: **SUPPORTS CORPORATE DECISION MAKING**
by
collecting, analyzing, summarizing, and disseminating external market information.

ESSENTIAL JOB RESULTS:

% of
time

% of
time

____ 1. **DETERMINES INTELLIGENCE REQUIREMENTS**
by
studying strategic business plans; identifying specific needs.

____ 2. **COLLECTS EXTERNAL COMPETITIVE AND REGULATOR INFORMATION**
by
identifying and searching sources of information; developing intelligence collection plans; establishing personal and leveraging networks; gathering and tracking data.

____ 3. **UNDERSTANDS EXTERNAL MARKET INFLUENCES**
by
analyzing competitor activities and changing market structure; tracking and anticipating government regulations; analyzing market observer opinions.

____ 4. **SUMMARIZES EXTERNAL MARKET INFLUENCES**
by
anticipating marketplace behavior and trends, and competitor technological and production capabilities; synthesizing information; drawing conclusions; providing recommendations; preparing reports; making presentations.

____ 5. **DISSEMINATES INTELLIGENCE**
by
identifying key decision makers and their decision-making processes and schedules.

____ 6. **MAINTAINS INFORMATION REFERENCE**
by
establishing and updating databases.

____ 7. **PROTECTS AGAINST CORPORATE ESPIONAGE**
by
identifying and closing potential information leaks.

____ 8. **COMPLIES WITH ETHICAL AND LEGAL REQUIREMENTS**
by
adhering to corporate standards and government regulations.

____ 9. **MAINTAINS PROFESSIONAL AND TECHNICAL KNOWLEDGE**
by
attending educational workshops; reviewing professional publications; establishing personal networks; benchmarking state-of-the-art practices; participating in professional societies.

____ 10. **CONTRIBUTES TO TEAM EFFORT**
by
accomplishing related results as needed.

JOB PURPOSE: RECOMMENDS CORPORATE OBJECTIVES
by
collecting, analyzing information; recommending actions; tracking results.

ESSENTIAL JOB RESULTS:

% of
time

_____ 1. **CONTRIBUTES TO ORGANIZATIONAL EFFECTIVENESS**
by
identifying short-term and long-range issues that must be addressed; providing information and commentary pertaining to deliberations.

_____ 2. **DEVELOPS PLANS**
by
analyzing and interpreting data; making comparable analyses; recommending options and courses of action; implementing directives.

_____ 3. **MONITORS PROJECTS**
by
selecting critical action plans; reviewing results; recommending corrective actions.

_____ 4. **PROVIDES STATUS OF CORPORATE FINANCIAL CONDITION AND ACHIEVES FINANCIAL OBJECTIVES**
by
collecting, interpreting, and reporting financial data; preparing business and subsidiary trendline analysis; preparing expense budgets and forecasts.

_____ 5. **PREPARES BUSINESS PLAN AND QUARTERLY REVIEWS**
by
completing economic and strategic assessments; analyzing premium and profit plans; streamlining budgeting.

% of
time

_____ 6. **CALCULATES INCENTIVES**
by
researching, accruing for, and maintaining incentive programs.

_____ 7. **PREPARES SPECIAL REPORTS**
by
completing surveys for outside information sources; preparing and maintaining corporate documents for the board of directors.

_____ 8. **PROTECTS OPERATIONS**
by
keeping company information confidential.

_____ 9. **MAINTAINS PROFESSIONAL AND TECHNICAL KNOWLEDGE**
by
attending educational workshops; reviewing professional publications; establishing personal networks; benchmarking state-of-the-art practices; participating in professional societies.

_____10. **CONTRIBUTES TO TEAM EFFORT**
by
accomplishing related results as needed.

JOB TITLE: CORPORATE SECRETARY

C104_M

JOB PURPOSE: ENHANCES EFFECTIVENESS OF PRESIDENT/CHIEF EXECUTIVE OFFICER AND BOARD OF DIRECTORS
by
managing information, schedules, and requirements.

ESSENTIAL JOB RESULTS:

% of
time

% of
time

____ 1. **PROVIDES SUPPORT TO BOARD OF DIRECTORS**
by
coordinating calendar and annual election process; recording minutes and maintaining legal recording requirements; coordinating and following up on committee assignments with board members and senior management; updating policy manual; compiling information for meeting agenda development; arranging educational development activities; preparing letters and memos.

____ 2. **PROVIDES SUPPORT TO PRESIDENT/CHIEF EXECUTIVE OFFICER**
by
welcoming and providing information to customers, vendors, or guests, either in person or by telephone; answering or directing inquiries; representing president/chief executive officer; maintaining relationships with board members, shareholders, competitors, industry representatives, legislators, and consumers; following up on project completion with vice presidents; coordinating executive committee action plan schedule; collecting and distributing information; scheduling, setting priorities, and conserving president/chief executive officer's time; preparing letters and memos.

____ 3. **ACHIEVES FINANCIAL OBJECTIVES**
by
assembling the annual budget; scheduling expenditures, analyzing variances, and initiating corrective action.

____ 4. **MAINTAINS CUSTOMER CONFIDENCE AND PROTECTS COMPANY**
by
keeping information confidential.

____ 5. **MAINTAINS PROFESSIONAL AND TECHNICAL KNOWLEDGE**
by
attending educational workshops; reviewing industry publications; establishing personal and industry networks; participating in industry organizations.

____ 6. **CONTRIBUTES TO TEAM EFFORT**
by
accomplishing related results as needed.

JOB PURPOSE: **ANALYZES GROSS PROFIT FROM HOME SALES**
by
collecting, tracking, and calculating cost information.

ESSENTIAL JOB RESULTS:

% of
time

% of
time

_____ 1. **PREPARES WORK TO BE ACCOMPLISHED**
by
gathering and sorting documents.

_____ 2. **ASSEMBLES CONSTRUCTION FINANCIAL DATA**
by
establishing methods, procedures, sources, and models.

_____ 3. **MONITORS CONSTRUCTION COSTS**
by
balancing critical path activity.

_____ 4. **CALCULATES SALES AND COST OF SALES**
by
comparing construction budget with variance calculations; scheduling job closing sessions; querying databases.

_____ 5. **MAINTAINS JOB COST SYSTEM**
by
preparing cost worksheets.

_____ 6. **PROVIDES JOB CLOSING FINANCIAL INFORMATION**
by
preparing residential closing work papers; completing monthly job closing routine; preparing financial statement data; preparing sales commissions, overhead, and marketing journal entries.

_____ 7. **INTERPRETS CONSTRUCTION FINANCIAL INFORMATION**
by
consolidating, studying, and analyzing data.

_____ 8. **DEVELOPS JOB COST RECOMMENDATIONS**
by
drawing conclusions from analyzed data.

_____ 9. **COMPLETES SPECIAL PROJECTS AND REPORTS**
by
gathering, organizing, and analyzing information.

_____ 10. **MAINTAINS CLOSEOUT HISTORICAL RECORDS**
by
filing documents.

_____ 11. **IMPROVES PROGRAM AND SERVICE QUALITY**
by
devising new applications; updating procedures; evaluating system results with users.

_____ 12. **ACHIEVES FINANCIAL OBJECTIVES**
by
anticipating requirements; submitting information for budget preparation; scheduling expenditures; monitoring costs; analyzing variances.

_____ 13. **PROTECTS OPERATIONS**
by
keeping financial information confidential.

ESSENTIAL JOB RESULTS:

% of
time

% of
time

____**14. MAINTAINS CONTINUITY AMONG CORPORATE, DIVISION, AND LOCAL WORK TEAMS**
by
documenting and communicating actions, irregularities, and continuing needs.

____**15. MAINTAINS TECHNICAL KNOWLEDGE**
by
attending educational workshops; reviewing publications.

____**16. CONTRIBUTES TO TEAM EFFORT**
by
accomplishing related results as needed.

JOB TITLE: COST ANALYST–LAND DEVELOPMENT   C107_M

JOB PURPOSE: **ANALYZES LAND ACQUISITION AND DEVELOPMENT COSTS**
by
collecting, tracking, and updating information.

ESSENTIAL JOB RESULTS:

% of
time

_____ 1. **ASSEMBLES LAND ACQUISITION AND DEVELOPMENT FINANCIAL DATA**
by
gathering transaction information.

_____ 2. **MAINTAINS RECORDS OF LAND ACQUISITIONS, IMPROVEMENTS, AND TRANSFERS**
by
tracking and allocating land improvement costs; inventorying lots; recording lot and land cost transfers.

_____ 3. **PAYS REAL AND PERSONAL PROPERTY TAXES**
by
maintaining schedules of property ownership and calculating prorations; tracking fixed assets.

_____ 4. **COMPLETES REPORTS**
by
gathering, organizing, and analyzing information.

_____ 5. **INTERPRETS LAND COST FINANCIAL DATA**
by
analyzing data; developing conclusions.

_____ 6. **DEVELOPS LAND COST RECOMMENDATIONS**
by
utilizing conclusions drawn from analyzed data.

% of
time

_____ 7. **MAINTAINS HISTORICAL RECORDS**
by
filing and retrieving documents.

_____ 8. **PROTECTS OPERATIONS**
by
keeping financial information confidential.

_____ 9. **MAINTAINS CONTINUITY AMONG CORPORATE, DIVISION, AND LOCAL WORK TEAMS**
by
documenting and communicating actions, irregularities, and continuing needs.

_____ 10. **MAINTAINS TECHNICAL KNOWLEDGE**
by
attending educational workshops; reviewing publications.

_____ 11. **CONTRIBUTES TO TEAM EFFORT**
by
accomplishing related results as needed.

JOB TITLE: COURIER

C108_M

JOB PURPOSE: FORWARDS INFORMATION
by
maintaining vehicles and pick-up and delivery schedules.

ESSENTIAL JOB RESULTS:

% of
time

% of
time

____ 1. **COMPLETES BANK TRANSACTIONS**
by
making deposits, cashing checks, and
picking up bank transactions.

____ 2. **DISTRIBUTES MATERIALS AND
INFORMATION**
by
delivering and picking up items for
accounts, vendors, subsidiaries, and
associates.

____ 3. **COMPLETES SPECIAL DELIVERIES
AND PICK-UPS**
by
responding to requests.

____ 4. **MAINTAINS SCHEDULED
DELIVERIES**
by
delivering items within the building.

____ 5. **MAINTAINS SERVICE VEHICLES**
by
completing inspections and operator
maintenance.

____ 6. **MAINTAINS QUALITY SERVICE**
by
following organization standards.

____ 7. **COMPLETES REPORTS**
by
entering required information.

____ 8. **CONTRIBUTES TO TEAM EFFORT**
by
accomplishing related results as
needed.

JOB PURPOSE: **DISPLAYS CRAFTS AND DEMONSTRATES TECHNIQUES**
by
planning and preparing exhibits; presenting demonstrations.

ESSENTIAL JOB RESULTS:

% of
time

1. PLANS DISPLAYS AND PROGRAMS
by
studying history, technical literature, and contemporary techniques; identifying visitor interests; developing calendar of events.

2. PROMOTES CENTER
by
writing descriptions of exhibits and activities; writing and placing advertisements.

3. PREPARES EXHIBITS
by
researching authenticity; assembling items, materials, and components; supervising installation and construction.

4. PRESENTS DEMONSTRATIONS
by
identifying, selecting, and contracting with craftspeople; guiding the development of presentations; scheduling and monitoring demonstrations.

5. OBTAINS REVENUE
by
collecting fees; selling items, supplies, and accessories.

6. MAINTAINS SUPPLIES INVENTORY
by
checking stock; anticipating needs; placing and expediting orders; verifying receipt.

% of
time

7. COMPLETES RECORDS
by
entering required information; approving and paying bills.

8. PREPARES REPORTS
by
collecting, analyzing, and summarizing information.

9. MAINTAINS FACILITY
by
contracting for maintenance and cleaning services; supervising repairs.

10. MAINTAINS PROFESSIONAL AND TECHNICAL KNOWLEDGE
by
attending educational workshops; reviewing professional publications; establishing personal networks; benchmarking state-of-the-art practices; participating in professional societies.

11. MAINTAINS CENTER SERVICES
by
accomplishing related results as needed.

JOB PURPOSE: **EXPLAINS CRAFTS AND DEMONSTRATES TECHNIQUES**
by
preparing and presenting programs.

ESSENTIAL JOB RESULTS:

% of
time

_____ 1. **DEVELOPS AUTHENTIC PRESENTATIONS**
by
researching history and technical literature; conferring with experts.

_____ 2. **PREPARES PRESENTATIONS**
by
writing scripts; assembling materials and equipment; setting up demonstrations; practicing delivery technique.

_____ 3. **PRESENTS PROGRAMS**
by
explaining crafts in terms of lifestyle and time period; demonstrating techniques; answering questions; guiding visitor participation.

_____ 4. **PROVIDES RESOURCES**
by
writing explanations; referring to other sources.

_____ 5. **MAINTAINS EXHIBITS AND EQUIPMENT**
by
completing or arranging for repairs; cleaning area.

% of
time

_____ 6. **OBTAINS REVENUE**
by
collecting fees; selling items, supplies, and accessories.

_____ 7. **MAINTAINS CENTER PROGRAMS**
by
accomplishing related results as needed.

_____ 8. **MAINTAINS TECHNICAL KNOWLEDGE**
by
attending educational workshops; reviewing publications.

_____ 9. **CONTRIBUTES TO TEAM EFFORT**
by
accomplishing related results as needed.

JOB TITLE: CRUISE SHIP CAPTAIN   C114_M

JOB PURPOSE: **DELIGHTS PASSENGERS**
by
maintaining staff; sailing ship to scheduled destinations; entertaining passengers; maintaining safe operations.

ESSENTIAL JOB RESULTS:

% of
time

% of
time

_____ 1. **MAINTAINS CRUISE SHIP STAFF**
by
orienting and training crew.

_____ 2. **ACCOMPLISHES STAFF RESULTS**
by
communicating job expectations; planning, monitoring, and appraising job results; coaching, counseling, and disciplining employees; initiating, coordinating, and enforcing systems, policies, and procedures.

_____ 3. **PREPARES FOR VOYAGE**
by
receiving sailing instructions; charting course.

_____ 4. **ENSURES OPERATION OF SHIP**
by
completing pre-voyage inspections; completing preventive maintenance requirements; arranging for repairs; maintaining equipment inventories; evaluating new equipment and techniques.

_____ 5. **MAINTAINS SUPPLIES INVENTORY**
by
anticipating requirements; checking stocks; placing and expediting orders; loading and verifying receipt.

_____ 6. **MAINTAINS SAFE AND HEALTHY ENVIRONMENT**
by
conducting drills; enforcing line standards and maritime regulations; directing emergency and rescue operations.

_____ 7. **COMPLETES CRUISE ITINERARY**
by
determining geographical location; sailing to ports; relinquishing command to pilots and tugboat captains.

_____ 8. **PROVIDES PASSENGER ENTERTAINMENT**
by
organizing and scheduling activities; visiting with passengers; recommending future activities.

_____ 9. **MAINTAINS SHIP'S LOG**
by
documenting required information.

_____ 10. **ACCOMPLISHES FINANCIAL OBJECTIVES**
by
forecasting requirements; analyzing budget variances; initiating corrective action.

_____ 11. **PREPARES REPORTS**
by
collecting, analyzing, and summarizing information.

_____ 12. **MAINTAINS PROFESSIONAL AND TECHNICAL KNOWLEDGE**
by
maintaining license; attending educational workshops; reviewing professional publications.

_____ 13. **CONTRIBUTES TO TEAM EFFORT**
by
accomplishing related results as needed.

JOB PURPOSE: **MAINTAINS CUSTOMERS' OPERATIONS**
by
maintaining equipment performance; providing training.

ESSENTIAL JOB RESULTS:

% of
time

____ 1. **PREPARES EQUIPMENT TECHNICIANS**
by
conducting training; helping assess work results.

____ 2. **COMPLETES OPERATIONS**
by
scheduling and assigning technicians.

____ 3. **PROVIDES CUSTOMER SUPPORT**
by
providing training; responding to requests; resolving problems both on-site and on the telephone.

____ 4. **SETS UP EQUIPMENT**
by
delivering, unpacking, assembling, and completing diagnostics; obtaining acceptance by customer.

____ 5. **MAINTAINS EQUIPMENT**
by
providing training; responding to requests; resolving problems both on-site and on the telephone.

% of
time

____ 6. **HELPS CUSTOMER ENGINEER**
by
designing modifications; implementing changes.

____ 7. **MAINTAINS REFERENCE MANUAL**
by
recording modifications and changes.

____ 8. **MAINTAINS PROFESSIONAL AND TECHNICAL KNOWLEDGE**
by
attending educational workshops; reviewing professional publications; establishing personal networks; benchmarking state-of-the-art practices; participating in professional societies.

____ 9. **CONTRIBUTES TO TEAM EFFORT**
by
accomplishing related results as needed.

| JOB TITLE: | DATA CENTER ANALYST | D119_M |

JOB PURPOSE: SERVES CUSTOMERS
by
maintaining system performance.

ESSENTIAL JOB RESULTS:

% of
time

% of
time

____ 1. **MAINTAINS PRODUCTION APPLICATION SYSTEMS**
by
monitoring system performance at master console; identifying and resolving problems.

____ 2. **MAINTAINS HARDWARE PRODUCTION**
by
identifying and resolving problems; coordinating resolution with vendors.

____ 3. **MAINTAINS NETWORK PERFORMANCE**
by
verifying availability of networks; identifying and resolving problems; coordinating resolution with internal support staff and vendors.

____ 4. **PREVENTS RECURRENCE OF PERFORMANCE PROBLEMS**
by
analyzing problem management records.

____ 5. **IMPROVES QUALITY, PRODUCTIVITY, AND PROCEDURES**
by
analyzing problems and changes; completing projects.

____ 6. **ACCOMPLISHES STAFF WORK RESULTS**
by
providing functional direction to junior operators; taking action in supervisor's absence.

____ 7. **MAINTAINS TECHNICAL KNOWLEDGE**
by
attending educational workshops; reviewing publications.

____ 8. **CONTRIBUTES TO TEAM EFFORT**
by
accomplishing related results as needed.

JOB TITLE:	DATA CENTER OPERATOR	D120_M

JOB PURPOSE: **SERVES CUSTOMERS**
by
operating and maintaining computer equipment.

ESSENTIAL JOB RESULTS:

% of
time

____ **1. PROVIDES DATA SERVICES**
by
operating a mainframe computer
including cartridge and tape drives,
automated library, impact and high-
speed printers.

____ **2. MAINTAINS OPERATING SYSTEM
ENVIRONMENT**
by
monitoring master console.

____ **3. MAINTAINS HIGH-SPEED PRINTER
AND CARTRIDGE DRIVE
PERFORMANCE**
by
identifying and resolving problems;
notifying vendors for assistance.

____ **4. FORWARDS INFORMATION**
by
distributing production and test reports.

____ **5. MAINTAINS PERFORMANCE
MANAGEMENT RECORDS**
by
recording production abends and
hardware failures.

% of
time

____ **6. MAINTAINS EQUIPMENT**
by
completing preventive maintenance
requirements.

____ **7. MAINTAINS SUPPLIES**
by
requesting scratch tape.

____ **8. PROTECTS INFORMATION**
by
sending tapes to off-site facility.

____ **9. MAINTAINS TECHNICAL
KNOWLEDGE**
by
attending educational workshops;
reviewing publications.

____**10. CONTRIBUTES TO TEAM EFFORT**
by
accomplishing related results as
needed.

JOB TITLE:	DATABASE ADMINISTRATOR	D123_M

JOB PURPOSE: **MAINTAINS DATABASE**
by
identifying and solving database requirements; supporting users.

ESSENTIAL JOB RESULTS:

% of
time

_____ 1. **IDENTIFIES DATABASE REQUIREMENTS**
by
interviewing customers; analyzing department applications, programming, and operations; evaluating existing systems and designing proposed systems.

_____ 2. **RECOMMENDS SOLUTIONS**
by
defining database physical structure and functional capabilities, database security, data back-up, and recovery specifications.

_____ 3. **INSTALLS REVISED OR NEW SYSTEMS**
by
proposing specifications and flowcharts; recommending optimum access techniques; coordinating installation requirements.

_____ 4. **MAINTAINS DATABASE PERFORMANCE**
by
calculating optimum values for database parameters; implementing new releases; completing maintenance requirements; evaluating computer operating systems and hardware products.

% of
time

_____ 5. **PREPARES USERS**
by
conducting training; providing information; resolving problems.

_____ 6. **PROVIDES INFORMATION**
by
answering questions and requests.

_____ 7. **SUPPORTS DATABASE FUNCTIONS**
by
designing and coding utilities.

_____ 8. **MAINTAINS QUALITY SERVICE**
by
establishing and enforcing organization standards.

_____ 9. **MAINTAINS PROFESSIONAL AND TECHNICAL KNOWLEDGE**
by
attending educational workshops; reviewing professional publications; establishing personal networks; benchmarking state-of-the-art practices; participating in professional societies.

_____ 10. **CONTRIBUTES TO TEAM EFFORT**
by
accomplishing related results as needed.

JOB PURPOSE: **MAINTAINS BUILDING DESIGN AND CONSTRUCTION**
by
supervising staff; producing and improving architectural plans.

ESSENTIAL JOB RESULTS:

% of
time

% of
time

____ 1. **MAINTAINS DESIGN SERVICES STAFF**
by
recruiting, selecting, orienting, and training employees; maintaining a safe and secure work environment; developing personal growth opportunities.

____ 2. **ACCOMPLISHES STAFF RESULTS**
by
communicating job expectations; planning, monitoring, and appraising job results; coaching, counseling, and disciplining employees; initiating, coordinating, and enforcing systems, policies, and procedures.

____ 3. **PRODUCES ARCHITECTURAL PLANS AND TAKE-OFFS**
by
scheduling and assigning employees; following up on work results; answering questions regarding construction, drafting, and structural situations; verifying work; conducting training.

____ 4. **IMPROVES BUILDING CONSTRUCTION AND REDUCES COSTS**
by
identifying ways that buildings can be constructed more effectively and efficiently.

____ 5. **RESOLVES DESIGN AND CONSTRUCTION PROBLEMS**
by
providing technical assistance to construction and sales departments.

____ 6. **MAINTAINS QUALITY SERVICE**
by
establishing and enforcing organization standards.

____ 7. **MAINTAINS CONTINUITY AMONG CORPORATE, DIVISION, AND LOCAL WORK TEAMS**
by
documenting and communicating actions, irregularities, and continuing needs.

____ 8. **MAINTAINS PROFESSIONAL AND TECHNICAL KNOWLEDGE**
by
attending educational workshops; reviewing professional publications; establishing personal networks; benchmarking state-of-the-art practices; participating in professional societies.

____ 9. **CONTRIBUTES TO TEAM EFFORT**
by
accomplishing related results as needed.

JOB TITLE: DESIGN TECHNICIAN–CONSTRUCTION   D128_M

JOB PURPOSE: **SUPPORTS BUILDING DESIGN AND CONSTRUCTION**
by
operating computer-aided design system to produce architectural plans;
negotiating design/construction issues.

ESSENTIAL JOB RESULTS:

% of
time

% of
time

____ 1. **PROVIDES ARCHITECTURAL PLANS**
by
operating computer-aided design
system; analyzing design options;
evaluating construction.

____ 2. **MAINTAINS COMPUTER-AIDED
DESIGN SYSTEM**
by
backing up data.

____ 3. **PREPARES TAKE-OFFS**
by
calculating construction costs.

____ 4. **CREATES STOCK PLANS**
by
identifying construction materials;
updating changes.

____ 5. **PREPARES BLUEPRINTS**
by
operating copying equipment;
forwarding to requesting parties.

____ 6. **RESOLVES DESIGN AND
CONSTRUCTION PROBLEMS**
by
providing technical assistance to
construction and sales departments.

____ 7. **MAINTAINS QUALITY SERVICE**
by
following organization standards.

____ 8. **MAINTAINS CONTINUITY AMONG
CORPORATE, DIVISION, AND
LOCAL WORK TEAMS**
by
documenting and communicating
actions, irregularities, and continuing
needs.

____ 9. **MAINTAINS PROFESSIONAL AND
TECHNICAL KNOWLEDGE**
by
attending educational workshops;
reviewing professional publications;
establishing personal networks;
participating in professional societies.

____10. **CONTRIBUTES TO TEAM EFFORT**
by
accomplishing related results as
needed.

JOB TITLE: DESKTOP TECHNICAL ANALYST D129_M

JOB PURPOSE: **MAINTAINS COMPUTER DESKTOP ENVIRONMENT**
by
analyzing requirements; resolving problems; installing hardware and software solutions.

ESSENTIAL JOB RESULTS:

% of
time

_____ 1. **IDENTIFIES ARCHITECTURAL REQUIREMENTS**
by
interviewing customers; analyzing applications, programming, and operations; evaluating existing and proposed systems; recommending solutions to infrastructure.

_____ 2. **ESTABLISHES AND UPGRADES SYSTEM**
by
installing hardware and software.

_____ 3. **MAINTAINS INSTALLATION RECORDS**
by
documenting procedures used.

_____ 4. **RESOLVES PROBLEMS**
by
conferring with vendors; consulting with and training users.

% of
time

_____ 5. **IMPROVES SYSTEM PERFORMANCE**
by
investigating current environment; recommending solutions; integrating standard solutions.

_____ 6. **MAINTAINS QUALITY SERVICE**
by
establishing and enforcing organization standards.

_____ 7. **MAINTAINS TECHNICAL KNOWLEDGE**
by
attending educational workshops; reviewing publications.

_____ 8. **CONTRIBUTES TO TEAM EFFORT**
by
accomplishing related results as needed.

JOB TITLE: DIRECT RESPONSE ANALYST — D133_M

JOB PURPOSE: SERVES CUSTOMERS
by
analyzing market results; recommending new strategies.

ESSENTIAL JOB RESULTS:

% of
time

% of
time

____ 1. **RECOMMENDS NEW OR REVISED MARKETING STRATEGIES AND PROFITABILITY RESULTS**
by
analyzing profitability studies; analyzing environmental and competitive trends; coordinating information with marketing and customer service coordinators.

____ 2. **PRESENTS ANALYSES TO CUSTOMERS**
by
assembling and analyzing results.

____ 3. **ACHIEVES MARKETING AND BUSINESS OBJECTIVES**
by
utilizing and updating the marketing database.

____ 4. **SECURES MARKETING DATABASE**
by
backing up information.

____ 5. **PURSUES SEGMENTATION OPPORTUNITIES**
by
maintaining modeling and segmentation processes.

____ 6. **MAINTAINS QUALITY SERVICE**
by
following organization standards.

____ 7. **MAINTAINS TECHNICAL KNOWLEDGE**
by
attending educational workshops; reviewing publications.

____ 8. **CONTRIBUTES TO DEPARTMENT EFFORT**
by
accomplishing related results as needed.

JOB PURPOSE: **MAINTAINS COMPANY FINANCIAL STRENGTH AND STABILITY**
by
directing and monitoring investments; maintaining controls.

ESSENTIAL JOB RESULTS:

% of
time

% of
time

____ 1. **EXECUTES A CAPITAL PLAN**
by
forecasting capital needs and cash
flows; monitoring capital and cash
positions; coordinating information
and actions with legal counsel, banks,
creditors, and investors;
recommending changes.

____ 2. **MAXIMIZES INVESTMENT
RETURNS**
by
recommending strategies and policies;
determining future portfolio purchase
duration needs; reviewing asset
allocations; analyzing alternative
investment opportunities; maintaining
product availability and price
information; managing portfolios;
selecting securities; evaluating results
of outside investment managers;
recommending changes.

____ 3. **RECOMMENDS FINANCIAL
ACTIONS**
by
developing financial and actuarial
models; collecting and interpreting
data.

____ 4. **MONITORS PERFORMANCE OF
EXTERNALLY MANAGED ASSETS**
by
establishing benchmarks for
performance measurement; reviewing
and analyzing actual results; making
reallocation decisions.

____ 5. **MAINTAINS RELATIONSHIPS WITH
COMMERCIAL BANKS AND
INVESTMENT BANKING FIRMS**
by
communicating financial and non-
financial information; responding to
inquiries related to the company's
financial results.

____ 6. **COMPLIES WITH INVESTMENT
GUIDELINES ESTABLISHED BY
STATE INSURANCE LAWS AND
RATING AGENCIES**
by
studying and reviewing existing and
new legislation; communicating with
the rating agencies; enforcing
adherence to requirements; advising
management on needed actions.

____ 7. **SUPPORTS CORPORATE
ACQUISITION DECISIONS**
by
analyzing the invested assets of the
target companies.

____ 8. **MAINTAINS ASSET MANAGEMENT
SYSTEM**
by
planning and implementing upgrades
and enhancements; communicating
with users; conducting training;
keeping up-to-date on new
developments.

ESSENTIAL JOB RESULTS:

% of
time

% of
time

____ 9. **MAINTAINS SAFEKEEPING AND CLEARANCE FUNCTIONS**
by
implementing and monitoring guidelines and controls for the execution of trades and the safekeeping and pledging of securities; maintaining broker and bank relationships.

____10. **PREPARES REPORTS**
by
collecting, analyzing, and summarizing information and trends.

____11. **PROTECTS OPERATIONS**
by
keeping financial information confidential.

____12. **MAINTAINS PROFESSIONAL AND TECHNICAL KNOWLEDGE**
by
attending educational workshops; reviewing professional publications; establishing personal networks; benchmarking state-of-the-art practices; participating in professional societies.

____13. **CONTRIBUTES TO TEAM EFFORT**
by
accomplishing related results as needed.

JOB TITLE: DIRECTOR OF QUALITY IMPROVEMENT   D135_M

JOB PURPOSE: **PROMOTES COMPANY QUALITY AND CUSTOMER SERVICE IMAGE**
by
supervising staff; forming, facilitating, and evaluating process improvement teams.

ESSENTIAL JOB RESULTS:

% of
time

____ **1. MAINTAINS QUALITY IMPROVEMENT STAFF**
by
recruiting, selecting, orienting, and training employees; maintaining a safe and secure work environment; developing personal growth opportunities.

____ **2. ACCOMPLISHES STAFF RESULTS**
by
communicating job expectations; planning, monitoring, and appraising job results; coaching, counseling, and disciplining employees; initiating, coordinating, and enforcing systems, policies, and procedures.

____ **3. DEVELOPS PROCESS IMPROVEMENT TEAMS**
by
promoting the value of teams; selecting, training, guiding, and monitoring team members; managing team projects; presenting assignments and recommendations to corporate quality steering group.

____ **4. IMPLEMENTS EMPLOYEE IMPROVEMENT SUGGESTIONS**
by
promoting the value of suggestions; soliciting, evaluating, and implementing improvements.

____ **5. MEASURES RESULTS**
by
collecting, maintaining, and interpreting quality performance data; tracking process improvement team project implementation; managing employee opinion survey.

% of
time

____ **6. INFORMS EMPLOYEES**
by
communicating quality measurements and results, and suggestions implemented; writing articles for quality newsletter.

____ **7. MANAGES AWARD AND RECOGNITION PROGRAMS**
by
establishing employee selection criteria; determining celebrations and prizes.

____ **8. ORIENTS NEW EMPLOYEES**
by
developing and maintaining interdisciplinary orientation training manuals; introducing employees to the organization's quality-focused concepts and programs.

____ **9. ACHIEVES FINANCIAL OBJECTIVES**
by
anticipating requirements; submitting information for budget preparation; scheduling expenditures; monitoring costs; analyzing variances.

____**10. MAINTAINS CONTINUITY AMONG CORPORATE, DIVISION, AND LOCAL WORK TEAMS**
by
documenting and communicating actions, irregularities, and continuing needs.

ESSENTIAL JOB RESULTS:

%
time

____11. **MAINTAINS PROFESSIONAL AND TECHNICAL KNOWLEDGE**
by
attending educational workshops;
reviewing professional publications;
establishing personal networks;
benchmarking state-of-the-art practices;
participating in professional societies.

%
time

____12. **CONTRIBUTES TO TEAM EFFORT**
by
accomplishing related results as
needed.

JOB TITLE: DISASTER RELIEF SERVICES DIRECTOR D136_M

JOB PURPOSE: **SUPPORTS DISASTER VICTIMS**
by
preparing for and implementing disaster plans.

ESSENTIAL JOB RESULTS:

% of
time

% of
time

____ **1. PREPARES DISASTER PLANS**
by
studying conditions and responses in previous disasters; developing preparedness plans; arranging interagency coordination; developing communication systems and procedures; determining and maintaining inventories; establishing standards and protocols; training personnel.

____ **2. ENSURES OPERATION OF EQUIPMENT**
by
directing preventive maintenance requirements; maintaining equipment inventories; evaluating new equipment and techniques.

____ **3. INITIATES DISASTER PLAN**
by
assessing situation; determining and communicating requirements; marshaling resources.

____ **4. COORDINATES EFFORTS**
by
maintaining communication with service agencies; integrating work schedules.

____ **5. MAINTAINS DISASTER SERVICES**
by
controlling distribution of aid; directing service personnel; recruiting and training volunteers.

____ **6. MAINTAINS SAFE AND HEALTHY ENVIRONMENT**
by
establishing and enforcing standards; determining risks.

____ **7. ACHIEVES RELIEF OBJECTIVES**
by
gathering pertinent information; identifying and evaluating options; choosing a course of action.

____ **8. CONTROLS COSTS**
by
monitoring expenditures.

____ **9. DEVELOPS RECOMMENDATIONS**
by
evaluating results of disaster efforts.

____ **10. MAINTAINS PROFESSIONAL AND TECHNICAL KNOWLEDGE**
by
attending educational workshops; reviewing professional publications; establishing personal networks; benchmarking state-of-the-art practices; participating in professional societies.

____ **11. CONTRIBUTES TO TEAM EFFORT**
by
accomplishing related results as needed.

<table>
<tr><td colspan="2">

JOB TITLE: **DISTRIBUTION MANAGER**   **D137_M**

</td></tr>
</table>

JOB PURPOSE: TRANSPORTS FINISHED GOODS AND MATERIALS
by
managing staff; establishing policies, procedures and methods.

ESSENTIAL JOB RESULTS:

% of
time

_____ 1. **MAINTAINS DISTRIBUTION STAFF**
by
recruiting, selecting, orienting, and
training employees; maintaining a safe
and secure work environment;
developing personal growth
opportunities.

_____ 2. **ACCOMPLISHES STAFF RESULTS**
by
communicating job expectations;
planning, monitoring, and appraising
job results; coaching, counseling, and
disciplining employees; initiating,
coordinating, and enforcing systems,
policies, and procedures.

_____ 3. **DIRECTS TRANSPORTATION OF**
FINISHED GOODS AND MATERIALS
by
developing methods and procedures for
transporting products and supplies to
customers and warehouses.

_____ 4. **DETERMINES ROUTING AND**
TRANSPORTATION METHODS
by
appraising current freight rates;
analyzing all modes of transportation.

_____ 5. **ISSUES CLAIMS**
by
investigating causes of damage,
shortages, and freight overcharges.

% of
time

_____ 6. **PREPARES REPORTS**
by
collecting, analyzing, and summarizing
information and trends.

_____ 7. **PROCESSES ORDERS**
by
supervising the scheduling of orders for
shipment.

_____ 8. **MAINTAINS BILLING OF ORDERS**
by
supervising the preparation and
verification of invoices.

_____ 9. **MAINTAINS PROFESSIONAL AND**
TECHNICAL KNOWLEDGE
by
attending educational workshops;
reviewing professional publications;
establishing personal networks;
benchmarking state-of-the-art practices;
participating in professional societies.

_____10. **CONTRIBUTES TO TEAM EFFORT**
by
accomplishing related results as
needed.

JOB TITLE: DISTRICT SALES MANAGER   D138_M

JOB PURPOSE: ACHIEVES DISTRIBUTOR SALES VOLUME
by
managing distributors; developing promotions; attaining sales quotas.

ESSENTIAL JOB RESULTS:

% of
time

% of
time

_____ 1. **MAINTAINS DISTRIBUTION CHANNELS**
by
recruiting, selecting, orienting, training, encouraging, and managing distributors.

_____ 2. **ACCOMPLISHES DISTRIBUTOR RESULTS**
by
communicating job expectations; planning, monitoring, and appraising job results; coaching, counseling, and disciplining distributors; initiating, coordinating, and enforcing systems, policies, and procedures.

_____ 3. **DEVELOPS PROMOTIONS**
by
setting goals with distributors.

_____ 4. **ACHIEVES SALES OBJECTIVES**
by
setting quotas with distributors; presenting products to accounts.

_____ 5. **ACHIEVES FINANCIAL OBJECTIVES**
by
staying within budgets for accrual and overhead costs.

_____ 6. **MAINTAINS SALES ACCOUNTS RECEIVABLE OPERATIONS**
by
submitting claims and/or deductions; communicating actions and irregularities.

_____ 7. **PROVIDES INFORMATION TO CORPORATE MANAGEMENT**
by
recapping promotional activity; reporting business opportunities, results, trends, and competitive information.

_____ 8. **MAINTAINS QUALITY SERVICE**
by
establishing and enforcing organization standards.

_____ 9. **MAINTAINS PROFESSIONAL AND TECHNICAL KNOWLEDGE**
by
attending educational workshops; reviewing professional publications; establishing personal networks; benchmarking state-of-the-art practices; participating in professional societies.

_____10. **CONTRIBUTES TO TEAM EFFORT**
by
accomplishing related results as needed.

JOB PURPOSE: **MAXIMIZES HUMAN RESOURCES DIVERSITY**
by
supervising staff; identifying diversity issues; providing training and guidance;
measuring program impact.

ESSENTIAL JOB RESULTS:

% of
time

% time

_____ 1. **MAINTAINS DIVERSITY STAFF**
by
recruiting, selecting, orienting, and
training employees; maintaining a safe,
secure, and legal work environment;
developing personal growth
opportunities.

_____ 2. **ACCOMPLISHES STAFF RESULTS**
by
communicating job expectations;
planning, monitoring, and appraising
job results; coaching, counseling, and
disciplining employees; developing,
coordinating, and enforcing systems,
policies, procedures, and productivity
standards.

_____ 3. **EXPLORES DIVERSITY ISSUES**
by
reviewing publications; benchmarking
state-of-the art thinking; forming focus
groups; conducting surveys; requesting
internal and external input from those in
a position to contribute; measuring
diversity tension.

_____ 4. **RECOMMENDS STRATEGIC
DIVERSITY GOALS**
by
gathering pertinent business, financial,
service, and operations information;
identifying and evaluating trends and
options; choosing a course of action;
defining objectives; evaluating
outcomes; conducting cost/benefit
analyses.

_____ 5. **DEVELOPS DIVERSITY
AWARENESS TRAINING**
by
preparing content, training media, and
intervention techniques.

_____ 6. **BALANCES INCREASED DIVERSITY
AND MAINTAINING QUALIFIED
WORKFORCE REQUIREMENTS**
by
studying essential work requirements;
identifying potential opportunities to
provide supplemental training to diverse
candidates who nearly meet those
requirements; identifying possible
facility and equipment modifications.

_____ 7. **MAINTAINS INTEGRATED TEAMS**
by
developing communication, problem
solving, and appreciation of differences
programs; evaluating attitudinal,
behavioral, and work-result outcomes.

_____ 8. **AVOIDS EMPLOYMENT
DISCRIMINATION LITIGATION**
by
identifying units within the organization
where minorities or women are
significantly underrepresented as
compared to the availability of qualified
candidates; determining whether there
is a reasonable explanation; exploring
whether active or passive discrimination
occurs.

ESSENTIAL JOB RESULTS:

% of
time

____ 9. PROVIDES TOOLS FOR MANAGING DIVERSITY
by
gathering information on the availability and hiring levels of minorities and women by organization unit or department; identifying working relationships on recruitment and promotion.

____10. ATTRACTS A WIDENING CUSTOMER BASE
by
retaining a diverse workforce mirroring the diversity of potential domestic and foreign markets; conducting business recognizing the diversity of the market.

____11. MAINTAINS QUALITY SERVICE
by
enforcing quality, diversity, and customer service standards; analyzing and resolving quality, diversity, and customer service problems; identifying trends; recommending system improvements.

% of
time

____12. MAINTAINS PROFESSIONAL AND TECHNICAL KNOWLEDGE
by
attending educational workshops; establishing personal networks; participating in professional societies; creating mentoring programs for minority employees.

____13. CONTRIBUTES TO TEAM EFFORT
by
accomplishing related results as needed.

JOB TITLE:	DIVISION PRESIDENT–HOME CONSTRUCTION	D140_M

JOB PURPOSE: **MAINTAINS PROFITABLE BUSINESS OF SATISFIED HOME BUYERS IN COMMUNITIES**
by
managing staff; acquiring and building quality homes; accomplishing financial objectives.

ESSENTIAL JOB RESULTS:

% of
time

_____ 1. **MAINTAINS DIVISION STAFF**
by
recruiting, selecting, orienting, and training employees; maintaining a safe and secure work environment; developing personal growth opportunities; building productive sub-contractor relationships.

_____ 2. **ACCOMPLISHES STAFF RESULTS**
by
communicating job expectations; planning, monitoring, and appraising job results; coaching, counseling, and disciplining employees; initiating, coordinating, and enforcing systems, policies, and procedures.

_____ 3. **PREPARES A STRATEGIC PLAN**
by
aligning with long-term corporate objectives; assessing growth opportunities; monitoring economic forecasts; planning product lines.

_____ 4. **ACQUIRES AND DEVELOPS LAND**
by
identifying suitable locations; negotiating purchases; developing building sites; opening communities.

_____ 5. **MARKETS HOMES**
by
identifying consumer requirements; developing marketing and advertising strategies and sales approaches; fostering broker relationships.

% of
time

_____ 6. **BUILDS QUALITY HOMES**
by
completing home construction; maintaining quality standards; finding ways to reduce construction cycle times.

_____ 7. **SATISFIES HOMEOWNERS**
by
completing home inspections; responding to customer requests; fulfilling home warranties; conducting customer satisfaction surveys.

_____ 8. **ACHIEVES FINANCIAL OBJECTIVES**
by
forecasting requirements; scheduling and monitoring expenditures; analyzing variances; initiating corrective action.

_____ 9. **MAINTAINS CONTINUITY AMONG CORPORATE, AREA, AND LOCAL WORK TEAMS**
by
documenting and communicating actions, irregularities, and continuing needs.

_____ 10. **MAINTAINS PROFESSIONAL AND TECHNICAL KNOWLEDGE**
by
attending educational workshops; benchmarking professional standards; reviewing professional publications; establishing personal networks.

_____ 11. **CONTRIBUTES TO TEAM EFFORT**
by
accomplishing related results as needed.

JOB TITLE: DOCUMENT CONTROL PROCESSOR   D141_M

JOB PURPOSE: MAINTAINS WORK FLOW
by
sorting and forwarding information; supporting operations.

ESSENTIAL JOB RESULTS:

% of
time

_____ 1. **PREPARES WORK TO BE ACCOMPLISHED**
by
sorting incoming documents.

_____ 2. **FORWARDS INFORMATION**
by
verifying document identification; distributing incoming documents; collecting and mailing outgoing documents.

_____ 3. **PROVIDES INFORMATION**
by
answering questions and requests.

_____ 4. **MAINTAINS QUALITY SERVICE**
by
maintaining and following procedure manuals; resolving processing problems; recording time measurements.

% of
time

_____ 5. **SUPPORTS OPERATIONS**
by
cross-training on related jobs.

_____ 6. **MAINTAINS SUPPLIES INVENTORY**
by
checking stock; anticipating needs; placing orders; verifying receipt.

_____ 7. **MAINTAINS TECHNICAL KNOWLEDGE**
by
attending educational workshops; reviewing publications.

_____ 8. **CONTRIBUTES TO TEAM EFFORT**
by
accomplishing related results as needed.

JOB TITLE: EMERGENCY MEDICAL TECHNICIAN   E149_M

JOB PURPOSE: PROVIDES EMERGENCY MEDICAL SUPPORT
by
responding to emergencies; stabilizing and transporting patients.

ESSENTIAL JOB RESULTS:

% of
time

% of
time

_____ 1. **PREPARES TO TRANSPORT PATIENTS**
by
completing operator vehicle inspections; inventorying supplies; correcting deficiencies.

_____ 2. **RESPONDS TO EMERGENCIES**
by
choosing route; observing traffic conditions; avoiding dangerous situations; maintaining communications with dispatcher.

_____ 3. **DETERMINES MEDICAL AND SAFETY REQUIREMENTS AT EMERGENCY SCENE**
by
assessing medical status of ill or injured persons; assessing prevailing circumstances; calling for support.

_____ 4. **STABILIZES ILL OR INJURED PERSONS**
by
rendering first aid; relaying status to medical personnel.

_____ 5. **MAINTAINS ORDER AT EMERGENCY SCENE**
by
controlling access; providing information to friends and relatives.

_____ 6. **MAINTAINS SAFE AND HEALTHY CONDITIONS**
by
following organization medical standards and legal regulations.

_____ 7. **CLEARS EMERGENCY SCENE**
by
transporting victims.

_____ 8. **COMPLETES REPORTS**
by
entering required information.

_____ 9. **ENSURES OPERATION OF EQUIPMENT**
by
completing preventive maintenance requirements; following manufacturer's instructions; troubleshooting malfunctions; calling for repairs; maintaining equipment inventories; evaluating new equipment and techniques.

_____ 10. **MAINTAINS PROFESSIONAL AND TECHNICAL KNOWLEDGE**
by
attending educational workshops; reviewing professional publications; establishing personal networks; benchmarking state-of-the-art practices; participating in professional societies.

_____ 11. **CONTRIBUTES TO TEAM EFFORT**
by
accomplishing related results as needed.

JOB TITLE: EMPLOYMENT CLERK   E151_M

JOB PURPOSE: **SUPPORTS EMPLOYMENT OPERATIONS**
by
entering information; completing interview arrangements; securing human resource data.

ESSENTIAL JOB RESULTS:

% of
time

____ 1. **PREPARES WORK TO BE ACCOMPLISHED**
by
gathering and sorting documents.

____ 2. **MAINTAINS APPLICANT COMPUTER SYSTEM**
by
entering resumes, applications, test results, and requisitions; routing or rejecting resumes; forwarding referral payment report to the payroll department.

____ 3. **COMPLETES INTERVIEW ARRANGEMENTS**
by
contacting applicants; scheduling tests and interviews; preparing agendas, travel arrangements, and hotel accommodations; photocopying and distributing background materials.

____ 4. **COMPLETES CORRESPONDENCE**
by
generating job postings; preparing recruiter memoranda; sending turndown letters.

____ 5. **VERIFIES APPLICANTS' QUALIFICATIONS**
by
administering and scoring tests; conducting preliminary reference checks.

____ 6. **PROCESSES INVOICES**
by
verifying vendor invoices and applicant travel and expense reports.

% of
time

____ 7. **SECURES HUMAN RESOURCES DATA**
by
completing database backups.

____ 8. **MAINTAINS HISTORICAL REFERENCE**
by
filing and retrieving applications.

____ 9. **MAINTAINS EMPLOYEE CONFIDENCE AND PROTECTS OPERATIONS**
by
keeping personnel data confidential.

____10. **MAINTAINS OPERATION OF EQUIPMENT**
by
following operator procedures; calling for repairs.

____11. **COMPLIES WITH FEDERAL, STATE, AND LOCAL REQUIREMENTS**
by
following policies and procedures.

____12. **MAINTAINS TECHNICAL KNOWLEDGE**
by
attending educational workshops; reviewing publications.

____13. **CONTRIBUTES TO TEAM EFFORT**
by
accomplishing related results as needed.

JOB PURPOSE: ENSURES EQUAL EMPLOYMENT OPPORTUNITIES FOR EMPLOYEES AND APPLICANTS
by
verifying compliance; training managers.

ESSENTIAL JOB RESULTS:

% of
time

% of
time

_____ 1. **VERIFIES COMPLIANCE**
by
conducting interviews; auditing procedures and actions; analyzing information.

_____ 2. **SUSTAINS KNOWLEDGE OF REGULATORY REQUIREMENTS**
by
studying current and proposed legislation and rulings; establishing personal networks with counterparts in other organizations.

_____ 3. **ADVOCATES EQUAL EMPLOYMENT POLICY, GOALS, AND ACTIONS**
by
studying regulatory requirements, organization goals, and compliance efforts; advising management; reviewing contracts.

_____ 4. **PROPOSES AFFIRMATIVE ACTION PLANS**
by
collecting data; preparing reports.

_____ 5. **HELPS MANAGERS ACCOMPLISH EQUAL EMPLOYMENT GOALS AND POLICIES**
by
conducting training programs.

_____ 6. **REPRESENTS THE ORGANIZATION**
by
obtaining, clarifying, and verifying documentation of situations; meeting with government representatives; studying and resolving complaints; recommending remedies.

_____ 7. **PREPARES REPORTS**
by
collecting, analyzing, and summarizing information.

_____ 8. **MAINTAINS PROFESSIONAL AND TECHNICAL KNOWLEDGE**
by
attending educational workshops; reviewing professional publications; establishing personal networks; benchmarking state-of-the-art practices; participating in professional societies.

_____ 9. **CONTRIBUTES TO TEAM EFFORT**
by
accomplishing related results as needed.

JOB PURPOSE: **PROJECTS AND CONTROLS CONSTRUCTION COSTS**
by
collecting and studying information; controlling construction costs.

ESSENTIAL JOB RESULTS:

% of
time

_____ 1. **PREPARES WORK TO BE ACCOMPLISHED**
by
gathering information and requirements; setting priorities.

_____ 2. **PREPARES CONSTRUCTION BUDGET**
by
studying home plans; updating specifications; identifying and projecting costs for each elevation.

_____ 3. **EVALUATES OFFERS TO PURCHASE**
by
costing changes, additions, and site requirements.

_____ 4. **OBTAINS BIDS FROM VENDORS AND SUBCONTRACTORS**
by
specifying materials; identifying qualified subcontractors; negotiating price.

_____ 5. **MAINTAINS COST KEYS AND PRICE MASTERS**
by
updating information.

_____ 6. **RESOLVES COST DISCREPANCIES**
by
collecting and analyzing information.

% of
time

_____ 7. **PREPARES SPECIAL REPORTS**
by
collecting, analyzing, and summarizing information and trends.

_____ 8. **MAINTAINS QUALITY SERVICE**
by
following organization standards.

_____ 9. **MAINTAINS CONTINUITY AMONG CORPORATE, DIVISION, AND LOCAL WORK TEAMS**
by
documenting and communicating actions, irregularities, and continuing needs.

_____10. **MAINTAINS PROFESSIONAL AND TECHNICAL KNOWLEDGE**
by
attending educational workshops; reviewing professional publications; establishing personal networks; participating in professional societies.

_____11. **CONTRIBUTES TO TEAM EFFORT**
by
accomplishing related results as needed.

JOB TITLE: FACILITIES AND TRANSPORTATION ASSISTANT   **F162_M**

JOB PURPOSE: **SUPPORTS OPERATIONS**
by
maintaining buildings, grounds, storage, and vehicles.

ESSENTIAL JOB RESULTS:

% of
time

% of
time

____ 1. **PREPARES WORK TO BE ACCOMPLISHED**
by
gathering requirements and information; establishing priorities.

____ 2. **MAINTAINS BUILDINGS AND GROUNDS**
by
ordering and stocking supplies; arranging for services and repairs; issuing and controlling keys; completing minor repairs; maintaining inventory.

____ 3. **PROVIDES VEHICLES**
by
negotiating price for purchase or lease; issuing purchase orders; arranging for maintenance, repairs, and cleaning; issuing credit cards; relocating trailers; disposing of vehicles; maintaining inventory.

____ 4. **PROVIDES STORAGE, SUPPLIES, AND OFFICE SERVICES**
by
renting warehouse space; storing records; supplying printers and copiers; monitoring mail delivery; maintaining inventory.

____ 5. **MAINTAINS TECHNICAL KNOWLEDGE**
by
attending educational workshops; reviewing publications.

____ 6. **CONTRIBUTES TO TEAM EFFORT**
by
accomplishing related results as needed.

JOB PURPOSE: PRODUCES PRODUCT
by
supervising crew; harvesting product; maintaining equipment.

ESSENTIAL JOB RESULTS:

% of
time

_____ 1. **DETERMINES CREW REQUIREMENTS**
by
studying production plan.

_____ 2. **MAINTAINS CREW**
by
recruiting, selecting, orienting, training, and transporting employees.

_____ 3. **ACCOMPLISHES CREW RESULTS**
by
communicating job expectations; planning, monitoring, and appraising job results; coaching, counseling, and disciplining employees; enforcing policies and procedures.

_____ 4. **ACCOMPLISHES FINANCIAL OBJECTIVES**
by
monitoring costs; completing payroll records.

_____ 5. **MAINTAINS SAFE AND HEALTHY ENVIRONMENT**
by
following organization standards and legal regulations; inspecting living quarters; arranging emergency medical treatment.

_____ 6. **ENSURES OPERATION OF EQUIPMENT**
by
completing preventive maintenance requirements; following manufacturer's instructions; troubleshooting malfunctions; calling for repairs; maintaining equipment inventories; evaluating new equipment and techniques.

% of
time

_____ 7. **PRODUCES PRODUCT**
by
cultivating ground; planting seeds; adding fertilizers and chemicals.

_____ 8. **IMPROVES PRODUCTION**
by
studying operations; recommending changes.

_____ 9. **HARVESTS PRODUCT**
by
establishing work schedules; assigning employees; inspecting, collecting, transporting, and storing product.

_____10. **COMPLETES RECORDS AND REPORTS**
by
entering required information.

_____11. **MAINTAINS TECHNICAL KNOWLEDGE**
by
attending educational workshops; reviewing publications.

_____12. **CONTRIBUTES TO TEAM EFFORT**
by
accomplishing related results as needed.

JOB PURPOSE: **PRODUCES PRODUCT**
by
supervising crew; planning, protecting, and harvesting crop.

ESSENTIAL JOB RESULTS:

% of
time

% of
time

_____ 1. **MAINTAINS CREW**
by
recruiting, selecting, orienting, and training employees; completing payroll requirements.

_____ 2. **ACCOMPLISHES CREW RESULTS**
by
communicating job expectations; planning, monitoring, and appraising job results; coaching, counseling, and disciplining employees.

_____ 3. **MAINTAINS OPERATIONS**
by
initiating and enforcing policies and procedures.

_____ 4. **DETERMINES GROWING REQUIREMENTS**
by
analyzing and estimating market conditions.

_____ 5. **PLANS GROWTH**
by
allocating acreage; calculating seed, fertilizer, and chemical requirements.

_____ 6. **ACCOMPLISHES FINANCIAL OBJECTIVES**
by
forecasting requirements; preparing an annual budget; scheduling expenditures; analyzing variances; initiating corrective action; recording costs.

_____ 7. **ENSURES OPERATION OF EQUIPMENT**
by
completing preventive maintenance requirements; following manufacturer's instructions; troubleshooting malfunctions; calling for repairs; maintaining equipment inventories; evaluating new equipment and techniques.

_____ 8. **PROTECTS GROWTH**
by
conducting inspections; anticipating adverse conditions; taking preventive action.

_____ 9. **HARVESTS GROWTH**
by
determining harvest date; moving, storing, and shipping product.

_____ 10. **MAINTAINS SAFE AND HEALTHY WORKING ENVIRONMENT**
by
establishing and enforcing organization standards; adhering to legal regulations.

_____ 11. **PREPARES REPORTS**
by
collecting, analyzing, and summarizing information.

ESSENTIAL JOB RESULTS:

% of
time

% of
time

____**12. MAINTAINS PROFESSIONAL AND TECHNICAL KNOWLEDGE**
by
attending educational workshops;
reviewing professional publications;
establishing personal networks;
benchmarking state-of-the-art practices;
participating in professional societies.

____**13. CONTRIBUTES TO TEAM EFFORT**
by
accomplishing related results as
needed.

JOB TITLE:	FAST-FOOD SERVER	F166_M

JOB PURPOSE: **SERVES CUSTOMERS**
by
taking and filling orders.

ESSENTIAL JOB RESULTS:

% of
time

% of
time

____ 1. **MAINTAINS SUPPLIES**
by
checking stock; anticipating needs;
restocking.

____ 2. **RECORDS CUSTOMER ORDERS**
by
clarifying selection; entering order into
cash register/ordering system; relaying
special orders.

____ 3. **OBTAINS REVENUE**
by
collecting and recording payment.

____ 4. **FILLS ORDERS**
by
retrieving items from prepared stock;
requesting items from kitchen; loading
containers.

____ 5. **FILLS STOCK ITEMS**
by
following recipes or instructions;
retrieving items from inventory.

____ 6. **MAINTAINS QUALITY SERVICE**
by
following organization standards.

____ 7. **MAINTAINS SAFE AND HEALTHY
WORK ENVIRONMENT**
by
following organization standards and
legal regulations; removing refuse;
cleaning tables, floors, and work area.

____ 8. **MAINTAINS TECHNICAL
KNOWLEDGE**
by
attending educational workshops;
reviewing publications.

____ 9. **CONTRIBUTES TO TEAM EFFORT**
by
accomplishing related results as
needed.

JOB PURPOSE: **SERVES CUSTOMERS**
by
establishing customer relationships; determining and documenting loss.

ESSENTIAL JOB RESULTS:

% of
time

_____ 1. **ESTABLISHES CUSTOMER RELATIONSHIPS**
by
initiating contacts; making appointments.

_____ 2. **DETERMINES COVERED LOSS**
by
meeting with insureds; inspecting losses; investigating incidents; interpreting policy coverages; explaining coverages; determining subrogation and salvage.

_____ 3. **PROVIDES CLAIMS INFORMATION**
by
documenting claims transactions; preparing and forwarding reports.

_____ 4. **DOCUMENTS REQUIRED REPAIRS**
by
obtaining costs and prices; preparing estimates.

_____ 5. **COMPLETES CLAIMS**
by
obtaining, providing, and exchanging information and agreements with contractors, public adjusters, attorneys, and other third parties.

% of
time

_____ 6. **DOCUMENTS CLAIMS MANAGEMENT ACTIONS**
by
writing letters to insureds; maintaining contact with accounts; keeping territory management informed.

_____ 7. **MAINTAINS PROFESSIONAL KNOWLEDGE**
by
attending educational workshops; reviewing professional publications; establishing personal networks; benchmarking state-of-the-art practices; participating in professional societies.

_____ 8. **CONTRIBUTES TO TEAM EFFORT**
by
accomplishing related results as needed.

JOB PURPOSE: **OBTAINS RAW PRODUCT FOR PROCESSING**
by
supervising staff; procuring raw product; building relationships with growers.

ESSENTIAL JOB RESULTS:

% of
time

_____ 1. **ACCOMPLISHES FIELD SERVICES STAFF RESULTS**
by
communicating job expectations; planning, monitoring, and appraising job results; coaching, counseling, and disciplining employees; initiating, coordinating, and enforcing systems, policies, and procedures.

_____ 2. **MAINTAINS STAFF**
by
recruiting, selecting, orienting, and training employees; maintaining a safe and secure work environment; developing personal growth opportunities.

_____ 3. **DEVELOPS POSITIVE IMAGE OF ORGANIZATION**
by
explaining capabilities and performance; establishing and maintaining communications with growers, warehouses, and industry; developing and conducting public relations campaigns.

_____ 4. **FOCUSES ADVERTISING AND MERCHANDISING PROGRAMS**
by
providing information and analysis of market from growers' point of view.

_____ 5. **LOCATES AND ENLISTS NEW GROWERS**
by
contacting potential suppliers; presenting and explaining value of relationship.

% of
time

_____ 6. **DETERMINES AMOUNT OF PRODUCT AVAILABLE FOR PROCESSING**
by
studying production and trends; obtaining information from growers, warehouses, and industry sources.

_____ 7. **PROCURES RAW PRODUCT**
by
negotiating contracts; specifying quality.

_____ 8. **MAINTAINS QUALITY SERVICE**
by
establishing and enforcing organization standards.

_____ 9. **MAINTAINS PROFESSIONAL AND TECHNICAL KNOWLEDGE**
by
attending educational workshops; reviewing professional publications; establishing personal networks; benchmarking state-of-the-art practices; participating in professional societies.

_____10. **CONTRIBUTES TO TEAM EFFORT**
by
accomplishing related results as needed.

JOB TITLE: FINANCE ACCOUNTING CLERK   F170_M

JOB PURPOSE: **SUPPORTS THE FINANCE DEPARTMENT**
by
collecting, reconciling, and summarizing information; entering data.

ESSENTIAL JOB RESULTS:

% of
time

_____ 1. **PREPARES FINANCE ACCOUNTING WORK TO BE ACCOMPLISHED**
by
gathering and sorting documents and related information.

_____ 2. **MAINTAINS SUBSIDIARY ACCOUNTS**
by
reconciling balances; preparing journal entries.

_____ 3. **MAINTAINS JOURNAL ENTRIES**
by
entering and editing data.

_____ 4. **PREPARES SPECIAL FINANCIAL REPORTS AND GRAPHS**
by
collecting and summarizing account information and trends.

_____ 5. **MAINTAINS SYSTEM CODES**
by
researching, collecting, and keying new or changed data.

_____ 6. **COMPLETES FINANCIAL TRANSACTIONS**
by
verifying and correcting transaction information; scheduling and preparing transactions; obtaining authorizations.

% of
time

_____ 7. **ENSURES ACCOUNT ACCURACY**
by
reconciling transactions; investigating and resolving discrepancies; following policies and procedures; keeping information confidential.

_____ 8. **PROTECTS OPERATIONS**
by
keeping financial information confidential.

_____ 9. **MAINTAINS HISTORICAL RECORDS**
by
preparing, sorting, and filing documents.

_____ 10. **MAINTAINS TECHNICAL KNOWLEDGE**
by
attending educational workshops; reviewing publications.

_____ 11. **CONTRIBUTES TO TEAM EFFORT**
by
accomplishing related results as needed.

JOB PURPOSE: **ANALYZES FINANCIAL STATUS**
by
collecting, monitoring, and studying data; recommending actions.

ESSENTIAL JOB RESULTS:

% of
time

____ 1. **DETERMINES COST OF OPERATIONS**
by
establishing standard costs; collecting operational data.

____ 2. **IDENTIFIES FINANCIAL STATUS**
by
comparing and analyzing actual results with plans and forecasts.

____ 3. **GUIDES COST ANALYSIS PROCESS**
by
establishing and enforcing policies and procedures; providing trends and forecasts; explaining processes and techniques; recommending actions.

____ 4. **IMPROVES FINANCIAL STATUS**
by
analyzing results; monitoring variances; identifying trends; recommending actions to management.

____ 5. **RECONCILES TRANSACTIONS**
by
comparing and correcting data.

____ 6. **MAINTAINS DATABASE**
by
entering, verifying, and backing up data.

% of
time

____ 7. **RECOMMENDS ACTIONS**
by
analyzing and interpreting data and making comparative analyses; studying proposed changes in methods and materials.

____ 8. **INCREASES PRODUCTIVITY**
by
developing automated accounting applications; coordinating information requirements.

____ 9. **PROTECTS OPERATIONS**
by
keeping financial information confidential.

____10. **MAINTAINS TECHNICAL KNOWLEDGE**
by
attending educational workshops; reviewing publications.

____11. **CONTRIBUTES TO TEAM EFFORT**
by
accomplishing related results as needed.

JOB PURPOSE: **SUPPORTS DEPARTMENT OPERATIONS**
by
processing invoices; entering and updating information.

ESSENTIAL JOB RESULTS:

% of
time

% of
time

____ 1. **MAINTAINS PAYABLES**
by
processing invoices.

____ 2. **MAINTAINS VENDOR DATABASE**
by
entering, updating, and backing up
data.

____ 3. **MAINTAINS CONTRACT FILES**
by
filing and updating contract information.

____ 4. **COMPLETES FINANCIAL TRANSACTIONS**
by
verifying, scheduling, preparing, and
correcting transaction information.

____ 5. **PROVIDES INFORMATION TO MANAGEMENT**
by
collecting and analyzing data; preparing
reports; gathering and reporting budget
and expense information.

____ 6. **MAINTAINS INVENTORY**
by
preparing worksheets.

____ 7. **IDENTIFIES TELEPHONE EXPENSES**
by
preparing worksheets.

____ 8. **PROTECTS OPERATIONS**
by
keeping financial information
confidential.

____ 9. **MAINTAINS TECHNICAL KNOWLEDGE**
by
attending educational workshops;
reviewing publications.

____10. **CONTRIBUTES TO TEAM EFFORT**
by
accomplishing related results as
needed.

JOB PURPOSE: **SUPPORTS MANAGEMENT PLANNING AND DECISION MAKING**
by
identifying, maintaining, and evaluating information; recommending actions.

ESSENTIAL JOB RESULTS:

% of
time

_____ 1. **DEFINES FINANCIAL SITUTATION**
by
completing quantitative analyses.

_____ 2. **EVALUATES OPTIONAL PLANS**
by
identifying outcomes and potential
returns.

_____ 3. **VALUES ASSETS**
by
appraising current condition; assessing
potential.

_____ 4. **RECOMMENDS DEBT STRUCTURES**
by
analyzing refinancing options.

_____ 5. **BUILDS FINANCIAL DATABASE**
by
identifying sources of information;
assembling, verifying, and backing up
data.

_____ 6. **RECOMMENDS FINANCIAL
ACTIONS**
by
assessing options in relation to
organization goals.

% of
time

_____ 7. **PREPARES FINANCIAL REPORTS**
by
collecting, formatting, analyzing, and
explaining information.

_____ 8. **PROTECTS OPERATIONS**
by
keeping financial information
confidential.

_____ 9. **MAINTAINS TECHNICAL
KNOWLEDGE**
by
attending educational workshops;
reviewing publications.

_____10. **CONTRIBUTES TO TEAM EFFORT**
by
accomplishing related results as
needed.

JOB PURPOSE: **PRODUCES MARINE PRODUCTS**
by
catching, loading, and unloading fish; operating equipment.

ESSENTIAL JOB RESULTS:

% of
time

____ **1. ENSURES OPERATION OF EQUIPMENT**
by
completing preventive maintenance requirements; following manufacturer's instructions; troubleshooting malfunctions; reporting repairs.

____ **2. PRODUCES PRODUCT**
by
transferring fish; sowing spat; providing feed.

____ **3. CATCHES FISH**
by
lowering and raising nets and baskets.

____ **4. UNLOADS FISH**
by
operating equipment; hand-picking unmarketable and illegal items.

____ **5. PACKS FISH**
by
loading fish and ice into containers.

% of
time

____ **6. ESTABLISHES AND MAINTAINS GROWING AREAS**
by
fencing perimeter; completing repairs; maintaining tanks.

____ **7. COMPLETES REPORTS**
by
entering required information.

____ **8. MAINTAINS TECHNICAL KNOWLEDGE**
by
attending educational workshops; reviewing publications.

____ **9. CONTRIBUTES TO TEAM EFFORT**
by
accomplishing related results as needed.

JOB TITLE: FIXED ASSET ACCOUNTANT   F177_M

JOB PURPOSE: **PROTECTS FIXED ASSETS**
by
maintaining schedules; entering and updating information.

ESSENTIAL JOB RESULTS:

% of
time

_____ **1. MAINTAINS FIXED ASSET SCHEDULES**
by
researching depreciation laws; recommending actions; completing depreciation transactions.

_____ **2. RESOLVES DISCREPANCIES**
by
investigating and reconciling transactions; maintaining suspense files.

_____ **3. COMPLETES FINANCIAL TRANSACTIONS**
by
processing fixed asset schedules; verifying and correcting transaction information; scheduling and preparing transactions.

_____ **4. CONTROLS EXPENSES**
by
preparing annual budgets for cost centers; monitoring monthly allocation system.

_____ **5. MAINTAINS DATABASE**
by
entering, verifying, and backing up data.

% of
time

_____ **6. MAINTAINS FINANCIAL HISTORICAL RECORDS**
by
preparing and securing accounting documents.

_____ **7. PROTECTS OPERATIONS**
by
keeping financial information confidential.

_____ **8. MAINTAINS CONTINUITY AMONG CORPORATE, DIVISION, AND LOCAL WORK TEAMS**
by
documenting and communicating actions, irregularities, and continuing needs.

_____ **9. MAINTAINS TECHNICAL KNOWLEDGE**
by
attending educational workshops; reviewing publications.

_____**10. CONTRIBUTES TO TEAM EFFORT**
by
accomplishing related results as needed.

JOB PURPOSE: **SERVES AND PROTECTS PASSENGERS**
by
greeting and directing them; preparing equipment and supplies; maintaining safe operations.

ESSENTIAL JOB RESULTS:

% of
time

% of
time

_____ **1. PREPARES FOR FLIGHT**
by
inspecting cabin; invontorying supplies; correcting deficiencies.

_____ **2. WELCOMES PASSENGERS**
by
greeting and directing them; verifying tickets; helping with luggage storage.

_____ **3. MAINTAINS SAFE OPERATIONS**
by
announcing and enforcing Federal Aviation Administration and company regulations; explaining and demonstrating use of equipment.

_____ **4. SERVES PASSENGERS**
by
taking meal and refreshment orders and delivering them; providing comfort items such as pillows and blankets; providing information.

_____ **5. AIDS ILL PASSENGERS**
by
providing first aid and comfort.

_____ **6. OBTAINS REVENUE**
by
collecting charges; recording receipts.

_____ **7. COMPLETES REPORTS**
by
entering required information.

_____ **8. MAINTAINS PROFESSIONAL AND TECHNICAL KNOWLEDGE**
by
attending educational workshops; completing proficiency tests; reviewing professional publications.

_____ **9. CONTRIBUTES TO TEAM EFFORT**
by
accomplishing related results as needed.

JOB TITLE: FOOD SAMPLING SPECIALIST   F179_M

JOB PURPOSE: **PROVIDES FOOD SAMPLES TO CUSTOMERS**
by
preparing and shipping items.

ESSENTIAL JOB RESULTS:

% of
time

____ 1. **ORGANIZES WORKLOAD**
by
routing requests; tracking responses.

____ 2. **MAINTAINS QUALITY**
by
verifying that food samples meet
organization standards.

____ 3. **DETERMINES METHOD OF SHIPMENT**
by
considering items to be shipped,
destination, route, rate, and time the
shipment is needed.

____ 4. **PREPARES SHIPMENTS**
by
assembling, packing, protecting, and
labeling containers.

____ 5. **DOCUMENTS FOOD SAMPLE ITEMS SHIPPED**
by
recording identifying information.

____ 6. **MAINTAINS DATABASE**
by
entering, verifying, and backing up
data.

% of
time

____ 7. **MAINTAINS SHIPPING AND RECEIVING MATERIALS**
by
checking stock to determine inventory
level; anticipating needs; placing and
expediting orders; verifying receipt.

____ 8. **MAINTAINS QUALITY SERVICE**
by
following organization standards.

____ 9. **MAINTAINS HISTORICAL RECORDS**
by
filing and retrieving documents.

____10. **MAINTAINS TECHNICAL KNOWLEDGE**
by
attending educational workshops;
reviewing publications.

____11. **CONTRIBUTES TO TEAM EFFORT**
by
accomplishing related results as
needed.

JOB TITLE: FOOD TECHNOLOGIST–PRODUCTION   F180_M

JOB PURPOSE: **SUPPORTS TECHNICAL, RESEARCH, ANALYTICAL, AND SENSORY PROJECTS**
by
maintaining quality consistency; preparing and testing samples.

ESSENTIAL JOB RESULTS:

% of
time

_____ 1. **ANALYZES PRODUCTION**
by
benchmarking projects; developing flowcharts; tracking labor hours.

_____ 2. **COMPLIES WITH REGULATORY REQUIREMENTS**
by
preparing samples for pesticide residue testing; developing data for authenticity and labeling requirements; preparing and testing samples for possible adulteration.

_____ 3. **MAINTAINS PRODUCT QUALITY CONSISTENCY**
by
providing assistance in the preparation, setup, and serving of samples for sensory evaluation panels and projects; aiding in the training of sensory panelists.

_____ 4. **MAINTAINS ANALYTICAL QUALITY CONSISTENCY**
by
monitoring the calibration of analytical equipment; tracking plant analytical capabilities and accuracy; solving analytical problems and discrepancies.

_____ 5. **SUPPORTS ANALYTICAL AND SENSORY RESEARCH**
by
preparing samples; participating in pilot plant projects; assisting in off-site research; participating in product shelf-life studies; entering information into computer databases; writing reports.

% of
time

_____ 6. **MAINTAINS DATABASE**
by
entering, verifying, and backing up data.

_____ 7. **MAINTAINS QUALITY SERVICE**
by
establishing and enforcing organization standards.

_____ 8. **MAINTAINS PROFESSIONAL AND TECHNICAL KNOWLEDGE**
by
attending educational workshops; reviewing professional publications; establishing personal networks; benchmarking state-of-the-art practices; participating in professional societies.

_____ 9. **CONTRIBUTES TO TEAM EFFORT**
by
accomplishing related results as needed.

JOB PURPOSE: **ASSURES QUALITY PRODUCT**
by
identifying, monitoring, and reporting quality status.

ESSENTIAL JOB RESULTS:

% of
time

% of
time

_____ 1. **IDENTIFIES RAW MATERIAL CONDITION**
by
collecting material samples; conducting inspections and physical tests of materials.

_____ 2. **IDENTIFIES FINISHED PRODUCT CONDITION**
by
collecting, classifying, analyzing, and interpreting quality data; judging product acceptability in comparison to specifications; conducting inspections and physical tests of materials.

_____ 3. **DOCUMENTS FINISHED PRODUCT STATUS**
by
recording and summarizing raw materials and finished product inspection and physical test data; updating quality assurance database.

_____ 4. **SECURES DATABASE**
by
backing up data.

_____ 5. **MAINTAINS QUALITY ASSURANCE OPERATIONS**
by
following policies and procedures; reporting needed changes.

_____ 6. **ENSURES OPERATION OF EQUIPMENT**
by
completing preventive maintenance; following calibration procedures; calling for repairs.

_____ 7. **PREPARES TECHNICAL REPORTS**
by
collecting, analyzing, and summarizing information and trends.

_____ 8. **CONTRIBUTES TO TEAM EFFORT**
by
accomplishing related results as needed.

JOB TITLE:	FOREST TECHNICIAN	F182_M

JOB PURPOSE: **MAINTAINS FOREST LANDS**
by
collecting data; planting; protecting resources.

ESSENTIAL JOB RESULTS:

% of
time

% of
time

_____ 1. **SURVEYS AND MAPS FOREST RESOURCES**
by
obtaining measurements; recording data.

_____ 2. **COLLECTS RESOURCE DATA**
by
recording topographical and environmental data, tree species and population, disease and pest damage, seedling mortality, and timber available for harvest; marking trees.

_____ 3. **COMPLETES FORESTATION AND REFORESTATION PROJECTS**
by
collecting seed cones; planting seedlings.

_____ 4. **PROTECTS RESOURCES**
by
patrolling area; identifying fire danger conditions; preparing fire breaks.

_____ 5. **RESCUES RESOURCES**
by
fighting fires.

_____ 6. **PREVENTS DAMAGE TO RESOURCES**
by
educating campers and hikers.

_____ 7. **COMPLETES WORK**
by
scheduling and assigning conservation workers; monitoring work results; conducting training.

_____ 8. **ENSURES OPERATION OF EQUIPMENT**
by
completing preventive maintenance requirements; following manufacturer's instructions; troubleshooting malfunctions; calling for repairs; maintaining equipment inventories; evaluating new equipment and techniques.

_____ 9. **MAINTAINS FACILITIES**
by
completing repairs and cleaning.

_____10. **COMPLETES REPORTS**
by
entering required information.

_____11. **MAINTAINS TECHNICAL KNOWLEDGE**
by
attending educational workshops; reviewing publications.

_____12. **CONTRIBUTES TO TEAM EFFORT**
by
accomplishing related results as needed.

JOB TITLE: FOREST WORKER   F183_M

JOB PURPOSE: **MAINTAINS FOREST LANDS**
by
maintaining and protecting resources.

ESSENTIAL JOB RESULTS:

% of
time

% of
time

_____ 1. **DEVELOPS FOREST RESOURCES**
by
planting seedlings.

_____ 2. **MAINTAINS RESOURCES**
by
pruning; cutting out undesirable trees;
applying herbicides.

_____ 3. **CLEARS AREA**
by
removing brush, limbs, and debris.

_____ 4. **PROTECTS RESOURCES**
by
patrolling area; identifying fire danger
conditions; preparing fire breaks.

_____ 5. **MAINTAINS FACILITIES**
by
completing construction, repairs, and
cleaning; replenishing supplies;
erecting signs.

_____ 6. **SURVEYS AND MAPS RESOURCES**
by
operating measurement instruments.

_____ 7. **RESCUES RESOURCES**
by
fighting fires.

_____ 8. **PREVENTS DAMAGE TO
RESOURCES**
by
educating campers and hikers.

_____ 9. **MAINTAINS TECHNICAL
KNOWLEDGE**
by
attending educational workshops;
reviewing publications.

_____10. **CONTRIBUTES TO TEAM EFFORT**
by
accomplishing related results as
needed.

JOB PURPOSE: **DEVELOPS FOREST LANDS**
by
planning and protecting resources.

ESSENTIAL JOB RESULTS:

% of
time

____ 1. **IDENTIFIES FOREST RESOURCES**
by
surveying and mapping forest areas;
estimating standing timber and future
growth.

____ 2. **MAINTAINS AND IMPROVES
RESOURCES**
by
planning forestation and reforestation
projects; planning cutting programs;
determining removal methods.

____ 3. **PROTECTS RESOURCES**
by
patrolling area; enforcing laws; training
firefighters; planning fire breaks.

____ 4. **PROTECTS ENVIRONMENT**
by
completing environmental studies;
implementing environmental control
programs.

____ 5. **PREVENTS DAMAGE TO
RESOURCES**
by
preparing fire prevention programs and
literature; educating campers and
hikers; implementing flood control, soil
erosion, tree disease, and pest control
programs.

____ 6. **RESCUES RESOURCES**
by
directing fire fighting and fighting fires.

% of
time

____ 7. **MAINTAINS FACILITIES**
by
designing and constructing roads,
paths, observation towers, and
recreational facilities; supervising repair
and cleaning.

____ 8. **OBTAINS REVENUE**
by
selling timber; collecting payment.

____ 9. **MAINTAINS HISTORICAL RECORDS**
by
filing documents.

____10. **PREPARES REPORTS**
by
collecting, analyzing, and summarizing
information.

____11. **MAINTAINS PROFESSIONAL AND
TECHNICAL KNOWLEDGE**
by
attending educational workshops;
reviewing professional publications;
establishing personal networks;
benchmarking state-of-the-art practices;
participating in professional societies.

____12. **CONTRIBUTES TO TEAM EFFORT**
by
accomplishing related results as
needed.

152

JOB TITLE:	FORM DESIGNER	F185_M

JOB PURPOSE: **CREATES FORMS**
by
designing and preparing documents to be printed.

ESSENTIAL JOB RESULTS:

% of
time

____ 1. **PRODUCES MATERIALS**
by
formatting and typesetting forms.

____ 2. **PASTES UP DOCUMENTS**
by
creating boards, adding cropmarks, and
trimming to required size; indicating
color separations and screens on final
print jobs; creating mock-ups; indicating
carbon stops, page sequence and
length, screens, and blockouts;
operating desktop publishing system.

____ 3. **ENSURES QUALITY OF
DOCUMENTS**
by
creating and revising typeset and
desktop publishing documents.

____ 4. **RESOLVES PRINTERS' INQUIRIES**
by
providing instruction and clarification
regarding mock-ups and printing jobs.

____ 5. **RESOLVES INTERNAL CUSTOMER
PROBLEMS**
by
collecting and analyzing information on
design and setup procedures;
furnishing instruction and clarification.

% of
time

____ 6. **PRODUCES GRAPHICS**
by
scanning half-tones and line art for
incorporation into documents.

____ 7. **MAINTAINS DATABASE DRIVEN
WORK-TRACKING PROGRAMS**
by
entering page-counting information.

____ 8. **ENSURES OPERATION OF
EQUIPMENT**
by
following manufacturer's instructions;
troubleshooting malfunctions; calling for
repair.

____ 9. **MAINTAINS PROFESSIONAL AND
TECHNICAL KNOWLEDGE**
by
attending educational workshops;
reviewing publications.

____ 10. **CONTRIBUTES TO TEAM EFFORT**
by
accomplishing related results as
needed.

JOB TITLE: FUNERAL HOME DIRECTOR

F188_M

JOB PURPOSE: **HELPS BEREAVED DEAL WITH THEIR LOSS**
by
supervising staff; removing and preparing body; preparing and conducting services.

ESSENTIAL JOB RESULTS:

% of
time

% of
time

____ 1. **MAINTAINS FUNERAL HOME STAFF**
by
recruiting, selecting, orienting, and training employees; developing personal growth opportunities.

____ 2. **ACCOMPLISHES STAFF RESULTS**
by
communicating job expectations; planning, monitoring, and appraising job results; coaching, counseling, and disciplining employees; initiating, coordinating, and enforcing systems, policies, and procedures.

____ 3. **REMOVES BODY TO MORTUARY**
by
responding to calls; dispatching drivers and vehicles; preparing mortuary staff to receive corpse.

____ 4. **MAINTAINS SAFE AND HEALTHY WORKING ENVIRONMENT**
by
establishing and enforcing organization standards; adhering to legal regulations.

____ 5. **ENSURES OPERATION OF EQUIPMENT**
by
completing preventive maintenance requirements; following manufacturer's instructions; troubleshooting malfunctions; calling for repairs; maintaining equipment inventories; evaluating new equipment and techniques.

____ 6. **COMFORTS FAMILY**
by
acknowledging their grief; offering condolences; identifying arrangements to be made; determining priorities; suggesting services available.

____ 7. **NOTIFIES THE COMMUNITY**
by
interviewing family members and others; reviewing news releases; summarizing the life of the departed; writing the obituary notice; notifying news services, newspapers, and others with the need to know; arranging for issuance of death certificates.

____ 8. **PLANS FINAL CEREMONIES**
by
assisting in selecting casket or urn; determining cemetery or alternative destination; arranging ceremony, including readings, songs, contemplations, messages, and religious rites.

____ 9. **ARRANGES VISITATION**
by
placing casket in parlor; adjusting lighting; arranging floral displays; greeting mourners; furnishing refreshments in visitor lounge.

ESSENTIAL JOB RESULTS:

% of
time

% of
time

_____10. **CONDUCTS FUNERAL SERVICES**
by
welcoming grieving friends and family;
offering condolences; speaking and
introducing others; closing casket;
supporting family and others close to
the deceased.

_____11. **ESCORTS DECEASED TO
INTERMENT**
by
instructing pallbearers how to lift and
carry casket; leading funeral cortege.

_____12. **ACCOMPLISHES FINANCIAL
OBJECTIVES**
by
forecasting requirements; preparing an
annual budget; scheduling
expenditures; analyzing variances;
initiating corrective action.

_____13. **MAINTAINS QUALITY SERVICE**
by
establishing and enforcing organization
standards.

_____14. **MAINTAINS PROFESSIONAL AND
TECHNICAL KNOWLEDGE**
by
attending educational workshops;
reviewing professional publications;
establishing personal networks;
benchmarking state-of-the-art practices;
participating in professional societies.

_____15. **CONTRIBUTES TO TEAM EFFORT**
by
accomplishing related results as
needed.

JOB PURPOSE: **OBTAINS PROFIT CONTRIBUTION**
by
managing staff; establishing and accomplishing business objectives.

ESSENTIAL JOB RESULTS:

% of
time

____ 1. **INCREASES MANAGEMENT'S EFFECTIVENESS**
by
recruiting, selecting, orienting, training, coaching, counseling, and disciplining managers; communicating values, strategies, and objectives; assigning accountabilities; planning, monitoring, and appraising job results; developing incentives; developing a climate for offering information and opinions; providing educational opportunities.

____ 2. **DEVELOPS STRATEGIC PLAN**
by
studying technological and financial opportunities; presenting assumptions; recommending objectives.

____ 3. **ACCOMPLISHES SUBSIDIARY OBJECTIVES**
by
establishing plans, budgets, and results measurements; allocating resources; reviewing progress; making mid-course corrections.

____ 4. **COORDINATES EFFORTS**
by
establishing procurement, production, marketing, field, and technical services policies and practices; coordinating actions with corporate staff.

% of
time

____ 5. **BUILDS COMPANY IMAGE**
by
collaborating with customers, government, community organizations, and employees; enforcing ethical business practices.

____ 6. **MAINTAINS QUALITY SERVICE**
by
establishing and enforcing organization standards.

____ 7. **MAINTAINS PROFESSIONAL AND TECHNICAL KNOWLEDGE**
by
attending educational workshops; reviewing professional publications; establishing personal networks; benchmarking state-of-the-art practices; participating in professional societies.

____ 8. **CONTRIBUTES TO TEAM EFFORT**
by
accomplishing related results as needed.

```
┌─────────────────────────────────────────────────────────────────────────┐
│  JOB TITLE:    GOLF CLUB MANAGER                          G190_M          │
└─────────────────────────────────────────────────────────────────────────┘
```

JOB PURPOSE: **PROVIDES GOLFING AND SOCIAL ENTERTAINMENT**
by
supervising staff; planning and maintaining grounds; planning and presenting
activities.

ESSENTIAL JOB RESULTS:

% of
time

_____ 1. **MAINTAINS GOLF CLUB STAFF**
by
recruiting, selecting, orienting, and
training employees; maintaining a safe
and secure work environment;
developing personal growth
opportunities.

_____ 2. **ACCOMPLISHES STAFF RESULTS**
by
communicating job expectations;
planning, monitoring, and appraising
job results; coaching, counseling, and
disciplining employees; initiating,
coordinating, and enforcing systems,
policies, and procedures.

_____ 3. **ACHIEVES WORK OBJECTIVES**
by
gathering pertinent information;
identifying and evaluating options;
choosing a course of action.

_____ 4. **ACCOMPLISHES FINANCIAL
OBJECTIVES**
by
forecasting requirements; preparing an
annual budget; scheduling
expenditures; analyzing variances;
initiating corrective action.

_____ 5. **KEEPS GOLF COURSE IN PLAYING
CONDITION**
by
maintaining grounds and turf;
overseeing tilling, cultivating, and
grading new turf areas; directing
applications of lime, fertilizer,
insecticide, and fungicide.

% of
time

_____ 6. **BEAUTIFIES GROUNDS**
by
adding landscaping enhancements.

_____ 7. **ATTRACTS NEW MEMBERS**
by
promoting services; anticipating golfing
trends; developing networks with those
in a position to recommend new
services; satisfying current members.

_____ 8. **MAINTAINS CLUB BUILDINGS**
by
identifying needed repairs; selecting
maintenance methods; utilizing external
resources as needed.

_____ 9. **PROVIDES FOOD AND BEVERAGE
SERVICES**
by
maintaining restaurant, grill, and
lounge; catering private parties.

_____10. **SELLS GOLF MERCHANDISE**
by
selecting goods; maintaining pro shop;
offering advice.

_____11. **IMPROVES MEMBERS' GOLF
GAMES**
by
providing services of a golf
professional.

_____12. **GENERATES REVENUES**
by
collecting membership, food and
beverage, pro shop, golf lesson, and
greens fees.

157

ESSENTIAL JOB RESULTS:

% of
time

% of
time

____13. **MAINTAINS HARMONY AMONG MEMBERS**
by
explaining rules of golf; settling member disputes; preventing unauthorized persons from using facilities; handling lost and found articles.

____14. **MAINTAINS PROFESSIONAL AND TECHNICAL KNOWLEDGE**
by
attending educational workshops; reviewing professional publications; establishing personal networks; benchmarking state-of-the-art practices; participating in professional societies.

____15. **CONTRIBUTES TO TEAM EFFORT**
by
accomplishing related results as needed.

JOB PURPOSE: **MAINTAINS REGULATION COMPLIANCE**
by
monitoring, analyzing, updating, and forwarding regulatory information.

ESSENTIAL JOB RESULTS:

% of
time

% of
time

_____ 1. **RESEARCHES GOVERNMENT AND PUBLIC AFFAIRS ISSUES**
by
monitoring and tracking legislative, regulatory, trade, and public affairs issues.

_____ 2. **INFORMS CUSTOMERS AND EMPLOYEES**
by
publishing government affairs newsletter and political action newsletter.

_____ 3. **MAINTAINS REGULATORY INFORMATION**
by
distributing new laws and regulations; coordinating information with applicable departments about changes; responding to requests for current and updated regulatory information.

_____ 4. **COMPLETES GOVERNMENT RELATIONS REPORTING REQUIREMENTS**
by
preparing responses for distribution to insurance departments, state and federal legislators and their staff; tracking political action contribution filings and reporting deadlines.

_____ 5. **DELIVERS PUBLIC AFFAIRS SERVICES**
by
developing brochures; preparing marketing statements; conducting surveys; maintaining company position paper manual; preparing responses to trade and non-trade media and to other external sources.

_____ 6. **MAINTAINS QUALITY SERVICE**
by
establishing and enforcing organization standards.

_____ 7. **ADVISES MANAGEMENT**
by
analyzing legislative and regulatory issues; attending hearings and conferences; providing technical, research, analytical, communications, and compliance support.

_____ 8. **COMPLIES WITH LEGAL REQUIREMENTS**
by
studying existing and new legislation; anticipating future legislation; enforcing adherence to requirements; advising executive management on needed actions.

_____ 9. **MAINTAINS PROFESSIONAL AND TECHNICAL KNOWLEDGE**
by
attending educational workshops; reviewing professional publications; establishing personal networks; benchmarking state-of-the-art practices; participating in professional societies.

_____ 10. **CONTRIBUTES TO TEAM EFFORT**
by
accomplishing related results as needed.

JOB TITLE: HAIR STYLIST   H193_M

JOB PURPOSE: **SERVES CUSTOMERS**
by
preparing, conditioning, and styling hair.

ESSENTIAL JOB RESULTS:

% of
time

% of
time

_____ 1. **MAINTAINS SUPPLIES**
by
checking stock; anticipating needs;
placing orders; verifying receipt.

_____ 2. **PREPARES HAIR FOR STYLING**
by
analyzing hair condition; shampooing
and treating hair.

_____ 3. **CONDITIONS HAIR AND SCALP**
by
applying treatments.

_____ 4. **PLANS DESIRED EFFECT**
by
studying facial features; examining
potential styles; conferring with
customer; making recommendations.

_____ 5. **PRODUCES DESIRED EFFECT**
by
arranging, shaping, curling, cutting,
trimming, setting, bleaching, dyeing,
and tinting hair.

_____ 6. **MAINTAINS QUALITY SERVICE**
by
following organization standards.

_____ 7. **MAINTAINS SAFE AND HEALTHY
CONDITIONS**
by
following organization standards and
legal regulations.

_____ 8. **OBTAINS REVENUE**
by
recording or collecting charges.

_____ 9. **MAINTAINS TECHNICAL
KNOWLEDGE**
by
attending educational workshops;
reviewing publications.

_____10. **CONTRIBUTES TO TEAM EFFORT**
by
accomplishing related results as
needed.

JOB TITLE: HEALTH AND WELLNESS INSTRUCTOR   H194_M

JOB PURPOSE: PROMOTES AND MAINTAINS HEALTH AND WELLNESS
by
developing fitness plans; providing training.

ESSENTIAL JOB RESULTS:

% of
time

% of
time

_____ 1. **ASSESSES FITNESS**
by
identifying short-term and long-term
fitness issues using submax stress test
and flexibility, strength, and body
composition assessments.

_____ 2. **DEVELOPS FITNESS PLANS**
by
interpreting assessment results;
designing exercise routines; providing
nutritional information; explaining
equipment.

_____ 3. **PROVIDES PERSONAL TRAINING**
by
consulting on proper technique;
adjusting weights; spotting.

_____ 4. **PRESENTS CLASSES**
by
identifying learning objectives; selecting
instructional methodologies; delivering
information (weight management,
fitness challenges, prenatal care).

_____ 5. **ACCOMPLISHES SPECIAL
PROJECTS**
by
designing and implementing fitness
games; ordering prizes.

_____ 6. **INFORMS EMPLOYEES**
by
publishing newsletter.

_____ 7. **MAINTAINS QUALITY SERVICE**
by
following organization standards.

_____ 8. **MAINTAINS RECORDS**
by
updating membership list.

_____ 9. **ENSURES OPERATION OF
EQUIPMENT**
by
following manufacturer's instructions;
troubleshooting malfunctions; calling for
repairs.

_____ 10. **MAINTAINS SAFE AND CLEAN
WORKING ENVIRONMENT**
by
complying with procedures, rules, and
regulations.

_____ 11. **MAINTAINS PROFESSIONAL AND
TECHNICAL KNOWLEDGE**
by
attending educational workshops;
reviewing publications.

_____ 12. **CONTRIBUTES TO TEAM EFFORT**
by
accomplishing related results as
needed.

JOB TITLE:	HOME DECORATOR	H198_M

JOB PURPOSE: **SATISFIES HOME BUYERS**
by
explaining design selections.

ESSENTIAL JOB RESULTS:

% of
time

% of
time

_____ 1. **WELCOMES HOME BUYERS**
by
scheduling appointments; giving
directions to design center.

_____ 2. **DETERMINES DESIGN
REQUIREMENTS**
by
interviewing home buyers.

_____ 3. **HELPS HOME BUYERS WITH
DESIGN SELECTIONS**
by
explaining design choices; giving
advice on materials, appliances, colors,
custom trims, and features; evaluating
home buyer's ability to add additional-
cost items; negotiating payment
options; verifying selections.

_____ 4. **RESEARCHES SPECIAL REQUESTS**
by
obtaining information on special
materials and verifying applicability with
construction manager.

_____ 5. **MAINTAINS HOME BUYER DESIGN
RECORDS**
by
recording and updating selections and
costs.

_____ 6. **PROVIDES INFORMATION**
by
gathering, analyzing, and forwarding
customer design requests and changes
to sales representatives and
construction manager.

_____ 7. **MAINTAINS DESIGN CENTERS**
by
gathering, organizing, and displaying
selections.

_____ 8. **CREATES SALES**
by
fostering and maintaining relationships
with area realtors; planning luncheons
and special events.

_____ 9. **IDENTIFIES CURRENT AND FUTURE
CUSTOMER DESIGN
REQUIREMENTS**
by
establishing personal rapport with
potential and actual customers and
other persons in a position to
understand design requirements.

_____ 10. **PREPARES REPORTS**
by
collecting, analyzing, and summarizing
data.

_____ 11. **MAINTAINS CONTINUITY AMONG
CORPORATE, DIVISION, AND
LOCAL WORK TEAMS**
by
documenting and communicating
actions, irregularities, and continuing
needs.

_____ 12. **MAINTAINS PROFESSIONAL AND
TECHNICAL KNOWLEDGE**
by
attending educational workshops;
reviewing publications.

_____ 13. **CONTRIBUTES TO TEAM EFFORT**
by
accomplishing related results as
needed.

_162_

JOB TITLE: HORTICULTURE SUPERVISOR   H199_M

JOB PURPOSE: DISPLAYS PLANTS
by
supervising staff; planning and constructing displays; generating revenue.

ESSENTIAL JOB RESULTS:

% of
time

____ 1. **MAINTAINS HORTICULTURE STAFF**
by
recruiting, selecting, orienting, and
training employees.

____ 2. **ACCOMPLISHES STAFF RESULTS**
by
communicating job expectations;
planning, monitoring, and appraising
job results; coaching, counseling, and
disciplining employees; initiating,
coordinating, and enforcing systems,
policies, and procedures.

____ 3. **MAINTAINS SAFE AND HEALTHY
WORKING ENVIRONMENT**
by
following organization standards and
legal regulations.

____ 4. **DEVELOPS DISPLAY PLAN**
by
evaluating display options;
preparing drawings; determining
specifications.

____ 5. **DETERMINES DISPLAY
REQUIREMENTS**
by
studying display concept, plan, and
specifications; providing
recommendations.

____ 6. **PRODUCES DISPLAY
REQUIREMENTS**
by
scheduling and supervising growing
activities; inspecting plants; correcting
problems.

% of
time

____ 7. **CONSTRUCTS DISPLAY**
by
scheduling and assigning employees;
installing design plan; monitoring work
results.

____ 8. **ENSURES OPERATION OF
EQUIPMENT**
by
completing preventive maintenance
requirements; following manufacturer's
instructions; troubleshooting
malfunctions; calling for repairs;
maintaining equipment inventories;
evaluating new equipment and
techniques.

____ 9. **PRODUCES REVENUE**
by
displaying and selling plants,
accessories, and supplies.

____ 10. **COMPLETES REPORTS**
by
entering required information.

____ 11. **MAINTAINS PROFESSIONAL AND
TECHNICAL KNOWLEDGE**
by
attending educational workshops;
reviewing professional publications;
establishing personal networks;
benchmarking state-of-the-art practices;
participating in professional societies.

____ 12. **CONTRIBUTES TO TEAM EFFORT**
by
accomplishing related results as
needed.

JOB PURPOSE: **PROVIDES ACCOMMODATIONS FOR RESIDENTS**
by
maintaining and securing facilities; managing residents.

ESSENTIAL JOB RESULTS:

% of
time

% of
time

____ **1. WELCOMES RESIDENTS**
by
assigning rooms; explaining occupancy rules; providing orientation to house, neighborhood, transportation, and services.

____ **2. MAINTAINS FACILITY**
by
inspecting premises; identifying problems; contracting with and supervising maintenance, cleaning, landscaping, and snow removal services; purchasing and repairing furniture; identifying need for renovations; ordering and maintaining supplies.

____ **3. SECURES FACILITY**
by
installing and maintaining security devices; enforcing house rules; monitoring security patrol services; enforcing safety and health rules; responding to emergencies.

____ **4. FORWARDS INFORMATION**
by
recording telephone messages; distributing mail.

____ **5. MAINTAINS ORDER**
by
investigating resident or neighbor complaints; counseling residents; resolving disputes; supervising social functions.

____ **6. COMPLETES REPORTS**
by
entering required information.

____ **7. HELPS RESIDENTS**
by
escorting them on trips; arranging recreational events; obtaining medical attention and social services.

____ **8. MAINTAINS TECHNICAL KNOWLEDGE**
by
attending educational workshops; reviewing publications.

____ **9. MAINTAINS HOUSE SERVICES**
by
accomplishing related results as needed.

JOB PURPOSE: **SUPPORTS HUMAN RESOURCES PROCESSES**
by
administering tests; scheduling appointments; conducting orientation;
maintaining records and information.

ESSENTIAL JOB RESULTS:

% of
time

% of
time

____ 1. **SUBSTANTIATES APPLICANTS' SKILLS**
by
administering and scoring tests.

____ 2. **SCHEDULES EXAMINATIONS**
by
coordinating appointments.

____ 3. **WELCOMES NEW EMPLOYEES TO THE ORGANIZATION**
by
conducting orientation.

____ 4. **PROVIDES PAYROLL INFORMATION**
by
collecting time and attendance records.

____ 5. **SUBMITS EMPLOYEE DATA REPORTS**
by
assembling, preparing, and analyzing data.

____ 6. **MAINTAINS EMPLOYEE INFORMATION**
by
entering and updating employment and status-change data.

____ 7. **PROVIDES SECRETARIAL SUPPORT**
by
entering, formatting, and printing information; organizing work; answering the telephone; relaying messages; maintaining equipment and supplies.

____ 8. **MAINTAINS EMPLOYEE CONFIDENCE AND PROTECTS OPERATIONS**
by
keeping human resource information confidential.

____ 9. **MAINTAINS QUALITY SERVICE**
by
following organization standards.

____10. **MAINTAINS TECHNICAL KNOWLEDGE**
by
attending educational workshops; reviewing publications.

____11. **CONTRIBUTES TO TEAM EFFORT**
by
accomplishing related results as needed.

JOB TITLE: HUMAN RESOURCES RECORDS CLERK H206_M

JOB PURPOSE: **SUPPORTS HUMAN RESOURCES OPERATIONS**
by
maintaining and updating information and records.

ESSENTIAL JOB RESULTS:

% of
time

_____ **1. PREPARES WORK TO BE ACCOMPLISHED**
by
gathering and sorting documents.

_____ **2. MAINTAINS HUMAN RESOURCES DATABASE AND RECORDS**
by
entering, updating, and retrieving information.

_____ **3. COMPLETES INSURANCE PAPERWORK**
by
preparing group insurance applications and billing transmittals; responding to enrollment and contact inquiries by employees and/or dependents.

_____ **4. PREPARES HUMAN RESOURCES REPORTS**
by
assembling and compiling data.

_____ **5. PROVIDING INFORMATION**
by
responding to telephone or written verifications of employment and other requests for information; answering questions and requests.

_____ **6. SECURES HUMAN RESOURCES DATA**
by
completing database backups.

% of
time

_____ **7. MAINTAINS EMPLOYEE CONFIDENCE AND PROTECTS OPERATIONS**
by
keeping personnel data confidential.

_____ **8. MAINTAINS OPERATION OF EQUIPMENT**
by
following operator procedures; calling for repairs.

_____ **9. COMPLIES WITH FEDERAL, STATE, AND LOCAL REQUIREMENTS**
by
following policies and procedures.

_____ **10. MAINTAINS TECHNICAL KNOWLEDGE**
by
attending educational workshops; reviewing publications.

_____ **11. CONTRIBUTES TO TEAM EFFORT**
by
accomplishing related results as needed.

JOB PURPOSE: **MARKETS PRODUCTS**
by
managing staff; maintaining response operations; maintaining quality ratings.

ESSENTIAL JOB RESULTS:

% of
time

% of
time

_____ 1. **MAINTAINS INBOUND MARKETING STAFF**
by
recruiting, selecting, orienting, and training employees; maintaining a safe and secure work environment; developing personal growth opportunities.

_____ 2. **ACCOMPLISHES STAFF RESULTS**
by
communicating job expectations; planning, monitoring, and appraising job results; coaching, counseling, and disciplining employees; initiating, coordinating, and enforcing systems, policies, and procedures.

_____ 3. **MAINTAINS CUSTOMER RESPONSE OPERATIONS**
by
establishing work schedules; assigning employees; providing back-up.

_____ 4. **MAINTAINS QUALITY SERVICE**
by
establishing and enforcing standards; training representatives; monitoring calls; surveying customers; evaluating outcomes.

_____ 5. **RESOLVES CUSTOMER PROBLEMS**
by
training telemarketing service representatives; maintaining reference manuals and dialogue guides; providing information; answering questions.

_____ 6. **MAINTAINS WORK PROCESS FLOWS**
by
coordinating information and requirements with related operational departments; participating with and providing resources to business improvement teams.

_____ 7. **KEEPS MANAGEMENT INFORMED**
by
preparing reports; making presentations; interpreting information; making recommendations.

_____ 8. **MAINTAINS EQUIPMENT**
by
coordinating requirements with telecommunications and information services departments; examining state-of-the-art technology; recommending upgrades; controlling installations.

_____ 9. **MAINTAINS PROFESSIONAL AND TECHNICAL KNOWLEDGE**
by
attending educational workshops; reviewing professional publications; establishing personal networks; benchmarking state-of-the-art practices; participating in professional societies.

_____10. **CONTRIBUTES TO TEAM EFFORT**
by
accomplishing related results as needed.

JOB TITLE: INFORMATION SECURITY SPECIALIST   I209_M

JOB PURPOSE: **SAFEGUARDS INFORMATION SYSTEM ASSETS**
by
identifying and solving potential and actual security problems.

ESSENTIAL JOB RESULTS:

% of
time

_____ **1. PROTECTS SYSTEM**
by
defining access privileges, control structures, and resources.

_____ **2. RECOGNIZES PROBLEMS**
by
identifying abnormalities; reporting violations.

_____ **3. IMPLEMENTS SECURITY IMPROVEMENTS**
by
assessing current situation; evaluating trends; anticipating requirements.

_____ **4. DETERMINES SECURITY VIOLATIONS AND INEFFICIENCIES**
by
conducting periodic audits.

_____ **5. UPGRADES SYSTEM**
by
implementing and maintaining security controls.

% of
time

_____ **6. KEEPS USERS INFORMED**
by
preparing performance reports; communicating system status.

_____ **7. MAINTAINS QUALITY SERVICE**
by
following organization standards.

_____ **8. MAINTAINS TECHNICAL KNOWLEDGE**
by
attending educational workshops; reviewing publications.

_____ **9. CONTRIBUTES TO TEAM EFFORT**
by
accomplishing related results as needed.

JOB TITLE: INFORMATION SYSTEMS MANAGER–MANUFACTURING   I211_M

JOB PURPOSE: **ACCOMPLISHES MANUFACTURING OBJECTIVES**
by
managing staff; designing and monitoring information systems.

ESSENTIAL JOB RESULTS:

% of
time

% of
time

____ **1. ACCOMPLISHES INFORMATION SYSTEMS STAFF RESULTS**
by
communicating job expectations; planning, monitoring, and appraising job results; coaching, counseling, and disciplining employees; initiating, coordinating, and enforcing systems, policies, and procedures.

____ **2. MAINTAINS STAFF**
by
recruiting, selecting, orienting, and training employees; developing personal growth opportunities.

____ **3. MAINTAINS SAFE AND HEALTHY WORKING ENVIRONMENT**
by
establishing and enforcing organization standards; adhering to legal regulations.

____ **4. SUSTAINS MANUFACTURING RESULTS**
by
defining, delivering, and supporting manufacturing systems; auditing application of systems.

____ **5. ASSESSES MANUFACTURING RESULTS**
by
auditing application of systems.

____ **6. ENHANCES MANUFACTURING RESULTS**
by
identifying information systems technology opportunities and developing application strategies in production planning, production tracking, cost management, and manufacturing.

____ **7. SAFEGUARDS ASSETS**
by
planning and implementing disaster recovery and back-up procedures and information security and control structures.

____ **8. ACCOMPLISHES FINANCIAL OBJECTIVES**
by
determining service level required; preparing an annual budget; scheduling expenditures; analyzing variances; initiating corrective action.

ESSENTIAL JOB RESULTS:

% of
time

% of
time

_____ 9. **MAINTAINS PROFESSIONAL AND TECHNICAL KNOWLEDGE**
by
attending educational workshops;
reviewing professional publications;
establishing personal networks;
benchmarking state-of-the-art practices;
participating in professional societies.

_____10. **CONTRIBUTES TO TEAM EFFORT**
by
accomplishing related results as
needed.

JOB TITLE: INFORMATION TECHNOLOGY MANAGER I212_M

JOB PURPOSE: **MAINTAINS INFORMATION TECHNOLOGY STRATEGIES**
by
managing staff; researching and implementing technological strategic solutions.

ESSENTIAL JOB RESULTS:

% of
time

% of
time

____ 1. **ACCOMPLISHES INFORMATION TECHNOLOGY STAFF RESULTS**
by
communicating job expectations; planning, monitoring, and appraising job results; coaching, counseling, and disciplining employees; initiating, coordinating, and enforcing systems, policies, and procedures.

____ 2. **MAINTAINS STAFF**
by
recruiting, selecting, orienting, and training employees; maintaining a safe and secure work environment; developing personal growth opportunities.

____ 3. **MAINTAINS ORGANIZATION'S EFFECTIVENESS AND EFFICIENCY**
by
defining, delivering, and supporting strategic plans for implementing information technologies.

____ 4. **DIRECTS TECHNOLOGICAL RESEARCH**
by
studying organization goals, strategies, practices, and user projects.

____ 5. **COMPLETES PROJECTS**
by
coordinating resources and timetables with user departments and data center.

____ 6. **VERIFIES APPLICATION RESULTS**
by
conducting system audits of technologies implemented.

____ 7. **PRESERVES ASSETS**
by
implementing disaster recovery and back-up procedures and information security and control structures.

____ 8. **RECOMMENDS INFORMATION TECHNOLOGY STRATEGIES, POLICIES, AND PROCEDURES**
by
evaluating organization outcomes; identifying problems; evaluating trends; anticipating requirements.

____ 9. **ACCOMPLISHES FINANCIAL OBJECTIVES**
by
forecasting requirements; preparing an annual budget; scheduling expenditures; analyzing variances; initiating corrective action.

____ 10. **MAINTAINS QUALITY SERVICE**
by
establishing and enforcing organization standards.

____ 11. **MAINTAINS PROFESSIONAL AND TECHNICAL KNOWLEDGE**
by
attending educational workshops; reviewing professional publications; establishing personal networks; benchmarking state-of-the-art practices; participating in professional societies.

____ 12. **CONTRIBUTES TO TEAM EFFORT**
by
accomplishing related results as needed.

JOB TITLE: INTERNATIONAL BUSINESS OPERATIONS COORDINATOR

I213_M

JOB PURPOSE: **SUPPORTS INTERNATIONAL OPERATIONS**
by
achieving financial objectives; resolving production, storage, and distribution problems; identifying current and future customer requirements.

ESSENTIAL JOB RESULTS:

% of
time

% of
time

_____ 1. **RESOLVES INTERNATIONAL PRODUCTION PROBLEMS**
by
collecting and analyzing information; altering production schedules to meet customers' needs; collaborating with production personnel to maximize utilization of resources.

_____ 2. **ACHIEVES INTERNATIONAL FINANCIAL OBJECTIVES**
by
forecasting requirements; preparing an annual budget; scheduling expenditures; analyzing variances; initiating corrective action; selling excess capacity.

_____ 3. **RESOLVES INTERNATIONAL STORAGE AND DISTRIBUTION PROBLEMS**
by
arranging special shipments; expediting orders; locating inventory; identifying temporary warehousing; negotiating with shippers.

_____ 4. **IDENTIFIES CURRENT AND FUTURE CUSTOMER REQUIREMENTS**
by
establishing personal rapport with potential and actual customers and other persons in a position to understand customer requirements.

_____ 5. **CONTRIBUTES TO OPERATIONS DIVISION EFFECTIVENESS**
by
identifying short-term and long-range issues that must be addressed; providing information and commentary pertinent to deliberations; recommending options and courses of action; implementing directives.

_____ 6. **PREPARES REPORTS**
by
determining information needs; collecting, analyzing, and summarizing information.

_____ 7. **MAINTAINS QUALITY SERVICE**
by
establishing and enforcing organization standards.

_____ 8. **MAINTAINS PROFESSIONAL AND TECHNICAL KNOWLEDGE**
by
attending educational workshops; reviewing professional publications; establishing personal networks; benchmarking state-of-the-art practices; participating in professional societies.

_____ 9. **CONTRIBUTES TO OPERATIONS TEAM EFFORT**
by
accomplishing related results as needed.

JOB PURPOSE: **ACHIEVES INTERNATIONAL OBJECTIVES**
by
developing and implementing marketing programs.

ESSENTIAL JOB RESULTS:

% of
time

% of
time

____ 1. **PROVIDES ACCOUNT INTERFACE FOR INTERNATIONAL MARKET OPPORTUNITIES**
by
establishing and developing new supporting products, marketing materials, and procedures; implementing strategies and action plans with internal/subsidiary resources; assisting in developing marketing plans for telemarketing, direct response, and country profile development campaigns.

____ 2. **CONTRIBUTES TO PRODUCT AND COUNTRY DEVELOPMENT BUSINESS PLANS**
by
outlining country-specific profiles; researching legal and foreign requirements; designing product program proposals, and supporting procedures, forms, pricing sheets; obtaining executive approvals.

____ 3. **SUPPORTS MARKETING CONTACT PROCESS OBJECTIVES**
by
developing and producing multilingual marketing materials for contact packages; obtaining approvals from functional areas; adhering to timelines.

____ 4. **ESTABLISHES CLIENT SETUP**
by
coordinating client setup process; assisting with proposal and contracting process.

____ 5. **IDENTIFIES TRAINING NEEDS**
by
analyzing international sales force, client requirements, plans, forecasts, and current training programs; verifying needs with sales force, subsidiary management, and clients.

____ 6. **SATISFIES TRAINING NEEDS**
by
researching, designing, or purchasing training programs and media; developing new point-of-sales training manuals and support materials.

____ 7. **PROVIDES CLIENT SERVICES**
by
researching and documenting issues and problems; forwarding necessary actions; leading client service team; providing response to client; guiding internal resources; measuring and ensuring results.

____ 8. **FINALIZES CONTRACT APPROVAL**
by
preparing business deal recapitulations; drafting contracts; obtaining approvals; verifying understanding among parties; monitoring status and quality.

____ 9. **RESOLVES AND PREVENTS CONTRACT PROBLEMS**
by
researching and documenting issues/problems; forwarding necessary actions; leading client service team; providing response to client.

ESSENTIAL JOB RESULTS:

% of
time

% of
time

_____10. **MAINTAINS CLIENTS' DATA INTEGRITY**
by
determining marketing and installation plans; reconciling pricing sheet expenses to services outlined in contract; controlling quality of data from sales through contracting setup process; communicating data to, and obtaining support and approvals from, functional areas.

_____11. **IMPLEMENTS INTERNAL, CLIENT-SPECIFIC BUSINESS PLANS**
by
establishing and developing plans with sales representatives; managing strategic and action plans with internal resources; analyzing profit and loss statements for trends; coordinating in-house activities.

_____12. **MAINTAINS PROFESSIONAL AND TECHNICAL KNOWLEDGE**
by
attending educational workshops; reviewing professional publications; establishing personal networks; benchmarking state-of-the-art practices; participating in professional societies.

_____13. **CONTRIBUTES TO TEAM EFFORT**
by
accomplishing related results as needed.

JOB PURPOSE: **ACHIEVES INTERNATIONAL OBJECTIVES**
by
identifying and developing business, marketing, and sales opportunities.

ESSENTIAL JOB RESULTS:

% of
time

% of
time

____ 1. **DEVELOPS MARKETING EFFECTIVENESS**
by
identifying short-term and long-range issues; developing internal discussions to prepare strategies and solutions; identifying options and courses of action; implementing customer programs.

____ 2. **EXPANDS CURRENT BUSINESS**
by
developing marketing and administrative strategies to offer niche products.

____ 3. **MEETS SALES AND ADMINISTRATIVE OBJECTIVES**
by
managing sales and administrative functions; developing budgets; providing staff.

____ 4. **ENSURES COMPLIANCE WITH REQUIREMENTS, POLICIES, AND REGULATIONS**
by
enforcing adherence to corporate systems, policies, and governmental regulations; coordinating filing and approval of products and lines of business with regulatory agencies; advising executive management on needed actions.

____ 5. **KEEPS MANAGEMENT INFORMED**
by
collecting, analyzing, and summarizing information; preparing reports including progress reviews and annual report.

____ 6. **ACCOMPLISHES STAFF WORK**
by
training sales and administrative representatives.

____ 7. **MAINTAINS PROFESSIONAL AND TECHNICAL KNOWLEDGE**
by
attending educational workshops; reviewing professional publications; establishing personal networks; benchmarking state-of-the-art practices; participating in professional societies.

____ 8. **CONTRIBUTES TO TEAM EFFORT**
by
accomplishing related results as needed.

JOB PURPOSE: DEVELOPS INTERNATIONAL EMPLOYEE RESOURCES
by
hiring and monitoring staff; developing and enforcing policies and procedures.

ESSENTIAL JOB RESULTS:

% of
time

____ **1. PROVIDES STAFF**
by
Interviewing candidates, completing offers of employment; conducting orientations.

____ **2. MONITORS WORK RESULTS**
by
enforcing job results planning, monitoring, and appraising by managers; counseling managers and employees; resolving grievances.

____ **3. IDENTIFIES CULTURAL REQUIREMENTS**
by
studying country history and morés; interviewing local resources and other companies doing business in the country; analyzing local practices as compared with U.S. practices.

____ **4. ESTABLISHES POLICIES, PROCEDURES, AND GUIDELINES**
by
adjusting corporate values to local requirements.

____ **5. ESTABLISHES COMPENSATION PROGRAM**
by
developing job descriptions; establishing internal equity; surveying market rates and benefits; maintaining expatriate policies; monitoring salaries.

% of
time

____ **6. COMPLIES WITH UNITED STATES AND LOCAL LEGAL REQUIREMENTS**
by
researching and adhering to statutory regulations.

____ **7. PROMOTES FOREIGN PLACEMENTS**
by
providing information to U.S. employees and families; developing relocation package and support; monitoring willingness of U.S. employees to relocate.

____ **8. MAINTAINS HISTORICAL HUMAN RESOURCE RECORDS**
by
designing a filing and retrieval system.

____ **9. MAINTAINS PROFESSIONAL AND TECHNICAL KNOWLEDGE**
by
attending educational workshops; reviewing professional publications; establishing personal networks; benchmarking state-of-the-art practices; participating in professional societies.

____**10. CONTRIBUTES TO TEAM EFFORT**
by
accomplishing related results as needed.

JOB TITLE: INTERNATIONAL MARKETING DIRECTOR I217_M

JOB PURPOSE: **ACHIEVES INTERNATIONAL MARKETING OBJECTIVES**
by
managing staff; developing and exploiting marketing opportunities.

ESSENTIAL JOB RESULTS:

% of
time

% of
time

____ 1. **MAINTAINS INTERNATIONAL MARKETING STAFF**
by
recruiting, selecting, orienting, and training employees; maintaining a safe and secure work environment; developing personal growth opportunities.

____ 2. **ACCOMPLISHES STAFF RESULTS**
by
communicating job expectations; planning, monitoring, and appraising job results; coaching, counseling, and disciplining employees; initiating, coordinating, and enforcing systems, policies, and procedures.

____ 3. **DEVELOPS MARKETING PROGRAMS**
by
identifying customer issues; providing information for deliberations; recommending courses of action; implementing directives.

____ 4. **EXPANDS CURRENT BUSINESS**
by
managing, directing, and supervising the development of international subsidiary markets.

____ 5. **OBTAINS MARKET SHARE**
by
developing marketing strategy and programs for international subsidiaries; developing marketing support concepts.

____ 6. **MAINTAINS RELATIONS WITH CUSTOMERS**
by
establishing rapport with prospects, clients, and business agents; organizing and developing customer relations programs; determining company presence within market.

____ 7. **PROVIDES SHORT-TERM AND LONG-RANGE MARKET FORECASTS AND REPORTS**
by
directing market research collection, analysis, and interpretation of market data.

____ 8. **DEVELOPS FUTURE PRODUCTS**
by
determining and evaluating future market trends; analyzing and participating in product development.

____ 9. **ACHIEVES FINANCIAL OBJECTIVES**
by
managing the subsidiary's budget; developing and implementing policy and action parameters for the subsidiary.

ESSENTIAL JOB RESULTS:

% of
time

% of
time

____**10. MAINTAINS PROFESSIONAL AND
TECHNICAL KNOWLEDGE**
by
attending educational workshops;
reviewing professional publications;
establishing personal networks;
benchmarking state-of-the-art practices;
participating in professional societies.

____**11. CONTRIBUTES TO TEAM EFFORT**
by
accomplishing related results as
needed.

JOB TITLE:	INVENTORY AND INVOICE CLERK	I218_M

JOB PURPOSE: **COMPLETES CUSTOMER ORDERS**
by
receiving, entering, and forwarding orders; preparing invoices.

ESSENTIAL JOB RESULTS:

% of
time

% of
time

____ 1. **RECEIVES AND PREPARES ORDERS FOR COMPUTER ENTRY**
by
calling for electronic messages; sorting faxes; bursting orders; calculating totals.

____ 2. **ENTERS ORDERS**
by
inputting data into order-entry system.

____ 3. **VERIFIES ORDERS**
by
reviewing "bill-to" and "ship-to" addresses; flagging for price, promotion problems, and credit limits.

____ 4. **FORWARDS ORDERS**
by
routing orders to supervisor for approval; routing orders to warehouse for filling.

____ 5. **VERIFIES ITEMS SHIPPED**
by
matching bills of lading; reconciling quantities; noting discrepancies.

____ 6. **PREPARES INVOICES**
by
calculating special charges; making necessary cuts; entering release numbers and correct shipping dates into computer system; placing orders in ready status.

____ 7. **PROCESSES CREDIT MEMORANDA AND CLAIMS**
by
generating credit memos and claims through computer system.

____ 8. **INITIATES INVOICES**
by
processing invoices through computer system; mailing invoices.

____ 9. **MAINTAINS TRAFFIC OPERATIONS AND ORGANIZES WORK**
by
reading and routing correspondence; collecting information; initiating telecommunications; following policies and procedures.

____ 10. **MAINTAINS PROFESSIONAL AND TECHNICAL KNOWLEDGE**
by
attending educational workshops and field trips.

____ 11. **CONTRIBUTES TO TEAM EFFORT**
by
accomplishing related results as needed.

JOB TITLE: INVENTORY SPECIALIST   I220_M

JOB PURPOSE: **RECONCILES INVENTORIES**
by
receiving, verifying, and processing orders.

ESSENTIAL JOB RESULTS:

% of
time

____ **1. PREPARES WORK TO BE ACCOMPLISHED**
by
gathering and sorting department documents and information.

____ **2. DISTRIBUTES MAIL**
by
retrieving mail from mailroom; opening and sorting by addressee and area or type; delivering items.

____ **3. VERIFIES AND COMPLETES RECEIVING REPORTS**
by
checking receiving document against sales order for quantities and items shipped, release number, and discrepancies; entering receiving information into database; correcting discrepancies.

____ **4. PROCESSES ORDERS**
by
entering and processing orders for outlet stores.

____ **5. AUDITS AND RECONCILES INVENTORY REPORTS**
by
examining distribution warehouse reports for inventory discrepancies; reconciling entries with inventory system from warehouse inventory reports, credit memos, and variances; completing physical counts.

____ **6. PAYS STORAGE BILLS**
by
verifying transaction information; scheduling and preparing disbursements; obtaining authorization for payment.

% of
time

____ **7. VERIFIES ACCOUNTS**
by
reconciling statements, transactions, and edits.

____ **8. PROVIDES INFORMATION**
by
answering questions; entering data; completing disposition forms.

____ **9. PREPARES REPORTS**
by
collecting and analyzing data; reporting information; initiating telecommunications.

____ **10. MAINTAINS DEPARTMENTAL HISTORICAL RECORDS**
by
filing documents and transferring inactive files; destroying obsolete records.

____ **11. MAINTAINS DISTRIBUTION INVENTORY OPERATIONS**
by
collecting information; following policies and procedures; reporting needed changes.

____ **12. MAINTAINS QUALITY SERVICE**
by
following organization standards.

____ **13. MAINTAINS PROFESSIONAL AND TECHNICAL KNOWLEDGE**
by
attending educational workshops; making field trips.

____ **14. CONTRIBUTES TO TEAM EFFORT**
by
accomplishing related results as needed.

JOB TITLE: INVESTMENT ACCOUNTANT I221_M

JOB PURPOSE: **SUPPORTS INVESTMENT OPERATIONS**
by
maintaining, verifying, and updating investment records; preparing tax returns.

ESSENTIAL JOB RESULTS:

% of
time

% of
time

____ 1. BALANCES SCHEDULE D FOR ALL COMPANIES
by
comparing general ledger balances to asset management Schedule D.

____ 2. VERIFIES INVESTMENT TRANSACTIONS
by
reviewing and correcting transactions.

____ 3. MAINTAINS ACCOUNTING LEDGERS
by
preparing cash transaction entries for general ledger.

____ 4. MAINTAINS FILING SYSTEM
by
compiling daily activity reports, bank reports, wire transfer payments, electronic payments, and tax payments.

____ 5. MAINTAINS SPECIAL MARKET ACCOUNTS
by
ensuring compliance with procedures for safekeeping, maintenance, and control of special market collateral; executing and maintaining investment accounts; maintaining records and control of investment accounts; completing accounting functions.

____ 6. MAINTAINS CONTROL DISBURSEMENT SYSTEM
by
downloading exceptions related to checks; researching and obtaining approvals for checks over dollar limit and "no issues"; determining payment action; notifying bank via electronic system.

____ 7. CONTROLS INVESTMENT INTERFACE
by
ensuring that accounts have been set up and approved prior to interface being submitted to the general ledger.

____ 8. VERIFIES ACCOUNTING TRANSACTIONS AND REPORTS
by
reviewing and controlling accounting activities, including generally accepted accounting practices changes to investment accounting practices.

____ 9. COMPLETES INVESTMENT REPORTS FOR TAX RETURN PREPARATION
by
completing required information.

____ 10. PROTECTS OPERATIONS
by
keeping financial information confidential.

____ 11. MAINTAINS PROFESSIONAL AND TECHNICAL KNOWLEDGE
by
attending educational workshops; reviewing professional publications; establishing personal networks; benchmarking state-of-the-art practices; participating in professional societies.

____ 12. CONTRIBUTES TO TEAM EFFORT
by
accomplishing related results as needed.

JOB PURPOSE: **SUPPORTS INVESTMENT OPERATIONS**
by
executing, recording, verifying, and reconciling investments.

ESSENTIAL JOB RESULTS:

% of
time

____ 1. **COMPLETES INVESTMENT TRADES**
by
executing transactions; communicating
with brokers and safekeeping banks.

____ 2. **MANAGES ASSET MANAGEMENT
SYSTEM**
by
recording transactions; completing cash
match function and interface with
general ledger.

____ 3. **COMPLETES ASSET MANAGEMENT
SYSTEM FUNCTIONS**
by
managing accounting and system
administration and system utilities.

____ 4. **OBTAINS VALUATIONS AND
DESIGNATIONS**
by
reporting newly acquired securities,
private placements, and subsidiaries.

____ 5. **RECONCILES ASSETS**
by
collecting security location information;
comparing asset information to records;
making adjustments.

____ 6. **PREPARES FINANCE COMMITTEE
REPORTS**
by
producing reports from the asset
management system; assembling
reports for distribution.

% of
time

____ 7. **ADMINISTERS LOAN PORTFOLIOS**
by
collecting payments; analyzing
portfolios; preparing documentation and
reports.

____ 8. **RECONCILES CORRESPONDING
ASSET AND LIABILITY ACCOUNTS**
by
comparing general ledger balances to
loan portfolios; analyzing and
researching information; resolving
problems.

____ 9. **PROTECTS OPERATIONS**
by
keeping financial information
confidential.

____10. **MAINTAINS PROFESSIONAL AND
TECHNICAL KNOWLEDGE**
by
attending educational workshops;
reviewing professional publications;
establishing personal networks;
benchmarking state-of-the-art practices;
participating in professional societies.

____11. **CONTRIBUTES TO TEAM EFFORT**
by
accomplishing related results as
needed.

JOB TITLE: INVESTMENT OPERATIONS ASSISTANT   I223_M

JOB PURPOSE: **SUPPORTS INVESTMENT OPERATIONS**
by
collecting, verifying, and recording information.

ESSENTIAL JOB RESULTS:

% of
time

_____ 1. **DEVELOPS AND MAINTAINS INVESTMENT REPORTS**
by
creating reports for the preparation of 10-Q, 10-K, and market tools for sale.

_____ 2. **PRICES PORTFOLIOS**
by
interfacing with the pricing source and downloading into the investment system.

_____ 3. **PRESENTS INVESTMENT INFORMATION TO SENIOR MANAGEMENT**
by
developing investment graphs.

_____ 4. **CREATES REPORTS**
by
accessing information from the investment system.

_____ 5. **SUPPORTS THE INVESTMENT SYSTEM**
by
assisting the manager and other clients in all functions of the investment system; developing backup resources.

% of
time

_____ 6. **PROJECTS INVESTMENT INCOME**
by
collecting and analyzing investment data.

_____ 7. **MAINTAINS DEBIT SYSTEM**
by
reconciling cash to reports generated by system; preparing deposits; keeping debit machines operational.

_____ 8. **PROTECTS OPERATIONS**
by
keeping financial information confidential.

_____ 9. **MAINTAINS PROFESSIONAL AND TECHNICAL KNOWLEDGE**
by
attending educational workshops; reviewing professional publications; establishing personal networks; benchmarking state-of-the-art practices; participating in professional societies.

_____10. **CONTRIBUTES TO TEAM EFFORT**
by
accomplishing related results as needed.

JOB PURPOSE: **CREATES INVESTOR INTEREST**
by
communicating company focus; maintaining rapport with the investment community.

ESSENTIAL JOB RESULTS:

% of
time

_____ 1. **COMMUNICATES THE ORGANIZATION'S GOALS, OBJECTIVES, AND STATUS**
by
developing, printing, and mailing the company's annual report, quarterly reports, financial press releases, and letters to shareholders.

_____ 2. **MONITORS INVESTMENTS IN THE ORGANIZATION'S STOCK**
by
tracking and analyzing the institutional and retail trading of major blocks of stock.

_____ 3. **INFORMS INVESTMENT COMMUNITY**
by
communicating and disseminating the organization's investment story and financial information; planning, developing, and implementing a strategy for target marketing to retail and institutional investors; providing information to external analysts for writing research reports.

_____ 4. **MAINTAINS RAPPORT WITH INVESTMENT COMMUNITY**
by
planning and coordinating visits by security analysts and brokers; planning and attending investment community presentations; writing and developing the president and chief executive officer's financial presentations.

% of
time

_____ 5. **PREPARES FOR ANNUAL SHAREHOLDER MEETING**
hy
writing the proxy statement and consulting with legal counsel; printing and distributing proxy solicitation; coordinating events.

_____ 6. **MAINTAINS THE ORGANIZATION'S REPUTATION**
by
complying with legal requirements; ensuring policy and procedure compliance; maintaining confidentiality.

_____ 7. **MAINTAINS RAPPORT WITH MEDIA REPRESENTATIVES**
by
communicating on financial matters, changes in senior management, major litigation and settlements, and major acquisitions and divestitures; working with executive management in the communication of new developments for public information.

_____ 8. **MAINTAINS RAPPORT WITH SHAREHOLDERS**
by
responding to correspondence, questions, and concerns.

ESSENTIAL JOB RESULTS:

% of
time

_____ 9. **ADVISES ON SECURITY AND EXCHANGE COMMISSION RULINGS**
by
preparing statistical reports; coordinating dividend payout activities with the accounting department and transfer agents; recommending actions.

_____ 10. **MAINTAINS HISTORICAL REFERENCE**
by
establishing and maintaining a filing and retrieval system.

% of
time

_____ 11. **MAINTAINS PROFESSIONAL AND TECHNICAL KNOWLEDGE**
by
attending educational workshops; reviewing professional publications; establishing personal networks; benchmarking state-of-the-art practices; participating in professional societies.

_____ 12. **CONTRIBUTES TO TEAM EFFORT**
by
accomplishing related results as needed.

JOB TITLE: JUDGE   J226_M

JOB PURPOSE: **ADJUDICATES CLAIMS**
by
preparing for and managing legal proceedings.

ESSENTIAL JOB RESULTS:

% of
time

_____ **1. ORGANIZES PROCEEDINGS**
by
enumerating rules and procedures;
planning schedules; arranging hearing
location, court personnel, and
accommodations; assembling potential
jurors.

_____ **2. DETERMINES PROBABLE CAUSE**
by
examining accusations, charges, and
evidence.

_____ **3. CONDUCTS PROCEEDINGS**
by
listening to arguments; ruling on
admissibility of evidence; resolving
objections; maintaining order.

_____ **4. PREPARES JURY**
by
conducting selection; issuing and
explaining instructions and rules.

_____ **5. RENDERS JUDGMENT**
by
weighing arguments and evidence;
studying relevant cases; polling jury,
writing and announcing opinion.

_____ **6. SENTENCES DEFENDANT**
by
applying statutes and guidelines;
considering extenuating and mitigating
circumstances; determining settlement.

% of
time

_____ **7. ENFORCES JUDGMENT**
by
following up and requiring compliance.

_____ **8. COMPLETES REPORTS**
by
entering required information.

_____ **9. IMPROVES JUDICIAL SYSTEM**
by
recommending changes in law,
guidelines, and procedures.

_____ **10. MAINTAINS PROFESSIONAL AND
TECHNICAL KNOWLEDGE**
by
attending educational workshops;
reviewing professional publications;
establishing personal networks;
benchmarking state-of-the-art practices;
participating in professional societies.

_____ **11. CONTRIBUTES TO TEAM EFFORT**
by
accomplishing related results as
needed.

JOB PURPOSE: **PROVIDES LOTS FOR CONSTRUCTION**
by
managing subcontractors; acquiring and improving land.

ESSENTIAL JOB RESULTS:

% of
time

____ 1. **MAINTAINS LAND-DEVELOPMENT SUBCONTRACTORS**
by
recruiting, selecting, orienting, and training subcontractors; developing subcontractor agreements; maintaining a safe and secure work environment; developing personal growth opportunities.

____ 2. **ACCOMPLISHES SUBCONTRACTOR RESULTS**
by
communicating job expectations; planning, monitoring, and appraising job results; coaching, counseling, and disciplining subcontractors; initiating, coordinating, and enforcing systems, policies, and procedures.

____ 3. **ACQUIRES LAND**
by
evaluating prospective properties; carrying out pre-purchase site investigation.

____ 4. **DEVELOPS LOT IMPROVEMENT STRATEGY**
by
consulting with sales and construction employees.

____ 5. **DIRECTS LAND DEVELOPMENT APPROVAL PROCESS**
by
providing information in rezoning cases; obtaining preliminary site plan approvals; obtaining full subdivision approvals; securing state and municipal approvals; helping sales in Veterans' Administration and Federal Housing Administration subdivision approvals.

% of
time

____ 6. **PREPARES LAND FOR LOT SUBDIVIDING**
by
consulting with engineer; developing proforma; soliciting, analyzing, and awarding bids; arranging for land grading; installing streets, curbs and gutters; providing utilities; controlling costs; scrutinizing contract extras; determining subcontractor retainage.

____ 7. **PROVIDES WELCOMING ENTRANCES TO COMMUNITIES**
by
constructing and landscaping entrance monuments.

____ 8. **IMPROVES PROGRAM AND SERVICE QUALITY**
by
devising new applications; updating procedures; evaluating system results with users.

____ 9. **ACHIEVES FINANCIAL OBJECTIVES**
by
anticipating requirements; submitting information for budget preparation; scheduling expenditures; approving payables; monitoring costs; analyzing variances.

____ 10. **MAINTAINS CONTINUITY AMONG CORPORATE, DIVISION, AND LOCAL WORK TEAMS**
by
documenting and communicating actions, irregularities, and continuing needs.

ESSENTIAL JOB RESULTS:

% of
time

% of
time

____11. **MAINTAINS PROFESSIONAL AND TECHNICAL KNOWLEDGE**
by
attending educational workshops;
benchmarking professional standards;
reviewing professional publications;
establishing personal networks.

____12. **CONTRIBUTES TO TEAM EFFORT**
by
accomplishing related results as needed.

JOB TITLE: LANDSCAPE ARCHITECT   L229_M

JOB PURPOSE: **BEAUTIFIES BUILDINGS AND GROUNDS**
by
developing and implementing landscape concepts.

ESSENTIAL JOB RESULTS:

% of
time

_____ **1. DEVELOPS LANDSCAPE CONCEPT**
by
conferring with clients; identifying requirements; examining design options.

_____ **2. DETERMINES SITE CONDITION**
by
studying location, soil, features, drainage; considering environmental impact.

_____ **3. DEVELOPS LANDSCAPE PLAN**
by
evaluating design options; providing recommendations; preparing drawings, specifications, and cost estimate.

_____ **4. HIRES CONTRACTOR**
by
evaluating competence; inspecting references.

_____ **5. MONITORS INSTALLATION**
by
inspecting materials; enforcing specifications; providing installation advice; adhering to budget.

% of
time

_____ **6. COLLECTS PAYMENT**
by
preparing and mailing invoice.

_____ **7. MAINTAINS HISTORICAL RECORDS**
by
filing plans and supporting data.

_____ **8. MAINTAINS PROFESSIONAL AND TECHNICAL KNOWLEDGE**
by
attending educational workshops; reviewing professional publications; establishing personal networks; benchmarking state-of-the-art practices; participating in professional societies.

_____ **9. CONTRIBUTES TO TEAM EFFORT**
by
accomplishing related results as needed.

JOB TITLE: LANDSCAPE CONTRACTOR   L230_M

JOB PURPOSE: **BEAUTIFIES BUILDINGS AND GROUNDS**
by
supervising staff; installing landscape plans.

ESSENTIAL JOB RESULTS:

% of
time

% of
time

____ **1. MAINTAINS STAFF**
by
recruiting, selecting, orienting, and
training employees.

____ **2. ACCOMPLISHES STAFF RESULTS**
by
communicating job expectations;
planning, monitoring, and appraising
job results; coaching, counseling, and
disciplining employees.

____ **3. MAINTAINS SAFE AND HEALTHY
WORK ENVIRONMENT**
by
inspecting work site; establishing and
enforcing organization standards;
adhering to legal regulations.

____ **4. DETERMINES INSTALLATION
REQUIREMENTS**
by
studying landscape concept, plans,
specifications, and site; conferring with
client and architect.

____ **5. PREPARES BID**
by
calculating labor, equipment, materials,
and overhead costs; obtaining
approval.

____ **6. PURCHASES MATERIALS**
by
identifying vendors; negotiating prices;
verifying quality; arranging for delivery.

____ **7. COMPLETES WORK**
by
scheduling jobs; scheduling and
assigning employees; monitoring work
results; conferring with client and
architect regarding actual placement.

____ **8. ENSURES OPERATION OF
EQUIPMENT**
by
completing preventive maintenance
requirements; following manufacturer's
instructions; troubleshooting
malfunctions; calling for repairs;
maintaining equipment inventories;
evaluating new equipment and
techniques.

____ **9. MAINTAINS HISTORICAL RECORDS**
by
filing plans and supporting data.

____**10. MAINTAINS PROFESSIONAL AND
TECHNICAL KNOWLEDGE**
by
attending educational workshops;
reviewing professional publications;
establishing personal networks;
benchmarking state-of-the-art practices;
participating in professional societies.

____**11. CONTRIBUTES TO TEAM EFFORT**
by
accomplishing related results as
needed.

JOB PURPOSE: **ENSURES DELIVERY OF LEGAL SERVICES**
by
supervising staff; identifying and developing business opportunities.

ESSENTIAL JOB RESULTS:

% of
time

% of
time

_____ 1. **MAINTAINS LEGAL STAFF**
by
recruiting and screening attorney candidates; orienting and training new hires; arranging professional growth opportunities.

_____ 2. **MAINTAINS PARALEGAL AND OTHER SUPPORT STAFF**
by
recruiting, selecting, orienting, and training staff.

_____ 3. **MAINTAINS LAW OFFICE STAFF JOB RESULTS**
by
communicating job expectations; planning, monitoring, and appraising job results; coaching, counseling, and disciplining employees; providing systems and controls.

_____ 4. **MAINTAINS OPERATIONS**
by
developing and enforcing program, operational, and personnel policies and procedures.

_____ 5. **PREPARES MARKETING PLAN**
by
developing fee policy strategies, objectives, plans, schedules, and assignments.

_____ 6. **OBTAINS MARKET SHARE**
by
planning, developing, implementing, and evaluating advertising and promotional programs.

_____ 7. **ESTABLISHES FUTURE CLIENT SERVICE REQUIREMENTS**
by
conducting and evaluating client satisfaction surveys; developing personal networks within the legal community; providing community service.

_____ 8. **PROMOTES THE LAW FIRM**
by
attending law events and educational workshops; maintaining news media relationships.

_____ 9. **PROVIDES QUALITY SERVICES**
by
establishing standards; developing and maintaining a collaborative environment among the legal, paralegal, and support staffs.

_____ 10. **IMPROVES PROFITABILITY**
by
preparing annual budget; controlling fiscal operations; recommending profit margins; conducting service analyses and cost studies.

_____ 11. **MAINTAINS BUILDING AND EQUIPMENT**
by
allocating space; planning renovations; planning expansions; determining equipment requirements.

ESSENTIAL JOB RESULTS:

% of
time

_____12. **COMPLIES WITH FEDERAL, STATE, AND LOCAL LEGAL REQUIREMENTS**
by
studying existing legislation; anticipating future legislation; enforcing adherence to requirements; advising the senior partners on needed actions.

_____13. **MAINTAINS PROFESSIONAL AND TECHNICAL KNOWLEDGE**
by
attending educational workshops; reviewing professional publications; establishing personal networks; benchmarking state-of-the-art practices; participating in professional societies.

% of
time

_____14. **CONTRIBUTES TO TEAM EFFORT**
by
accomplishing related results as needed.

JOB PURPOSE: **SUPPORTS LAW OFFICE OPERATIONS**
by
supervising staff; planning and monitoring operations.

ESSENTIAL JOB RESULTS:

% of
time

_____ 1. **ACCOMPLISHES LAWYERS' REQUIREMENTS**
by
recruiting, selecting, orienting, and training administrative staff; scheduling and assigning staff to cases; monitoring court dockets; following up on work output.

_____ 2. **MAINTAINS STAFF JOB RESULTS**
by
communicating job expectations; planning, monitoring, and appraising job results; coaching, counseling, and disciplining employees; initiating, coordinating, and enforcing systems, policies, and procedures; maintaining a safe and secure work environment; developing personal growth opportunities.

_____ 3. **COMPLIES WITH LEGAL REQUIREMENTS**
by
ensuring policy and procedure compliance.

_____ 4. **IDENTIFIES FUTURE CLIENT SERVICE REQUIREMENTS**
by
establishing personal rapport with clients and potential clients; conducting and interpreting client satisfaction surveys.

_____ 5. **REDUCES OPERATING COSTS**
by
monitoring annual budget; scheduling expenditures; analyzing variances; studying service mix; determining profitable service; recommending guidelines for pro bono case acceptance.

% of
time

_____ 6. **MAINTAINS DATABASES**
by
developing information requirements; procuring data services; implementing filing structures; controlling database backups.

_____ 7. **MAINTAINS CLIENT RECORDS**
by
following legal retention requirements; determining storage and retrieval requirements; supervising filing operations; keeping information confidential.

_____ 8. **MAINTAINS LAW REFERENCE SOURCES**
by
evaluating and purchasing hard copy, software, and on-line services; keeping indexes up-to-date.

_____ 9. **MAINTAINS SUPPLIES**
by
checking inventory levels; anticipating needed supplies; placing, expediting and receiving orders.

_____10. **KEEPS EQUIPMENT OPERATIONAL**
by
following manufacturer's instructions; troubleshooting malfunctions; maintaining inventories; evaluating new equipment and techniques.

ESSENTIAL JOB RESULTS:

% of
time

____**11. MAINTAINS PROFESSIONAL AND
TECHNICAL KNOWLEDGE**
by
attending educational workshops;
reviewing professional publications;
establishing personal networks;
benchmarking state-of-the-art practices;
participating in professional societies.

% of
time

____**12. CONTRIBUTES TO TEAM EFFORT**
by
accomplishing related results as
needed.

JOB TITLE: LETTER CARRIER   L234_M

JOB PURPOSE: **SERVES POSTAL CUSTOMERS**
by
sorting, delivering, and protecting mail; maintaining vehicle.

ESSENTIAL JOB RESULTS:

% of
time

_____ 1. SORTS MAIL FOR DELIVERY
by
assembling mail for route; sorting
according to address; packing for
delivery.

_____ 2. DELIVERS MAIL
by
following route to addresses; placing
mail in mail box or designated location;
obtaining required signatures.

_____ 3. OBTAINS REVENUE
by
collecting charges.

**_____ 4. COMPLETES REPORTS AND
DOCUMENTS ACTIONS**
by
entering required information.

_____ 5. MAINTAINS VEHICLE
by
completing operator preventive
maintenance requirements; following
manufacturer's instructions;
troubleshooting malfunctions; reporting
problems; calling for repairs.

% of
time

_____ 6. MAINTAINS QUALITY SERVICE
by
following postal standards.

**_____ 7. MAINTAINS SAFE WORKING
CONDITIONS**
by
following postal standards and legal
regulations.

**_____ 8. MAINTAINS TECHNICAL
KNOWLEDGE**
by
attending educational workshops;
reviewing publications.

_____ 9. CONTRIBUTES TO TEAM EFFORT
by
accomplishing related results as
needed.

JOB TITLE:	LIBRARIAN	L235_M

JOB PURPOSE: **SERVES PATRONS**
by
planning and maintaining collection; locating resources.

ESSENTIAL JOB RESULTS:

% of
time

_____ 1. **BUILDS COLLECTION**
by
selecting, recommending, and ordering
reference and circulation resources.

_____ 2. **ORGANIZES COLLECTION**
by
classifying, cataloguing, marking, and
displaying resources; developing
location guides; maintaining research
and locator systems; reshelving
resources.

_____ 3. **EXPLAINS COLLECTION**
by
describing resources and research and
locator systems and methods;
developing training materials.

_____ 4. **LOCATES RESOURCES**
by
clarifying requests; identifying and
searching resources; training patrons to
use facilities and systems.

% of
time

_____ 5. **ISSUES RESOURCES**
by
obtaining and entering identification.

_____ 6. **PROTECTS PATRONS'
CONCENTRATION**
by
maintaining order.

_____ 7. **MAINTAINS PROFESSIONAL AND
TECHNICAL KNOWLEDGE**
by
attending educational workshops;
reviewing professional publications;
establishing personal networks;
benchmarking state-of-the-art practices;
participating in professional societies.

_____ 8. **CONTRIBUTES TO TEAM EFFORT**
by
accomplishing related results as
needed.

JOB PURPOSE: **MAINTAINS MAINFRAME OPERATING ENVIRONMENT**
by
monitoring and upgrading operations.

ESSENTIAL JOB RESULTS:

% of
time

% of
time

____ 1. **COMPLETES PROJECTS**
by
planning, organizing, and monitoring
assignments; aligning decisions and
actions with corporate technology
directions.

____ 2. **ESTABLISHES AND UPGRADES
SYSTEM**
by
evaluating and implementing operating
systems and subsystems, utility
programs, monitoring and diagnostic
software, and hardware products.

____ 3. **MAINTAINS OPERATIONAL
EFFECTIVENESS AND EFFICIENCY**
by
monitoring, evaluating, and adjusting
mainframe operating systems.

____ 4. **MAINTAINS QUALITY SERVICE**
by
establishing and enforcing organization
standards.

____ 5. **MAINTAINS INSTALLATION
RECORDS**
by
documenting procedures used; filing
and retrieving documentation.

____ 6. **RESOLVES PROBLEMS**
by
determining cause; providing technical
assistance to applications and other
support staff.

____ 7. **PREPARES REPORTS**
by
collecting, analyzing, and summarizing
information.

____ 8. **MAINTAINS TECHNICAL
KNOWLEDGE**
by
attending educational workshops;
reviewing publications.

____ 9. **CONTRIBUTES TO TEAM EFFORT**
by
accomplishing related results as
needed.

JOB PURPOSE: **MAINTAINS INVENTORY**
by
purchasing, verifying, and recording items.

ESSENTIAL JOB RESULTS:

% of
time

% of
time

_____ 1. **PURCHASES PARTS AND MATERIALS**
by
investigating potential suppliers; researching parts, equipment, and material availability; preparing and submitting purchase requisitions.

_____ 2. **MAINTAINS HISTORICAL REFERENCE OF SUPPLIES, EQUIPMENT, AND SERVICES**
by
keeping records of items and services purchased, prices, delivery and shipping costs, and product or service acceptability.

_____ 3. **MAINTAINS SHIPPING AND RECEIVING MATERIALS**
by
checking stock to determine inventory level; anticipating needed materials; placing and expediting orders for materials; verifying receipt of materials.

_____ 4. **PROVIDES INFORMATION**
by
answering questions; entering and generating data; completing forms.

_____ 5. **RECEIVES MERCHANDISE**
by
checking merchandise for damage; verifying freight bills.

_____ 6. **MAINTAINS MASTER STOCK OF ITEMS**
by
assigning number to new stock item; updating specification files; recording reorder point information.

_____ 7. **VERIFIES WAREHOUSE INVENTORY**
by
entering and adding supplies received to current inventory levels.

_____ 8. **SUPERVISES A SAFE AND CLEAN WORK ENVIRONMENT**
by
ensuring compliance with collective bargaining agreements, safety procedures, good manufacturing practices, and federal regulations.

_____ 9. **MAINTAINS TECHNICAL KNOWLEDGE**
by
attending educational workshops; reviewing publications.

_____10. **CONTRIBUTES TO TEAM EFFORT**
by
accomplishing related results as needed.

┌───┐
│ **JOB TITLE: MANAGER (MODEL)**   **M245_M** │
└───┘

JOB PURPOSE: ACCOMPLISHES DEPARTMENT OBJECTIVES
by
managing staff; planning and evaluating department activities.

ESSENTIAL JOB RESULTS:

% of
time

____ 1. **MAINTAINS (DEPARTMENT) STAFF**
by
recruiting, selecting, orienting, and
training employees; maintaining a safe,
secure, and legal work environment;
developing personal growth
opportunities.

____ 2. **ACCOMPLISHES STAFF RESULTS**
by
communicating job expectations;
planning, monitoring, and appraising
job results; coaching, counseling, and
disciplining employees; developing,
coordinating, and enforcing systems,
policies, procedures, and productivity
standards.

____ 3. **ESTABLISHES (DEPARTMENT)
STRATEGIC GOALS**
by
gathering pertinent business, financial,
service, and operations information;
identifying and evaluating trends and
options; choosing a course of action;
defining objectives; evaluating
outcomes.

____ 4. **ACCOMPLISHES FINANCIAL
OBJECTIVES**
by
forecasting requirements; preparing an
annual budget; scheduling
expenditures; analyzing variances;
initiating corrective actions.

% of
time

____ 5. **(ENTER JOB-SPECIFIC RESULTS)**
by
(enter job-specific duties)

____ 6. **MAINTAINS QUALITY SERVICE**
by
enforcing quality and customer service
standards; analyzing and resolving
quality and customer service problems;
identifying trends; recommending
system improvements.

____ 7. **MAINTAINS PROFESSIONAL AND
TECHNICAL KNOWLEDGE**
by
attending educational workshops;
reviewing professional publications;
establishing personal networks;
benchmarking state-of-the-art practices;
participating in professional societies.

____ 8. **CONTRIBUTES TO TEAM EFFORT**
by
accomplishing related results as
needed.

JOB TITLE: MARINA MANAGER   M248_M

JOB PURPOSE: SERVES CUSTOMERS
by
supervising staff; maintaining marina facilities and services.

ESSENTIAL JOB RESULTS:

% of
time

% of
time

____ 1. **MAINTAINS MARINA STAFF**
by
recruiting, selecting, orienting, and
training employees.

____ 2. **ACCOMPLISHES STAFF RESULTS**
by
communicating job expectations;
planning, monitoring, and appraising
job results; coaching, counseling, and
disciplining employees; initiating,
coordinating, and enforcing systems,
policies, and procedures.

____ 3. **MAINTAINS FACILITIES**
by
identifying requirements; completing
preventive maintenance; arranging for
maintenance, cleaning, and repairs.

____ 4. **MAINTAINS SUPPLIES INVENTORY**
by
checking stock; anticipating needs;
placing and expediting orders; verifying
receipt.

____ 5. **RENTS ACCOMMODATIONS**
by
advertising and explaining services;
obtaining fees; assigning berths and
rooms.

____ 6. **PROVIDES SERVICES**
by
arranging for fuel delivery, power, trash
collection, mechanical, electrical, and
structural repairs, laundry, cleaning,
communications, and storage.

____ 7. **ARRANGES LAND
TRANSPORTATION**
by
contracting with livery service.

____ 8. **OFFERS RECREATION SERVICES**
by
renting boats, water skis, diving
equipment, and fishing tackle;
arranging tours.

____ 9. **ACCOMPLISHES FINANCIAL
OBJECTIVES**
by
forecasting requirements; preparing an
annual budget; scheduling
expenditures; analyzing variances;
initiating corrective action.

____10. **MAINTAINS A SAFE AND HEALTHY
ENVIRONMENT**
by
establishing and enforcing organization
standards; adhering to legal
regulations.

____11. **PREPARES REPORTS**
by
collecting, analyzing, and summarizing
information.

____12. **MAINTAINS PROFESSIONAL AND
TECHNICAL KNOWLEDGE**
by
attending educational workshops;
reviewing professional publications;
establishing personal networks;
benchmarking state-of-the-art practices;
participating in professional societies.

____13. **CONTRIBUTES TO TEAM EFFORT**
by
accomplishing related results as
needed.

JOB PURPOSE: **DEVELOPS MARKETING STRATEGY**
by
managing staff; researching marketing opportunities and competition; developing sales programs.

ESSENTIAL JOB RESULTS:

% of
time

% of
time

____ 1. **MAINTAINS MARKETING STAFF**
by
recruiting, selecting, orienting, and training employees; maintaining a safe and secure work environment; developing personal growth opportunities.

____ 2. **ACCOMPLISHES STAFF RESULTS**
by
communicating job expectations; planning, monitoring, and appraising job results; coaching, counseling, and disciplining employees; initiating, coordinating, and enforcing systems, policies, and procedures.

____ 3. **CONTRIBUTES TO MARKETING EFFECTIVENESS**
by
supporting corporate officers and divisions in identifying short-term and long-range issues that must be addressed; providing information and commentary pertinent to deliberations; recommending options and courses of action; implementing directives.

____ 4. **HELPS DIVISION PRESIDENTS ASSESS LAND OPPORTUNITIES AND PRODUCT SELECTION**
by
conducting marketing research; organizing focus groups on existing plans, new plans, new models; conducting exit interviews with buyers and non-buyers; identifying new product opportunities; contributing to plan designs and consumer and prototype tests; developing resources that will direct land purchase opportunities to the company.

____ 5. **DETERMINES HOME BUILDING TRENDS**
by
maintaining active presence with home builders' associations; gaining informal trade information.

ESSENTIAL JOB RESULTS:

% of
time

% of
time

_____ 6. **OBTAINS MARKET SHARE**
by
preparing annual reviews of market
opportunities in each division; providing
competitive shopping of communities;
obtaining information from local
planning staffs; determining proposed
and approved but non-existing
competitive subdivisions; obtaining
and analyzing roadway and utilities
plans affecting site and area's growth
potential.

_____ 7. **INCREASES SALES AND IMPROVES
PROFITS**
by
facilitating initiatives and helping launch
required programs.

_____ 8. **PREPARES SUMMARY REPORTS
FOR EACH DIVISION**
by
gathering and analyzing demographic,
lead card, and closing data.

_____ 9. **STANDARDIZES SALES OFFICES**
by
creating a model for merchandising;
arranging collateral materials.

_____ 10. **IMPROVES PROGRAM AND
SERVICE QUALITY**
by
devising new applications; updating
procedures; evaluating system results
with users.

_____ 11. **ACHIEVES FINANCIAL OBJECTIVES**
by
anticipating requirements; submitting
information for budget preparation;
scheduling expenditures; monitoring
costs; analyzing variances.

_____ 12. **MAINTAINS CONTINUITY AMONG
CORPORATE, DIVISION, AND
LOCAL WORK TEAMS**
by
documenting and communicating
actions, irregularities, and continuing
needs.

_____ 13. **MAINTAINS PROFESSIONAL AND
TECHNICAL KNOWLEDGE**
by
attending educational workshops;
reviewing professional publications;
establishing personal networks;
benchmarking state-of-the-art practices;
participating in professional societies.

_____ 14. **CONTRIBUTES TO TEAM EFFORT**
by
accomplishing related results as
needed.

JOB PURPOSE: **ACHIEVES ORGANIZATION BUSINESS DEVELOPMENT OBJECTIVES**
by
researching and developing marketing opportunities and plans.

ESSENTIAL JOB RESULTS:

% of
time

1. IDENTIFIES MARKETING OPPORTUNITIES
by
identifying consumer requirements; defining market, competitors' share, and competitors' advantages and weaknesses; forecasting projected business; establishing targeted company share.

2. IMPROVES PRODUCT MARKETABILITY AND PROFITABILITY
by
researching, identifying, and capitalizing on market opportunities; improving product packaging; coordinating new product development with research & development associates.

3. ESTABLISHES MARKETING PLAN
by
developing sales and pricing strategies, objectives, action plans, schedules, and assignments.

4. SUSTAINS RAPPORT WITH KEY ACCOUNTS
by
making periodic visits; exploring specific needs; anticipating new opportunities.

5. OBTAINS MARKET SHARE
by
planning, developing, implementing, and evaluating advertising, merchandising, and trade promotion programs.

% of
time

6. ACHIEVES FINANCIAL OBJECTIVES
by
preparing and managing an annual budget.

7. MAINTAINS QUALITY SERVICE
by
establishing and enforcing organization standards.

8. PREPARES REPORTS
by
collecting, analyzing, and presenting information.

9. MAINTAINS PROFESSIONAL AND TECHNICAL KNOWLEDGE
by
attending educational workshops; reviewing professional publications; establishing personal networks; benchmarking state-of-the-art practices; participating in professional societies.

10. CONTRIBUTES TO TEAM EFFORT
by
accomplishing related results as needed.

JOB PURPOSE: **MAINTAINS COMPETITIVE ADVANTAGE**
by
researching competition.

ESSENTIAL JOB RESULTS:

% of
time

_____ 1. **RESEARCHES COMPETITION**
by
identifying locations of competitors;
developing maps of competitors;
conducting competitive shopping.

_____ 2. **PREPARES REPORTS**
by
compiling analysis of competitive
shopping.

_____ 3. **PRESENTS INFORMATION**
by
developing primary competition graphs.

_____ 4. **MAINTAINS LIBRARY**
by
obtaining and compiling information on
best sellers and plans of the
competition.

% of
time

_____ 5. **MAINTAINS QUALITY SERVICE**
by
following organization standards.

_____ 6. **MAINTAINS PROFESSIONAL AND
TECHNICAL KNOWLEDGE**
by
attending educational workshops;
reviewing publications.

_____ 7. **CONTRIBUTES TO TEAM EFFORT**
by
accomplishing related results as
needed.

JOB TITLE: MARKETING SUPPORT REPRESENTATIVE   M254_M

JOB PURPOSE: ACCOMPLISHES MARKETING OBJECTIVES
by
collecting, verifying, and analyzing information.

ESSENTIAL JOB RESULTS:

% of
time

____ 1. **IDENTIFIES PROJECT REQUIREMENTS**
by
interviewing customers; analyzing data; documenting results.

____ 2. **RESOLVES PROBLEMS**
by
studying issues; reviewing documents; analyzing alternative solutions; making recommendations.

____ 3. **COMPILES INFORMATION**
by
researching data; reviewing account deficits in conjunction with credit and collections.

____ 4. **ADMINISTERS SALES FORCE COMPENSATION PROGRAMS**
by
researching and compiling data towards determination of incentive payments; administrating contracts and payments of commissions to sales force; reviewing contracts for compliance with guidelines; analyzing commission statements/payments; assisting legal department in litigated commission issues/cases; recommending alternatives.

____ 5. **DEVELOPS AGREEMENTS**
by
creating new agreements, addenda, or modifications to existing agreements in conjunction with legal department; reviewing nonstandard agreements; reporting and making recommendations to president on substantial items.

% of
time

____ 6. **ENSURES COMPLIANCE WITH REGULATIONS**
by
initiating contract setup for business processed in various locations.

____ 7. **DETERMINES CRITERIA FOR MARKETING INITIATIVE AWARD PROGRAMS**
by
researching and compiling data.

____ 8. **PREPARES REPORTS**
by
compiling data and producing reports; tracking business plans.

____ 9. **MAINTAINS QUALITY SERVICE**
by
establishing and enforcing organization standards.

____ 10. **MAINTAINS TECHNICAL KNOWLEDGE**
by
attending educational workshops; reviewing publications.

____ 11. **CONTRIBUTES TO TEAM EFFORT**
by
accomplishing related results as needed.

JOB TITLE:	MASSEUR/MASSEUSE	M255_M

JOB PURPOSE: **SERVES CUSTOMERS**
by
anticipating client needs; planning and administering massages.

ESSENTIAL JOB RESULTS:

% of
time

% of
time

_____ 1. **MAINTAINS SUPPLIES**
by
checking stock; anticipating needs;
placing orders; verifying receipt.

_____ 2. **PLANS TREATMENT**
by
assessing customer's condition, history,
and complaints; reviewing medical
orders; determining treatment
objectives.

_____ 3. **MASSAGES BODY**
by
applying rubbing solutions; applying
hand techniques or using vibrating
equipment.

_____ 4. **REHABILITATES BODY**
by
administering treatments.

_____ 5. **IMPROVES BODY CONDITION**
by
providing exercise instructions to
customer.

_____ 6. **COMPLETES REPORTS**
by
entering required information.

_____ 7. **MAINTAINS QUALITY SERVICE**
by
following organization standards.

_____ 8. **MAINTAINS SAFE AND HEALTHY
CONDITIONS**
by
following organization standards and
legal regulations.

_____ 9. **OBTAINS REVENUE**
by
collecting fees.

_____10. **MAINTAINS TECHNICAL
KNOWLEDGE**
by
attending educational workshops;
reviewing publications.

_____11. **CONTRIBUTES TO TEAM EFFORT**
by
accomplishing related results as
needed.

JOB TITLE:	MEDIA LIBRARY SPECIALIST	M259_M

JOB PURPOSE: **MAINTAINS COMPUTER OPERATIONS**
by
inventorying and providing media.

ESSENTIAL JOB RESULTS:

% of
time

____ **1. SUPPORTS USERS AND REMOTE SITES**
by
responding to requests and problems; training personnel.

____ **2. MAINTAINS MEDIA INVENTORY**
by
classifying and cataloguing files; maintaining logs of media movement; providing scratch media.

____ **3. CONTROLS MEDIA QUALITY**
by
cleaning and replacing media; following organization standards.

____ **4. MAINTAINS PRODUCTION**
by
determining and forecasting media usage; preparing media for off-shift processing.

____ **5. RESOLVES BAD MEDIA**
by
analyzing problems; implementing solutions.

% of
time

____ **6. MAINTAINS MEDIA CLEANING EQUIPMENT**
by
completing preventive maintenance requirements; troubleshooting malfunctions; calling for repairs; maintaining equipment inventories.

____ **7. MAINTAINS TECHNICAL KNOWLEDGE**
by
attending educational workshops; reviewing publications.

____ **8. CONTRIBUTES TO TEAM EFFORT**
by
accomplishing related results as needed.

<table>
<tr><td colspan="2">**JOB TITLE:**   **MEETING AND PROMOTION SERVICES DIRECTOR**</td><td>**M264_M**</td></tr>
</table>

JOB PURPOSE: **PRESENTS SERVICES TO CUSTOMERS**
by
managing staff; planning and conducting sales promotions and meetings.

ESSENTIAL JOB RESULTS:

% of
time

% of
time

____ 1. **MAINTAINS MEETINGS AND PROMOTIONAL SERVICES STAFF**
by
recruiting, selecting, orienting, and training employees; maintaining a safe and secure work environment; developing personal growth opportunities.

____ 2. **ACCOMPLISHES STAFF RESULTS**
by
communicating job expectations; planning, monitoring, and appraising job results; coaching, counseling, and disciplining employees; initiating, coordinating, and enforcing systems, policies, and procedures.

____ 3. **ACCOMPLISHES PROMOTIONAL SERVICES BUSINESS OBJECTIVES**
by
gathering information and making business plan recommendations; comparing progress to quarterly plan; completing action plans and assignments.

____ 4. **ACHIEVES FINANCIAL OBJECTIVES**
by
forecasting functional requirements; preparing an annual budget; scheduling expenditures; analyzing variances; initiating corrective actions; providing information for monthly financial control meetings.

____ 5. **PROVIDES QUALITY SERVICE**
by
enforcing meeting and promotional services quality and customer service standards; analyzing quality and customer service problems; initiating audits; identifying trends; recommending system improvements.

____ 6. **COMPLETES OPERATIONS**
by
managing meetings and promotional services process; evaluating work results; enforcing meeting and promotional services productivity standards; analyzing production problems; initiating audits; identifying trends; identifying new technology.

____ 7. **CONDUCTS SALES PROMOTION CAMPAIGNS**
by
developing strategies; supervising production of promotional materials; analyzing results.

____ 8. **PRODUCES CONVENTIONS AND MEETINGS**
by
preparing budgets; negotiating fees and arrangements; managing requirements; approving expenditures.

ESSENTIAL JOB RESULTS:

% of
time

% of
time

_____ 9. **PROVIDES MEALS AND OTHER HOSPITALITY SERVICES**
by
contracting with vendors; evaluating results.

_____10. **MAINTAINS PROFESSIONAL AND TECHNICAL KNOWLEDGE**
by
attending educational workshops; reviewing professional publications; establishing personal networks; benchmarking state-of-the-art practices; participating in professional societies.

_____11. **CONTRIBUTES TO TEAM EFFORT**
by
accomplishing related results as needed.

JOB PURPOSE: PRODUCES CONVENTIONS AND MEETINGS
by
developing programs; arranging for facilities, speakers, services, and printed materials.

ESSENTIAL JOB RESULTS:

% of
time

_____ 1. **DETERMINES CONVENTION AND MEETING REQUIREMENTS**
by
establishing personal rapport with potential and actual customers and other persons in a position to understand requirements.

_____ 2. **ATTRACTS ATTENTION TO EVENT**
by
preparing promotional materials.

_____ 3. **DESIGNS PROGRAM CONTENT**
by
focusing on and expanding client theme; following educational and entertainment principles; obtaining client approvals.

_____ 4. **ENGAGES SPEAKERS AND ENTERTAINERS**
by
matching presenter talents to program design requirements.

_____ 5. **PREPARES EXHIBITION HALL SPACE**
by
assembling vendor booths according to requirements; arranging for delivery; determining electrical requirements; contracting for electrical installation.

_____ 6. **PREPARES PRINTED MATERIALS**
by
identifying requirements; arranging for printing and delivery.

% of
time

_____ 7. **ARRANGES FOOD AND BEVERAGE SERVICES**
by
selecting vendors; designing menus; tasting selections.

_____ 8. **MAINTAINS ATTENDANCE COUNT FOR CONVENTIONS AND MEETINGS**
by
recording reservations and cancellations.

_____ 9. **ACHIEVES MEETING PLANNING FINANCIAL OBJECTIVES**
by
reviewing and paying invoices; controlling expenses.

_____10. **MAINTAINS PROFESSIONAL AND TECHNICAL KNOWLEDGE**
by
attending educational workshops; reviewing professional publications; establishing personal networks; benchmarking state-of-the-art practices; participating in professional societies.

_____11. **MAINTAINS CLIENT SATISFACTION**
by
accomplishing related results as needed.

JOB PURPOSE: **ACCOMPLISHES MICROCOMPUTER OBJECTIVES**
by
managing staff; procuring, installing, and maintaining hardware and software.

ESSENTIAL JOB RESULTS:

% of
time

% of
time

____ 1. **ACCOMPLISHES MICROCOMPUTER SERVICES STAFF RESULTS**
by
communicating job expectations; planning, monitoring, and appraising job results; coaching, counseling, and disciplining employees; initiating, coordinating, and enforcing systems, policies, and procedures.

____ 2. **MAINTAINS STAFF**
by
recruiting, selecting, orienting, and training employees; maintaining a safe and secure work environment; developing personal growth opportunities.

____ 3. **MEETS USER REQUIREMENTS**
by
surveying market for new user-friendly microcomputer hardware and software products; selecting, acquiring, installing, and maintaining products.

____ 4. **DEVELOPS INFORMATION SYSTEMS STRATEGIES**
by
developing organization tactics, policies, and procedures.

____ 5. **APPLIES SUITABLE RESOURCES**
by
monitoring use of installed base of microcomputer resources; recommending foremost applications; implementing disaster recovery and backup procedures; installing information security and control structures.

____ 6. **TRAINS USERS**
by
documenting procedures; designing and conducting training programs.

____ 7. **MAINTAINS INVENTORY**
by
recording and updating service and location of microcomputer resources.

____ 8. **PREPARES REPORTS**
by
collecting and analyzing project results and progress.

____ 9. **MAINTAINS QUALITY SERVICE**
by
establishing and enforcing organization standards.

____ 10. **MAINTAINS PROFESSIONAL AND TECHNICAL KNOWLEDGE**
by
attending educational workshops; reviewing professional publications; establishing personal networks; benchmarking state-of-the-art practices; participating in professional societies.

____ 11. **CONTRIBUTES TO TEAM EFFORT**
by
accomplishing related results as needed.

JOB TITLE: MICROCOMPUTER SYSTEMS ANALYST M268_M

JOB PURPOSE: **MAINTAINS WORKSTATION ENVIRONMENT**
by
installing hardware, software, and printers; maintaining workstation performance.

ESSENTIAL JOB RESULTS:

% of
time

_____ 1. **IDENTIFIES WORKSTATION SOLUTIONS**
by
interviewing customers; analyzing functions, applications, programming, and operations; evaluating existing and proposed solutions; recommending applicable solutions.

_____ 2. **ESTABLISHES WORKSTATION PERFORMANCE**
by
installing hardware, software, and printers.

_____ 3. **MAINTAINS NETWORK PERFORMANCE**
by
performing second-level problem determination; resolving problems.

_____ 4. **OPTIMIZES WORKSTATION PERFORMANCE**
by
modifying workstation resources.

_____ 5. **MAINTAINS QUALITY SERVICE**
by
following organization standards.

% of
time

_____ 6. **MAINTAINS RECORDS**
by
documenting procedures used.

_____ 7. **PREPARES REPORTS**
by
collecting, analyzing, and summarizing information, including project estimates.

_____ 8. **MAINTAINS WORKSTATION INVENTORY**
by
recording location and status.

_____ 9. **MAINTAINS PROFESSIONAL AND TECHNICAL KNOWLEDGE**
by
attending educational workshops; reviewing professional publications; establishing personal networks; benchmarking state-of-the-art practices; participating in professional societies.

_____10. **CONTRIBUTES TO TEAM EFFORT**
by
accomplishing related results as needed.

JOB TITLE: MICROFILM PROCESSOR   M269_M

JOB PURPOSE: **MAINTAINS HISTORICAL RECORDS**
by
operating equipment to process microfilm.

ESSENTIAL JOB RESULTS:

% of
time

% of
time

_____ 1. **PROCESSES MICROFILM**
by
operating equipment.

_____ 2. **DETECTS REFILMING NEEDS**
by
checking illegible documents; pulling
original documents for refilming.

_____ 3. **FORWARDS MICROFILM TO
CUSTOMERS**
by
preparing cartridges and labels;
distributing to customers.

_____ 4. **FORWARDS MICROFILM TO
STORAGE**
by
labeling security roll; entering on
archives box; sending full boxes to
outside storage facility.

_____ 5. **DESIGNATES DOCUMENTS FOR
DESTRUCTION**
by
marking film and verifying documents
for destruction.

_____ 6. **MAINTAINS FILM SUPPLIES
INVENTORY**
by
checking stock; anticipating needs;
placing orders; verifying receipt.

_____ 7. **MAINTAINS EQUIPMENT**
by
following manufacturer's instructions;
completing preventive maintenance;
calling for repairs.

_____ 8. **MAINTAINS SAFE AND CLEAN
WORK ENVIRONMENT**
by
completing daily cleanup; complying
with procedures, rules, and regulations.

_____ 9. **MAINTAINS TECHNICAL
KNOWLEDGE**
by
attending educational workshops;
reviewing publications.

_____10. **CONTRIBUTES TO TEAM EFFORT**
by
accomplishing related results as
needed.

JOB PURPOSE: **EXTRACTS PRODUCT**
by
managing staff; planning and maintaining productive and safe operations.

ESSENTIAL JOB RESULTS:

% of
time

% of
time

_____ 1. **MAINTAINS MINING STAFF**
by
recruiting, selecting, orienting, and training employees; developing personal growth opportunities.

_____ 2. **ACCOMPLISHES STAFF RESULTS**
by
communicating job expectations; planning, monitoring, and appraising job results; coaching, counseling, and disciplining employees; initiating, coordinating, and enforcing systems, policies, and procedures.

_____ 3. **PLANS MINE DEVELOPMENT**
by
studying geological surveys, maps, reports, and tests.

_____ 4. **MAINTAINS SAFE AND HEALTHY WORK ENVIRONMENT**
by
establishing and enforcing mine standards; adhering to legal regulations; conducting inspections.

_____ 5. **ACCOMPLISHES FINANCIAL OBJECTIVES**
by
estimating income; forecasting costs and requirements; preparing an annual budget; scheduling expenditures; analyzing variances; initiating corrective action.

_____ 6. **ACHIEVES OBJECTIVES**
by
gathering pertinent information; identifying and evaluating options; choosing a course of action.

_____ 7. **MAINTAINS OPERATIONS**
by
accessing, obtaining, hauling, and storing product.

_____ 8. **ENSURES OPERATION OF EQUIPMENT**
by
monitoring preventive maintenance and repair; maintaining inventories; evaluating new equipment and techniques.

_____ 9. **PREPARES REPORTS**
by
maintaining records; collecting, analyzing, and summarizing information.

_____10. **MAINTAINS PROFESSIONAL AND TECHNICAL KNOWLEDGE**
by
attending educational workshops; reviewing professional publications; establishing personal networks; benchmarking state-of-the-art practices; participating in professional societies.

_____11. **CONTRIBUTES TO TEAM EFFORT**
by
accomplishing related results as needed.

JOB TITLE: MUSEUM EDUCATION DIRECTOR   M272_M

JOB PURPOSE: **EDUCATES VISITORS**
by
developing, publicizing, and presenting programs.

ESSENTIAL JOB RESULTS:

% of
time

_____ 1. **ESTABLISHES EDUCATIONAL PROGRAMS**
by
studying and researching museum inventory; identifying potential visitors' interests; reviewing board of trustees' policy; reviewing budgets; coordinating resources with other institutions.

_____ 2. **PREPARES PROGRAMS**
by
developing concepts; evaluating and selecting media; writing scripts; designing displays and graphics; selecting display makers; supervising construction.

_____ 3. **PREPARES PROGRAM PRESENTATION**
by
selecting and training lecturers; approving materials; assisting lecturers.

_____ 4. **PUBLICIZES PROGRAMS**
by
developing and placing advertising and announcements; speaking before community groups; responding to inquiries.

_____ 5. **PRESENTS PROGRAMS**
by
supervising arrangements and events; monitoring tours and lectures.

% of
time

_____ 6. **EVALUATES PROGRAMS**
by
conducting surveys; analyzing and interpreting results; enhancing programs and presentations.

_____ 7. **ACCOMPLISHES FINANCIAL OBJECTIVES**
by
forecasting requirements; preparing an annual budget; scheduling expenditures; analyzing variances; initiating corrective action; writing and submitting grant proposals.

_____ 8. **PREPARES REPORTS**
by
collecting, analyzing, and summarizing information.

_____ 9. **MAINTAINS PROFESSIONAL AND TECHNICAL KNOWLEDGE**
by
attending educational workshops; reviewing professional publications; establishing personal networks; benchmarking state-of-the-art practices; participating in professional societies.

_____10. **CONTRIBUTES TO TEAM EFFORT**
by
accomplishing related results as needed.

JOB PURPOSE: **SERVES CUSTOMERS**
by
shaping, lengthening, strengthening, and dressing fingernails and toenails.

ESSENTIAL JOB RESULTS:

% of
time

_____ 1. **MAINTAINS SUPPLIES**
by
checking stock; anticipating needs;
placing orders; verifying receipt.

_____ 2. **PREPARES FINGERNAILS AND TOENAILS**
by
removing polish; cleaning and softening
nails and tissue.

_____ 3. **SHAPES NAILS**
by
cutting and filing ends.

_____ 4. **LENGTHENS FINGERNAILS**
by
applying nail wraps and tips.

_____ 5. **DRESSES NAILS**
by
applying polish or sculpture design.

_____ 6. **MAINTAINS QUALITY SERVICE**
by
following organization standards.

% of
time

_____ 7. **MAINTAINS SAFE AND HEALTHY CONDITIONS**
by
following aseptic standards; adhering to
legal regulations.

_____ 8. **OBTAINS REVENUE**
by
recording or collecting charges.

_____ 9. **MAINTAINS TECHNICAL KNOWLEDGE**
by
attending educational workshops;
reviewing publications.

_____ 10. **CONTRIBUTES TO TEAM EFFORT**
by
accomplishing related results as
needed.

JOB TITLE: NATIONAL ACCOUNT REPRESENTATIVE

N274_M

JOB PURPOSE: **OBTAINS NATIONAL MARKET SHARE**
by
serving current customers; identifying and developing new customers.

ESSENTIAL JOB RESULTS:

% of
time

____ 1. **SERVICES CURRENT CUSTOMERS**
by
maintaining rapport; making periodic visits; auditing stores for new opportunities; responding to requests; resolving problems.

____ 2. **IDENTIFIES NEW CUSTOMERS**
by
studying sales statistics; estimating sales volume; qualifying potential customers.

____ 3. **DEVELOPS NEW CUSTOMERS**
by
establishing new distribution channels; explaining product potential to retailers; identifying possibilities for product improvements and new products.

____ 4. **MAINTAINS DISTRIBUTOR NETWORK**
by
explaining promotions; training personnel; attending presentations; supporting efforts; answering questions.

____ 5. **ACCOMPLISHES SALES OBJECTIVES**
by
obtaining and maintaining dominant shelf position; negotiating contracts.

% of
time

____ 6. **INCREASES MARKET SHARE**
by
designing and presenting national and local promotions.

____ 7. **PROVIDES HISTORICAL INFORMATION**
by
completing records.

____ 8. **PREPARES REPORTS**
by
collecting, preparing, and analyzing information.

____ 9. **MAINTAINS PROFESSIONAL AND TECHNICAL KNOWLEDGE**
by
attending educational workshops; reviewing professional publications; establishing personal networks; benchmarking state-of-the-art practices; participating in professional societies.

____ 10. **CONTRIBUTES TO TEAM EFFORT**
by
accomplishing related results as needed.

JOB TITLE: NETWORK ANALYST   N275_M

JOB PURPOSE: **MAINTAINS COMMUNICATIONS NETWORK ENVIRONMENT**
by
analyzing and maintaining performance.

ESSENTIAL JOB RESULTS:

% of
time

____ 1. **IDENTIFIES NETWORK REQUIREMENTS**
by
interviewing customers; analyzing departments, applications, programming, and operations involving networks, operating systems, file servers, and equipment (including voice, data, local and wide area networks, and video communications).

____ 2. **DESIGNS NETWORK OPERATIONS AND RESOURCES**
by
preparing proposals; developing implementation projects.

____ 3. **MAINTAINS NETWORK PERFORMANCE**
by
installing, maintaining, and repairing network and equipment.

____ 4. **OPTIMIZES NETWORK RESOURCE PERFORMANCE**
by
analyzing operating system; recommending improved methodologies.

% of
time

____ 5. **PREPARES USERS TO ACCOMPLISH JOB RESULTS**
by
developing and conducting training sessions.

____ 6. **PREPARES REPORTS**
by
collecting, analyzing, and summarizing information.

____ 7. **MAINTAINS QUALITY SERVICE**
by
following organization standards.

____ 8. **MAINTAINS TECHNICAL KNOWLEDGE**
by
attending educational workshops; reviewing publications.

____ 9. **CONTRIBUTES TO TEAM EFFORT**
by
accomplishing related results as needed.

JOB PURPOSE: **SUPPORTS COMMUNICATIONS NETWORK TECHNOLOGY**
by
installing facilities; maintaining performance.

ESSENTIAL JOB RESULTS:

% of
time

____ 1. **ESTABLISHES NETWORK PERFORMANCE**
by
installing voice, data, local and wide area networks, communications software, equipment, and network facilities.

____ 2. **MAINTAINS NETWORK PERFORMANCE**
by
repairing equipment and network software.

____ 3. **OPTIMIZES NETWORK PERFORMANCE**
by
researching software and equipment.

____ 4. **MAINTAINS RECORDS**
by
documenting procedures used.

% of
time

____ 5. **HELPS PREPARE REPORTS**
by
collecting information.

____ 6. **MAINTAINS QUALITY SERVICE**
by
following organization standards.

____ 7. **MAINTAINS TECHNICAL KNOWLEDGE**
by
attending educational workshops; reviewing publications.

____ 8. **CONTRIBUTES TO TEAM EFFORT**
by
accomplishing related results as needed.

JOB PURPOSE: **PRODUCES PLANTS**
by
managing staff; developing and implementing a nursery production plan.

ESSENTIAL JOB RESULTS:

% of
time

% of
time

____ **1. MAINTAINS NURSERY STAFF**
by
recruiting, selecting, orienting, and
training employees.

____ **2. ACCOMPLISHES STAFF RESULTS**
by
communicating job expectations;
planning, monitoring, and appraising
job results; coaching, counseling, and
disciplining employees.

____ **3. MAINTAINS SAFE AND HEALTHY
WORK ENVIRONMENT**
by
following organization standards and
legal regulations.

____ **4. MAINTAINS PRODUCTION**
by
scheduling and assigning employees;
inspecting crops and growing
conditions; monitoring quality; taking
corrective action.

____ **5. EVALUATES GROWING LOCATION**
by
analyzing soil condition and drainage.

____ **6. ESTABLISHES PRODUCTION PLAN**
by
determining type, quantity, and quality
of plants.

____ **7. PREPARES PRODUCTION PLAN**
by
purchasing seed, nutrients, and
disease-control chemicals.

____ **8. ENSURES OPERATION OF
EQUIPMENT**
by
completing preventive maintenance
requirements; following manufacturer's
instructions; troubleshooting
malfunctions; calling for repairs;
maintaining equipment inventories;
evaluating new equipment and
techniques.

____ **9. ACCOMPLISHES FINANCIAL
OBJECTIVES**
by
forecasting requirements; preparing an
annual budget; scheduling
expenditures; analyzing variances;
initiating corrective action.

____**10. COMPLETES REPORTS**
by
entering required information.

____**11. PREPARES REPORTS**
by
collecting, analyzing, and summarizing
information.

ESSENTIAL JOB RESULTS:

% of
time

% of
time

____12. **MAINTAINS PROFESSIONAL AND TECHNICAL KNOWLEDGE**
by
attending educational workshops;
reviewing professional publications;
establishing personal networks;
benchmarking state-of-the-art practices;
participating in professional societies.

____13. **CONTRIBUTES TO TEAM EFFORT**
by
accomplishing related results as
needed.

JOB PURPOSE: SERVES PATIENTS
by
managing staff; developing and enforcing nursing policies and services.

ESSENTIAL JOB RESULTS:

% of
time

% of
time

____ 1. **DEFINES NURSING PRACTICES**
by
encouraging and supporting research
and potential quality improvement
efforts.

____ 2. **INFLUENCES MEDICAL CENTER
POLICY**
by
providing nursing services perspective.

____ 3. **ACCOMPLISHES THE FINANCIAL
GOALS OF THE MEDICAL CENTER**
by
improving the quality and cost-
effectiveness of nursing services.

____ 4. **MAINTAINS MEDICAL CENTER
LEGAL REQUIREMENTS**
by
interpreting hospital policy and state
nursing laws; investigating potential
breaches; studying existing and new
legislation; anticipating legislation;
advising medical center chief executive
officer on needed actions.

____ 5. **IDENTIFIES FUTURE NURSING
SERVICES REQUIREMENTS**
by
establishing rapport across
interdisciplinary services; interpreting
information from potential and actual
patients and families; conferring with
people in a position to understand
service requirements.

____ 6. **MAINTAINS NURSING STAFF**
by
determining strategic recruiting focus;
reviewing and developing selection
criteria; establishing hiring practices;
evaluating effectiveness of newly hired
nurses.

____ 7. **MAINTAINS CREDENTIALED STAFF**
by
keeping abreast of advances and
specialty opportunities in new and
emerging nursing services and
technologies.

____ 8. **MAINTAINS NURSING SERVICES
OPERATIONS**
by
defining required program and
operational and personnel policies;
implementing a nursing strategy.

____ 9. **MAINTAINS A COLLABORATIVE
PATIENT SERVICES WORK
ENVIRONMENT**
by
fostering a spirit of interdisciplinary
cooperation among nursing services,
medical staff, and support and ancillary
services.

ESSENTIAL JOB RESULTS:

% of
time

____10. **CONTRIBUTES TO MEDICAL CENTER EFFECTIVENESS**
    by
    identifying short-term and long-range issues that must be addressed; providing information and commentary pertinent to deliberations; recommending options and courses of action; implementing directives.

____11. **REPRESENTS THE MEDICAL CENTER**
    by
    establishing and maintaining relationships with community groups and health and support services; communicating with news media; collecting data and presenting information at hearings.

% of
time

____12. **MAINTAINS PROFESSIONAL AND TECHNICAL KNOWLEDGE**
    by
    attending educational workshops; reviewing professional publications; establishing personal networks; benchmarking state-of-the-art practices; participating in professional societies.

____13. **CONTRIBUTES TO TEAM EFFORT**
    by
    accomplishing related results as needed.

JOB TITLE: OCCUPATIONAL PHYSICIAN   O281_M

JOB PURPOSE: **FOSTERS EMPLOYEE HEALTH**
by
supervising staff; promoting employee health; providing health care services.

ESSENTIAL JOB RESULTS:

% of
time

% of
time

_____ 1. **ACCOMPLISHES OCCUPATIONAL HEALTH STAFF RESULTS**
by
communicating job expectations; planning, monitoring, and appraising job results; coaching, counseling, and disciplining employees; initiating, coordinating, and enforcing systems, policies, and procedures.

_____ 2. **MAINTAINS STAFF**
by
recruiting, selecting, orienting, and training employees; maintaining a safe and secure work environment; developing personal growth opportunities.

_____ 3. **PROMOTES WELLNESS**
by
researching, developing, and implementing programs and policies.

_____ 4. **PREVENTS WORK ILLNESSES AND INJURIES**
by
conducting employment and periodic physical examinations.

_____ 5. **PROVIDES SUBSTANCE ABUSE CONTROL PROGRAMS**
by
coordinating interventions; utilizing available social services; referring patients to the employee assistance program and other professional resources.

_____ 6. **MAINTAINS EMOTIONAL WELL-BEING PROGRAMS**
by
recognizing emotionally induced or related illnesses; making appropriate referrals to employee assistance program and other professional resources.

_____ 7. **TREATS OCCUPATIONAL INJURIES AND ILLNESSES**
by
diagnosing and treating employees; referring cases to hospitals and rehabilitation centers, outside physicians, and specialists.

_____ 8. **MINIMIZES WORKERS' COMPENSATION COSTS**
by
keeping abreast of work simulation rehabilitative techniques; utilizing assessment centers to identify alternative work assignments and company work accommodation possibilities.

_____ 9. **SUSTAINS OCCUPATIONAL SAFETY AND HEALTH ADMINISTRATION COMPLIANCE**
by
maintaining first-aid log; reporting serious incidents or trends to safety manager.

ESSENTIAL JOB RESULTS:

% of
time

% of
time

____10. **ASSESSES COMPANY HEALTH CARE BENEFITS**
by
keeping abreast of health care delivery system trends; evaluating managed care, self-insurance, and other alternative health care delivery mechanisms.

____11. **EVALUATES HEALTH CARE BENEFIT CLAIMS**
by
studying case management for appropriateness of care.

____12. **MAINTAINS EMPLOYEE TRUST AND PROTECTS OPERATIONS**
by
keeping medical information confidential; establishing medical record maintenance, retention, and access protocols.

____13. **DEFINES MEDICAL STANDARDS**
by
preparing standard treatment orders for shift occupational health nurses and employee first-aid designees.

____14. **PREPARES MEDICAL REPORTS**
by
collecting, analyzing, and summarizing information and trends.

____15. **MAINTAINS STABILITY AND REPUTATION OF COMPANY**
by
complying with medical standards and legal requirements.

____16. **MAINTAINS PROFESSIONAL AND TECHNICAL KNOWLEDGE**
by
attending educational workshops; reviewing professional publications; establishing personal networks; benchmarking state-of-the-art practices; participating in professional societies.

____17. **CONTRIBUTES TO TEAM EFFORT**
by
accomplishing related results as needed.

JOB PURPOSE: **ACCOMPLISHES BUSINESS OBJECTIVES**
by
identifying and solving customer information and processing problems.

ESSENTIAL JOB RESULTS:

% of
time

_____ 1. **IDENTIFIES PROJECT REQUIREMENTS**
by
interviewing customers; analyzing operations; determining project scope; documenting results; preparing customer contracts.

_____ 2. **DEVELOPS PROBLEM SOLUTIONS**
by
describing requirements in a work-flowchart and diagram; studying system capabilities; analyzing alternative solutions; preparing system specifications; writing programs.

_____ 3. **DEVELOPS PROJECT ESTIMATES**
by
identifying phases and elements, personnel requirements, and costs.

_____ 4. **VERIFIES RESULTS**
by
completing tests.

_____ 5. **PREPARES CUSTOMERS TO USE SYSTEM**
by
conducting training.

_____ 6. **PROVIDES REFERENCE FOR CUSTOMERS**
by
writing documentation; providing support and help.

% of
time

_____ 7. **MAINTAINS SYSTEMS**
by
researching and resolving problems; maintaining system integrity and security.

_____ 8. **MAINTAINS QUALITY SERVICE**
by
establishing and enforcing organization standards.

_____ 9. **PREPARES REPORTS**
by
collecting, analyzing, and summarizing information.

_____10. **MAINTAINS PROFESSIONAL AND TECHNICAL KNOWLEDGE**
by
attending educational workshops; reviewing professional publications; establishing personal networks; benchmarking state-of-the-art practices; participating in professional societies.

_____11. **CONTRIBUTES TO TEAM EFFORT**
by
accomplishing related results as needed.

JOB PURPOSE: **CONTROLS PRODUCT FLOW THROUGH INVENTORY**
by
managing staff; receiving, storing, securing, and distributing product.

ESSENTIAL JOB RESULTS:

% of
time

_____ 1. **MAINTAINS INVENTORY CONTROL STAFF**
by
recruiting, selecting, orienting, and training employees; developing personal growth opportunities.

_____ 2. **ACCOMPLISHES STAFF RESULTS**
by
communicating job expectations; planning, monitoring, and appraising job results; coaching, counseling, and disciplining employees; initiating, coordinating, and enforcing systems, policies, and procedures.

_____ 3. **MAINTAINS SAFE AND HEALTHY WORK ENVIRONMENT**
by
enforcing safety and health policies and procedures.

_____ 4. **SECURES PRODUCT IN STORAGE FACILITIES**
by
maintaining security guard force.

_____ 5. **PROVIDES PRODUCT WHEN AND WHERE NEEDED**
by
controlling product flow into, through, and out of the distribution facility.

_____ 6. **MAINTAINS STORAGE LEVELS**
by
adjusting production.

% of
time

_____ 7. **REDUCES COST OF INVENTORY**
by
maximizing just-in-time product completions.

_____ 8. **MAINTAINS QUALITY SERVICE**
by
establishing and enforcing organization standards; minimizing inventory levels; recommending new material handling systems.

_____ 9. **PREPARES REPORTS**
by
collecting, analyzing, and summarizing information.

_____10. **COMPLIES WITH FEDERAL, STATE, AND LOCAL LEGAL REQUIREMENTS**
by
enforcing regulations.

_____11. **MAINTAINS PROFESSIONAL AND TECHNICAL KNOWLEDGE**
by
attending educational workshops; reviewing professional publications; establishing personal networks; benchmarking state-of-the-art practices; participating in professional societies.

_____12. **CONTRIBUTES TO TEAM EFFORT**
by
accomplishing related results as needed.

JOB TITLE: ORDER PROCESSING REPRESENTATIVE

O288_M

JOB PURPOSE: **DELIVERS MERCHANDISE TO CUSTOMERS**
by
shipping from inventory; processing orders.

ESSENTIAL JOB RESULTS:

% of
time

% of
time

_____ 1. **ARRANGES SHIPMENT OF INVENTORIES TO OUTSIDE WAREHOUSE FACILITIES**
by
checking stock to determine inventory levels; anticipating needed product; placing and expediting orders for customers.

_____ 2. **DETERMINES METHOD OF SHIPMENT**
by
examining items to be shipped, destination, route, rate, and time of delivery; dispatching carriers.

_____ 3. **KEEPS CUSTOMERS INFORMED**
by
notifying customers of shipping and stock availability issues; answering questions; responding to requests.

_____ 4. **PROCESSES ORDERS**
by
editing for price, promotional problems, customer comment requirements, and weight compliance; sorting orders.

_____ 5. **VERIFIES ITEMS SHIPPED**
by
matching bills of lading; reconciling quantities; noting discrepancies.

_____ 6. **MAINTAINS TRAFFIC OPERATIONS AND ORGANIZES WORK**
by
reading and routing correspondence; collecting information; initiating telecommunications; following policies and procedures.

_____ 7. **REPLACES DAMAGED ITEMS, SHORTAGES, AND MIS-SHIPMENTS**
by
informing customer, shipper, and transporter of damage, shortage, or mis-shipped items; returning refused product; issuing credit for damage and/or shortages.

_____ 8. **MAINTAINS CARRIER/CUSTOMER CONFIDENCE**
by
keeping rate and carrier information confidential; maintaining confidentiality of price, promotions, purchase orders, and credit limit information.

_____ 9. **SUPPORTS NEW PROJECTS**
by
developing project procedures; analyzing operational functions.

_____10. **MAINTAINS QUALITY SERVICE**
by
following organization standards.

_____11. **PREPARES REPORTS**
by
collecting and analyzing data; reporting information; initiating telecommunications.

_____12. **MAINTAINS PROFESSIONAL AND TECHNICAL KNOWLEDGE**
by
attending educational workshops and field trips.

_____13. **CONTRIBUTES TO TEAM EFFORT**
by
accomplishing related results as needed.

JOB PURPOSE: **SAVES ATTORNEY'S TIME**
by
researching, obtaining, compiling, and preparing information.

ESSENTIAL JOB RESULTS:

% of
time

% of
time

____ **1. RESEARCHES LAW SOURCES**
by
identifying applicable statutes, judicial
decisions, and codes; initiating patent
and trademark searches.

____ **2. COMPILES EVIDENCE AND
SUPPORTING INFORMATION**
by
searching records, discovery
documents, transcripts, libraries, and
databases; interviewing clients, third
parties, and expert witnesses.

____ **3. PREPARES LEGAL DOCUMENTS
FOR ATTORNEY'S APPROVAL AND
USE**
by
identifying forms and formats;
producing text; proofreading;
maintaining document control system.

____ **4. BEGINS LEGAL ACTIONS**
by
arranging for notice and subpoena
service.

____ **5. OVERSEES CASES**
by
managing files and documents;
coordinating with support services and
clients, opposing law firms, and courts;
managing court docket calendar;
expediting paper flow; maintaining
schedules and deadlines; generating
status reports, logs, and indexes;
processing settlement papers and
payments.

____ **6. PREPARES FOR TRIAL**
by
preparing trial notebooks, exhibits, and
witness files; obtaining jury list and
background information; preparing
questions for jury selection.

____ **7. PREPARES WITNESSES**
by
detailing background information;
interviewing witnesses; preparing
interview summaries and statements.

____ **8. COMPOSES LEGAL ABSTRACTS**
by
summarizing deposition, arbitration,
hearing, trial, and other transcripts.

____ **9. DRAFTS APPEALS**
by
researching legal basis for appeal.

____ **10. MAINTAINS DATABASE**
by
organizing document control; designing
retrieval systems; summarizing, coding,
and storing documents; updating
system.

____ **11. COMPLETES REAL AND
PERSONAL PROPERTY
TRANSACTIONS**
by
inventorying and appraising assets;
arranging sales; establishing payment
mechanisms.

ESSENTIAL JOB RESULTS:

% of
time

% of
time

____**12. MAINTAINS LAW LIBRARY**
by
receiving and updating law service
reporting systems.

____**13. MAINTAINS TECHNICAL
KNOWLEDGE**
by
attending educational workshops;
reviewing publications.

____**14. CONTRIBUTES TO TEAM EFFORT**
by
accomplishing related results as
needed.

JOB TITLE:	PATIENT CARE COORDINATOR	P293_M

JOB PURPOSE: PROVIDES COORDINATED CARE TO (AGE-SPECIFIC) PATIENTS
by
developing, monitoring, and evaluating interdisciplinary care.

ESSENTIAL JOB RESULTS:

% of
time

_____ 1. **ORIENTS AND EDUCATES PATIENTS AND THEIR FAMILIES**
by
meeting them; explaining the role of the patient care coordinator; initiating the care plan; providing educational information in conjunction with direct care providers related to treatments, procedures, medications, and continuing care requirements.

_____ 2. **DEVELOPS INTERDISCIPLINARY CARE PLAN AND OTHER CASE MANAGEMENT TOOLS**
by
participating in meetings; coordinating information and care requirements with other care providers; resolving issues that could affect smooth care progression; fostering peer support; providing education to others regarding the case management process.

_____ 3. **MONITORS DELIVERY OF CARE**
by
completing patient rounds; documenting care; identifying progress toward desired care outcomes; intervening to overcome deviations in the expected plan of care; reviewing the care plan with patients in conjunction with the direct care providers; interacting with involved departments to negotiate and expedite scheduling and completion of tests, procedures, and consults; reporting personnel and performance issues to the unit manager; maintaining ongoing communication with utilization review staff regarding variances from the care plan or transfer/discharge plan.

% of
time

_____ 4. **EVALUATES OUTCOMES OF CARE WITH THE INTERDISCIPLINARY TEAM**
by
measuring intervention effectiveness with the team; implementing team recommendations.

_____ 5. **COMPLIES WITH HOSPITAL AND LEGAL REQUIREMENTS**
by
fostering nursing practices that adhere to the hospital's and nursing division's philosophy, goals, and standards of care; requiring adherence to Nurse Practice Act and other governing regulations.

_____ 6. **PROTECTS SELF, CO-WORKERS, AND PATIENTS**
by
following policies and procedures to prevent the spread of bloodborne and/or airborne diseases.

_____ 7. **RESPECTS PATIENTS**
by
recognizing their rights; maintaining confidentiality.

_____ 8. **MAINTAINS QUALITY SERVICE**
by
establishing and enforcing organization standards.

_____ 9. **MAINTAINS PATIENT CARE DATABASE**
by
entering new information as it becomes available; verifying findings and reports; backing up data.

ESSENTIAL JOB RESULTS:

% of
time

% of
time

____10. **MAINTAINS PROFESSIONAL AND TECHNICAL KNOWLEDGE**
by
attending educational workshops; reviewing professional publications; establishing personal networks; benchmarking state-of-the-art practices; participating in professional societies.

____11. **CONTRIBUTES TO TEAM EFFORT**
by
accomplishing related results as needed.

JOB PURPOSE: IMPROVES ORGANIZATION RESULTS
by
selecting, applying, and evaluating intervention strategies.

ESSENTIAL JOB RESULTS:

% of
time

% of
time

____ 1. **CLARIFIES ORGANIZATION TRAINING AND DEVELOPMENT RESULTS TO BE OBTAINED**
by
studying organization goals and strategies; interviewing executives; anticipating changes.

____ 2. **SELECTS ORGANIZATION INTERVENTION STRATEGIES**
by
assessing requirements; identifying resources; evaluating training and development options.

____ 3. **APPLIES INTERVENTION STRATEGIES**
by
studying unit and individual objectives and needs.

____ 4. **IMPROVES PERFORMANCE**
by
providing or conducting training.

____ 5. **PROMOTES GROWTH AND DEVELOPMENT**
by
offering and encouraging participation in educational opportunities; reviewing and recommending development policies and practices.

____ 6. **EVALUATES TRAINING AND DEVELOPMENT EFFECTIVENESS**
by
studying organization performance data, individual performance appraisals, disciplinary and counseling actions, job postings, promotions, and hiring requests; interviewing managers and employees.

____ 7. **MAINTAINS PROFESSIONAL AND TECHNICAL KNOWLEDGE**
by
attending educational workshops; reviewing professional publications; establishing personal networks; benchmarking state-of-the-art practices; participating in professional societies.

____ 8. **CONTRIBUTES TO TEAM EFFORT**
by
accomplishing related results as needed.

| JOB TITLE: | PILOT PLANT TECHNICIAN | P303_M |

JOB PURPOSE: **DEVELOPS PRODUCTION SAMPLES**
by
preparing, completing, and evaluating production tests.

ESSENTIAL JOB RESULTS:

% of
time

_____ **1. IDENTIFIES PRODUCT AND EQUIPMENT REQUIREMENTS**
by
conferring with operations, engineering, and research and development personnel.

_____ **2. PREPARES EQUIPMENT FOR TEST PRODUCTION**
by
setting tolerances.

_____ **3. ESTABLISHES QUALITY PRODUCTION**
by
following standards; establishing methods.

_____ **4. DOCUMENTS TESTS**
by
entering required information.

_____ **5. KEEPS EQUIPMENT OPERATIONAL**
by
completing maintenance requirements.

_____ **6. MAINTAINS PARTS AND EQUIPMENT INVENTORY**
by
checking and determining inventory levels; anticipating required parts and materials; placing and expediting orders for supplies; verifying receipt.

% of
time

_____ **7. MAINTAINS SAFE AND CLEAN WORK ENVIRONMENT**
by
complying with good manufacturing practices and sanitation procedures and standards.

_____ **8. PREPARES REPORTS**
by
collecting, analyzing, and summarizing information.

_____ **9. MAINTAINS TECHNICAL KNOWLEDGE**
by
attending educational workshops; reviewing publications.

_____**10. CONTRIBUTES TO TEAM EFFORT**
by
accomplishing related results as needed.

JOB TITLE: PIPELINE MANAGER P304_M

JOB PURPOSE: TRANSPORTS PRODUCT
by
managing crew; constructing and maintaining pipeline.

ESSENTIAL JOB RESULTS:

% of
time

____ 1. **MAINTAINS PIPELINE CREW**
by
recruiting, selecting, orienting, and
training employees; scheduling work
shifts.

____ 2. **ACCOMPLISHES CREW RESULTS**
by
communicating job expectations;
planning, monitoring, and appraising
job results; coaching, counseling, and
disciplining employees; initiating,
coordinating, and enforcing systems,
policies, and procedures.

____ 3. **DETERMINES PIPELINE
REQUIREMENTS**
by
studying customer demand estimates.

____ 4. **DEVELOPS PIPELINE
CONSTRUCTION PLAN**
by
preparing specifications; conducting
surveys; establishing access rights.

____ 5. **CONSTRUCTS PIPELINE**
by
hiring and supervising contractors;
inspecting work progress.

____ 6. **MAINTAINS SAFE AND HEALTHY
WORK ENVIRONMENT**
by
establishing and enforcing pipeline
standards; adhering to legal
regulations; conducting inspections.

____ 7. **SUSTAINS OPERATIONS**
by
measuring and regulating flow of
product.

% of
time

____ 7. **SUSTAINS OPERATIONS**
by
measuring and regulating flow of
product.

____ 8. **MAINTAINS PIPELINE**
by
establishing inspection and testing
policies, procedures, and schedules.

____ 9. **IMPROVES OPERATIONS**
by
conducting studies; benchmarking
state-of-the-art practices.

____10. **ENSURES OPERATION OF
EQUIPMENT**
by
completing preventive maintenance
requirements; following manufacturer's
instructions; troubleshooting
malfunctions; calling for repairs;
maintaining equipment inventories;
evaluating new equipment and
techniques.

____11. **ACCOMPLISHES FINANCIAL
OBJECTIVES**
by
forecasting requirements; preparing an
annual budget; scheduling
expenditures; analyzing variances;
initiating corrective action.

____12. **PREPARES REPORTS**
by
collecting, analyzing, and summarizing
information.

ESSENTIAL JOB RESULTS:

% of
time

____13. **MAINTAINS PROFESSIONAL AND TECHNICAL KNOWLEDGE**
by
attending educational workshops;
reviewing professional publications;
establishing personal networks;
participating in professional societies.

% of
time

____14. **CONTRIBUTES TO TEAM EFFORT**
by
accomplishing related results as
needed.

JOB TITLE: POWER LINE OPERATOR   P307_M

JOB PURPOSE: **PROVIDES ELECTRIC POWER**
by
operating equipment for constructing and maintaining power lines.

ESSENTIAL JOB RESULTS:

% of
time

_____ 1. **LOCATES WORK SITE**
by
reading detail maps.

_____ 2. **PREPARES EQUIPMENT**
by
loading and unloading vehicles;
assembling and disassembling line
equipment.

_____ 3. **CONSTRUCTS POWER LINES**
by
reading staking sheets; framing and
setting poles and anchors; adjusting
sagging wire; connecting transformer
banks on energized and de-energized
lines.

_____ 4. **SUPPORTS POWER LINE
CONSTRUCTION AND
MAINTENANCE**
by
operating equipment.

_____ 5. **COMPLETES PREVENTIVE
MAINTENANCE REQUIREMENTS**
by
inspecting power lines.

_____ 6. **MAINTAINS ELECTRIC SERVICE**
by
reading and setting meters; checking
voltage; completing paperwork.

% of
time

_____ 7. **MAINTAINS ASSIGNED VEHICLE**
by
completing inspections and operator's
repairs; reporting problems to vehicle
maintenance.

_____ 8. **SERVES MEMBER/CONSUMERS**
by
providing service requested; answering
questions; offering assistance.

_____ 9. **MAINTAINS RECORDS**
by
completing paperwork.

_____10. **MAINTAINS A SAFE WORK
ENVIRONMENT**
by
adhering to policies, procedures, and
regulations.

_____11. **MAINTAINS TECHNICAL
KNOWLEDGE**
by
attending educational workshops;
reviewing publications.

_____12. **CONTRIBUTES TO TEAM EFFORT**
by
accomplishing related results as
needed.

JOB PURPOSE: **SUPPORTS MARKETING OPERATIONS**
by
verifying, entering, and communicating pricing information.

ESSENTIAL JOB RESULTS:

% of
time

% of
time

____ 1. **MAINTAINS PRICING DATABASE**
by
verifying and updating freight rates,
charges, and allowances; entering and
backing up data.

____ 2. **COMMUNICATES PRICING**
by
publishing price schedules internally
and externally.

____ 3. **PAYS BROKERS**
by
processing broker statements; verifying
brokerage deductions and transfers.

____ 4. **MAINTAINS HISTORICAL RECORDS**
by
filing sales and contribution reports and
pricing records.

____ 5. **MAINTAINS QUALITY SERVICE**
by
following organization standards.

____ 6. **MAINTAINS TECHNICAL
KNOWLEDGE**
by
attending educational workshops;
reviewing publications.

____ 7. **CONTRIBUTES TO TEAM EFFORT**
by
accomplishing related results as
needed.

JOB TITLE:	PROCUREMENT MANAGER	P310_M

JOB PURPOSE: **SUPPORTS MANUFACTURING**
by
managing staff; pricing, evaluating, negotiating, and obtaining materials.

ESSENTIAL JOB RESULTS:

% of
time

% of
time

____ 1. **MAINTAINS PROCUREMENT STAFF**
by
recruiting, selecting, orienting, and training employees; maintaining a safe and secure work environment; developing personal growth opportunities.

____ 2. **ACCOMPLISHES STAFF RESULTS**
by
communicating job expectations; planning, monitoring, and appraising job results; coaching, counseling, and disciplining employees; initiating, coordinating, and enforcing systems, policies, and procedures.

____ 3. **MAINTAINS VENDOR CERTIFICATION PROGRAM**
by
establishing standards; conducting site visits; monitoring compliance.

____ 4. **SUSTAINS COMPETITIVE PRODUCT PRICING**
by
negotiating material costs; discovering new sources.

____ 5. **PROCURES MATERIALS AND SUPPLIES**
by
establishing optimum inventory levels; reordering quantities.

____ 6. **CONTROLS PACKAGING SPECIFICATIONS**
by
developing standards; updating packaging manual.

____ 7. **REDUCES PACKAGING COSTS**
by
researching new concepts; contracting with new suppliers.

____ 8. **PREPARES REPORTS**
by
collecting, analyzing, and summarizing information and trends.

____ 9. **MAINTAINS QUALITY SERVICE**
by
following organization standards.

____10. **MAINTAINS TECHNICAL KNOWLEDGE**
by
attending educational workshops; reviewing publications.

____11. **CONTRIBUTES TO TEAM EFFORT**
by
accomplishing related results as needed.

239

JOB PURPOSE: **ANALYZES PLANT PRODUCTION**
by
collecting, entering, and sorting information.

ESSENTIAL JOB RESULTS:

% of
time

____ 1. **INPUTS SOURCE DATA TO COMPUTER**
by
compiling and sorting information; establishing entry priorities; completing input.

____ 2. **REVISES SYSTEMS AND PROCEDURES**
by
analyzing operating and recording systems; controlling forms; implementing changes.

____ 3. **PREPARES PRODUCTION AND FINANCE REPORTS**
by
collecting, analyzing, and summarizing data, information, and trends.

____ 4. **PREPARES BUDGETS AND FORECASTS FOR PLANT OPERATIONS**
by
coordinating, collecting, consolidating, and inputting budget and cost data.

____ 5. **MAINTAINS DATABASE**
by
entering, verifying, and backing up data.

% of
time

____ 6. **PROVIDES INFORMATION TO PLANT EMPLOYEES**
by
posting data and charts; updating plant performance data; answering questions and requests; attending team and problem-solving meetings.

____ 7. **MAINTAINS QUALITY SERVICE**
by
following organization standards.

____ 8. **MAINTAINS TECHNICAL KNOWLEDGE**
by
attending educational workshops; reviewing publications.

____ 9. **CONTRIBUTES TO TEAM EFFORT**
by
accomplishing related results as needed.

JOB TITLE: PRODUCTION CLERK   P313_M

JOB PURPOSE: **PROVIDES PRODUCTION INFORMATION AND PAYS EMPLOYEES**
by
collecting, entering, analyzing, calculating, and maintaining information.

ESSENTIAL JOB RESULTS:

% of
time

_____ **1. COMPILES PRODUCTION INFORMATION**
by
collecting and sorting production records.

_____ **2. MAINTAINS PRODUCTION DATABASE**
by
entering, verifying, and backing up data.

_____ **3. RESOLVES PRODUCTION DISCREPANCIES**
by
collecting and analyzing information.

_____ **4. EXTENDS AND SUMMARIZES DATA**
by
calculating items produced, materials used, production rates.

_____ **5. MAINTAINS PAYROLL INFORMATION**
by
collecting, calculating, entering, verifying, and backing up data.

_____ **6. RESOLVES PAYROLL DISCREPANCIES**
by
collecting and analyzing information.

% of
time

_____ **7. PROVIDES PAYROLL INFORMATION**
by
answering questions and requests; locating employee files; searching files for misplaced items; retrieving files.

_____ **8. UPDATES PAYROLL RECORDS**
by
entering changes in exemptions, insurance coverage, savings deductions, and job title transfers.

_____ **9. PAYS EMPLOYEES**
by
distributing checks.

_____ **10. MAINTAINS EMPLOYEE CONFIDENCE AND PROTECTS PAYROLL OPERATIONS**
by
keeping information confidential.

_____ **11. MAINTAINS TECHNICAL KNOWLEDGE**
by
attending educational workshops; reviewing publications.

_____ **12. CONTRIBUTES TO TEAM EFFORT**
by
accomplishing related results as needed.

JOB PURPOSE: **SERVES CLIENTS**
by
inventorying and mailing printed pieces.

ESSENTIAL JOB RESULTS:

% of
time

% of
time

____ 1. **COMPLETES MAILING**
   REQUIREMENTS
   by
   preplanning and scheduling mailings;
   verifying printed materials and tape
   counts; keeping client coordinator
   informed; verifying return of tape data
   from vendor to client.

____ 2. **ENSURES MAILING QUALITY**
   by
   verifying vendor reports; resolving
   inconsistencies with vendors; obtaining
   approvals of mailing kit.

____ 3. **COMPLETES MAILING REPORTS**
   by
   gathering information.

____ 4. **MEETS MAILING QUALITY**
   REQUIREMENTS AND TARGET
   DATES
   by
   coordinating mailings and production
   schedules.

____ 5. **MAINTAINS INVENTORY**
   by
   recording printed pieces; authorizing
   reprints.

____ 6. **PROVIDES CLIENTS WITH MAILING**
   RESULTS
   by
   maintaining job file information.

____ 7. **ENSURES COMPLETE DATA**
   by
   coordinating incoming client data and
   autoname tapes with information
   services and direct response analysts.

____ 8. **MAINTAINS TECHNICAL**
   KNOWLEDGE
   by
   attending educational workshops;
   reviewing publications.

____ 9. **CONTRIBUTES TO TEAM EFFORT**
   by
   accomplishing related results as
   needed.

JOB PURPOSE: **MANUFACTURES PRODUCTS**
by
supervising staff; organizing and monitoring work flow.

ESSENTIAL JOB RESULTS:

% of
time

____ 1. **ACCOMPLISHES MANUFACTURING STAFF RESULTS**
by
communicating job expectations; planning, monitoring, and appraising job results; coaching, counseling, and disciplining employees; initiating, coordinating, and enforcing systems, policies, and procedures.

____ 2. **MAINTAINS STAFF**
by
recruiting, selecting, orienting, and training employees; developing personal growth opportunities.

____ 3. **MAINTAINS WORK FLOW**
by
monitoring steps of the process; setting processing variables; observing control points and equipment; monitoring personnel and resources; studying methods; implementing cost reductions; developing reporting procedures and systems; facilitating corrections to malfunctions within process control points; initiating and fostering a spirit of cooperation within and between departments.

____ 4. **COMPLETES PRODUCTION PLAN**
by
scheduling and assigning personnel; accomplishing work results; establishing priorities; monitoring progress; revising schedules; resolving problems; reporting results of the processing flow on shift production summaries.

% of
time

____ 5. **MAINTAINS QUALITY SERVICE**
by
establishing and enforcing organization standards.

____ 6. **ENSURES OPERATION OF EQUIPMENT**
by
calling for repairs; evaluating new equipment and techniques.

____ 7. **PROVIDES MANUFACTURING INFORMATION**
by
compiling, initiating, sorting, and analyzing production performance records and data; answering questions and responding to requests.

____ 8. **CREATES AND REVISES SYSTEMS AND PROCEDURES**
by
analyzing operating practices, record-keeping systems, forms of control, and budgetary and personnel requirements; implementing change.

____ 9. **MAINTAINS SAFE AND CLEAN WORK ENVIRONMENT**
by
educating and directing personnel on the use of all control points, equipment, and resources; maintaining compliance with established policies and procedures.

____10. **MAINTAINS WORKING RELATIONSHIP WITH THE UNION**
by
following the terms of the collective bargaining agreement.

ESSENTIAL JOB RESULTS:

% of
time

____11. **RESOLVES PERSONNEL PROBLEMS**
by
analyzing data, investigating issues; identifying solutions; recommending action.

____12. **MAINTAINS PROFESSIONAL AND TECHNICAL KNOWLEDGE**
by
attending educational workshops; reviewing professional publications; establishing personal networks; benchmarking state-of-the-art practices; participating in professional societies.

% of
time

____13. **CONTRIBUTES TO TEAM EFFORT**
by
accomplishing related results as needed.

JOB PURPOSE:　　**MAINTAINS COMPUTER PRODUCTION QUALITY**
by
analyzing procedures and output; recommending improvements.

ESSENTIAL JOB RESULTS:

% of
time

____ 1. **IMPLEMENTS NEW APPLICATIONS**
by
coordinating quality activities; analyzing
impact on current processing schedules
and service levels.

____ 2. **MAINTAINS COST-EFFECTIVE PRODUCTION**
by
reviewing corporate output, mainframe
print and fiche, distributed print, and
tape creation.

____ 3. **OPTIMIZES PRODUCTIVITY AND PERFORMANCE**
by
investigating exploitation of
infrastructure tools.

____ 4. **ENFORCES QUALITY STANDARDS**
by
recommending resolution of outages;
developing new procedures and
standards; implementing automated
software version control; implementing
automated distribution software
procedures to remote servers and
workstations.

____ 5. **PROTECTS ASSETS**
by
analyzing vaulting procedures;
reviewing disaster recovery procedures;
ensuring compliance with Internal
Revenue Service regulations.

% of
time

____ 6. **COMPLETES PROJECTS**
by
planning, organizing, and monitoring
assignments.

____ 7. **PREPARES REPORTS**
by
collecting, analyzing, and summarizing
information.

____ 8. **MAINTAINS PROFESSIONAL AND TECHNICAL KNOWLEDGE**
by
attending educational workshops;
reviewing professional publications;
establishing personal networks;
benchmarking state-of-the-art practices;
participating in professional societies.

____ 9. **CONTRIBUTES TO TEAM EFFORT**
by
accomplishing related results as
needed.

JOB TITLE: QUALITY ASSURANCE COORDINATOR– HOME CONSTRUCTION — Q328_M

JOB PURPOSE: **SATISFIES HOMEOWNERS**
by
identifying and correcting warranty problems.

ESSENTIAL JOB RESULTS:

% of
time

_____ 1. **IDENTIFIES HOMEOWNER COMPLAINTS**
by
interviewing homeowners.

_____ 2. **IDENTIFIES CORRECTIVE SOLUTIONS**
by
following warranty guidelines.

_____ 3. **CORRECTS WARRANTY PROBLEMS**
by
scheduling work with subcontractor; providing instructions; monitoring and evaluating work; verifying satisfaction with homeowner.

_____ 4. **KEEPS HOMEOWNERS INFORMED**
by
forwarding messages; communicating status of service; providing liaison between homeowners and subcontractors.

_____ 5. **KEEPS STAFF INFORMED**
by
answering questions and communicating changes regarding warranty policies and procedures.

_____ 6. **PREPARES REPORTS**
by
collecting and summarizing information; entering new tracking information; updating current files.

_____ 7. **PREPARES INVOICES**
by
completing required information; obtaining approvals; forwarding completed invoice.

% of
time

_____ 8. **MAINTAINS HOMEOWNER AND VENDOR FILES**
by
creating files; updating information.

_____ 9. **MAINTAINS DATABASE**
by
entering, verifying, and backing up data.

_____10. **SUPPORTS OPERATIONS**
by
completing administrative and clerical assignments.

_____11. **MAINTAINS QUALITY SERVICE**
by
following organization standards.

_____12. **MAINTAINS CONTINUITY AMONG CORPORATE, DIVISION, AND LOCAL WORK TEAMS**
by
documenting and communicating actions, irregularities, and continuing needs.

_____13. **MAINTAINS PROFESSIONAL AND TECHNICAL KNOWLEDGE**
by
attending educational workshops; reviewing professional publications.

_____14. **CONTRIBUTES TO TEAM EFFORT**
by
accomplishing related results as needed.

JOB TITLE: QUALITY ASSURANCE SPECIALIST– TELEMARKETING

Q330_M

JOB PURPOSE: **ENSURES ACCURACY OF INFORMATION AND QUALITY OF DELIVERY**
by
monitoring telephone calls; recommending improvements.

ESSENTIAL JOB RESULTS:

% of
time

____ 1. **DETERMINES TELEMARKETING QUALITY STANDARDS**
by
studying inbound and outbound calls and customer service presentations; conducting test calls to telemarketing service representatives on new products.

____ 2. **VERIFIES TELEMARKETING RESULTS**
by
measuring skills in use of scripts, product knowledge, sales and service ability, greeting, diction, listening, etiquette, objection handling, efficiency, and courteous close of call.

____ 3. **PROVIDES FEEDBACK TO TELEMARKETERS**
by
monitoring calls; monitoring feedback for external vendor programs; conducting monthly help sessions.

____ 4. **EVALUATES TELEMARKETING APPROACHES**
by
rating effectiveness of telemarketing service representatives; providing quality ratings; identifying training needs; developing training programs; conducting training.

% of
time

____ 5. **DIRECTS QUALITY INITIATIVES**
by
requiring adherence to quality assurance policies and procedures; developing new models; implementing changes.

____ 6. **MAINTAINS PROFESSIONAL AND TECHNICAL KNOWLEDGE**
by
attending educational workshops; reviewing professional publications; establishing personal networks; benchmarking state-of-the-art practices; participating in professional societies.

____ 7. **CONTRIBUTES TO TEAM EFFORT**
by
accomplishing related results as needed.

JOB PURPOSE: **PROVIDES STATISTICAL INFORMATION FOR QUALITY IMPROVEMENT**
by
identifying testing methods and samples.

ESSENTIAL JOB RESULTS:

% of
time

% of
time

____ 1. **DETERMINES QUALITY IMPROVEMENT PARAMETERS**
by
identifying statistical methods relevant to manufacturing processes.

____ 2. **ESTABLISHES STATISTICAL CONFIDENCE**
by
identifying sample size and acceptable error; determining levels of confidence.

____ 3. **ESTABLISHES STATISTICAL RELIABILITY**
by
using mean time before failure, Weibull 3-parameter distribution, reliability modeling, and reliability demonstration tests.

____ 4. **DEVELOPS EXPERIMENTS**
by
applying full and fractional factorial techniques.

____ 5. **DEVELOPS SAMPLING PLANS**
by
applying attribute, variable, and sequential sampling methods.

____ 6. **MAINTAINS STATISTICAL PROCESS CONTROLS**
by
applying demerit/unit, zone charting, X^2 charts for distributions and individual-medial/range for multistream processes.

____ 7. **ANALYZES DATA**
by
completing hypothesis, normal distribution, and process capability analysis tests.

____ 8. **PREPARES REPORTS**
by
collecting, analyzing, and summarizing data; making recommendations.

____ 9. **MAINTAINS PROFESSIONAL AND TECHNICAL KNOWLEDGE**
by
attending educational workshops; reviewing professional publications; establishing personal networks; benchmarking state-of-the-art practices; participating in professional societies; maintaining American Society of Quality Control Certified Quality Engineer qualification.

____10. **CONTRIBUTES TO TEAM EFFORT**
by
accomplishing related results as needed.

JOB TITLE: QUALITY IMPROVEMENT FACILITATOR   Q333_M

JOB PURPOSE: **PROMOTES ORGANIZATION QUALITY IMAGE**
by
forming and guiding process management teams.

ESSENTIAL JOB RESULTS:

% of
time

_____ 1. **PREPARES QUALITY IMPROVEMENT TEAM MEMBERS**
by
identifying training needs; training employees in analytical, problem-solving, communication, and presentation skills.

_____ 2. **RESOLVES QUALITY ISSUES**
by
identifying problems; examining solution options; implementing action plans; providing resources.

_____ 3. **RECOMMENDS QUALITY POLICIES**
by
identifying problems; studying standards; evaluating quality outcomes.

_____ 4. **PROMOTES INTEREST IN QUALITY IMPROVEMENT EFFORTS**
by
publicizing project results.

% of
time

_____ 5. **RECOGNIZES IMPROVEMENTS**
by
developing rewards.

_____ 6. **ADVISES MANAGEMENT**
by
summarizing data; preparing reports; explaining proposals; counseling managers.

_____ 7. **MAINTAINS TECHNICAL KNOWLEDGE**
by
attending educational workshops; reviewing publications.

_____ 8. **CONTRIBUTES TO TEAM EFFORT**
by
accomplishing related results as needed.

<table>
<tr><td colspan="2">

JOB TITLE:

</td><td>

**QUALITY MANAGER–
HOME CONSTRUCTION**

</td><td>

Q334_M

</td></tr>
</table>

JOB PURPOSE: **SATISFIES CUSTOMERS**
by
monitoring homeowner satisfaction; identifying and resolving problems.

ESSENTIAL JOB RESULTS:

% of
time

_____ 1. **TRACKS HOMEOWNER
SATISFACTION**
by
recording surveys; tracking warranty
claims; verifying, entering, and backing
up data.

_____ 2. **IDENTIFIES HOMEOWNER
COMPLAINTS**
by
obtaining and investigating facts of
each situation; completing special
inquiries.

_____ 3. **INFORMS MANAGEMENT AND
EMPLOYEES OF COMPANY
QUALITY STATUS**
by
compiling and updating homeowner
satisfaction information; producing and
distributing key quality measurement
charts.

_____ 4. **MAINTAINS CORPORATE QUALITY
AND CUSTOMER SERVICE IMAGE**
by
training quality assurance technicians;
exploring new systems, policies,
and procedures; recommending
new ways to expedite homeowner
concerns.

% of
time

_____ 5. **PROVIDES QUALITY AND SERVICE
RESOURCES**
by
maintaining warranty and product
information library; distributing
information materials.

_____ 6. **PROVIDES ADMINISTRATIVE
SUPPORT**
by
coordinating information and special
requirements.

_____ 7. **MAINTAINS CONTINUITY AMONG
CORPORATE, DIVISION, AND
LOCAL WORK TEAMS**
by
documenting and communicating
actions, irregularities, and continuing
needs.

_____ 8. **MAINTAINS PROFESSIONAL AND
TECHNICAL KNOWLEDGE**
by
attending educational workshops;
reviewing publications.

_____ 9. **CONTRIBUTES TO TEAM EFFORT**
by
accomplishing related results as
needed.

JOB TITLE: QUALITY PROCESSING LABORATORY TECHNICIAN   Q335_M

JOB PURPOSE: VERIFIES PRODUCT COMPLIANCE TO QUALITY STANDARD
by
maintaining equipment; monitoring production.

ESSENTIAL JOB RESULTS:

% of
time

% of
time

____ 1. **MAINTAINS COMPUTERIZED SCALE SYSTEM**
by
keeping units operational and current with formulations; monitoring and verifying records.

____ 2. **MAINTAINS FACTORY PROCESSES AND PROCEDURES TO STANDARD**
by
using statistical methods for monitoring and charting; notifying production supervisor of noncompliance.

____ 3. **PREPARES EXPERIMENTAL DESIGN PROJECTS**
by
mixing test batches in laboratory banbury or mill method.

____ 4. **RELEASES MATERIALS**
by
evaluating all results and visual inspection methods; determining status of nonshippable or usable material.

____ 5. **MAINTAINS QUALITY SERVICE**
by
following organization standards.

____ 6. **MAINTAINS STOCK OF FORMS AND SPARE PARTS**
by
verifying inventory of items; notifying laboratory manager when items are needed.

____ 7. **MAINTAINS SAFE AND HEALTHY WORK ENVIRONMENT**
by
following organization standards and legal regulations.

____ 8. **MAINTAINS TECHNICAL KNOWLEDGE**
by
attending educational workshops; reviewing publications.

____ 9. **CONTRIBUTES TO TEAM EFFORT**
by
accomplishing related results as needed.

JOB PURPOSE: **ENSURES QUALITY PRODUCTS AND PROCESSES**
by
conducting sensory tests; reporting results.

ESSENTIAL JOB RESULTS:

% of
time

____ 1. **IDENTIFIES QUALITY STANDARDS**
by
determining customer expectations for
products; evaluating competitor
products.

____ 2. **CONDUCTS SENSORY TESTS**
by
recruiting and training sensory
panelists; enhancing panelist sensory
skill; analyzing sensory data;
summarizing findings; making
recommendations.

____ 3. **COMPLIES WITH REGULATORY
REQUIREMENTS**
by
developing data for product authenticity
and labeling requirements; developing
data to support responses to pesticide
and food safety issues.

____ 4. **PREPARES TECHNICAL REPORTS**
by
collecting, analyzing, and summarizing
research and project data.

% of
time

____ 5. **MAINTAINS CLEAN AND SAFE
WORK ENVIRONMENT**
by
adhering to safety regulations;
maintaining sensory kitchen.

____ 6. **COMPLETES PROJECTS**
by
benchmarking practices; developing
flowcharts; tracking man-hours.

____ 7. **MAINTAINS PROFESSIONAL AND
TECHNICAL KNOWLEDGE**
by
attending educational workshops;
reviewing professional publications;
establishing personal networks;
participating in professional societies.

____ 8. **CONTRIBUTES TO TEAM EFFORT**
by
accomplishing related results as
needed.

252

JOB TITLE: REAL ESTATE CLOSING COORDINATOR R338_M

JOB PURPOSE: SUPPORTS HOME CLOSINGS
by
monitoring and completing contract requirements.

ESSENTIAL JOB RESULTS:

% of
time

____ 1. **PREPARES TO ACCOMPLISH WORK RESULTS**
by
gathering information and requirements; setting priorities.

____ 2. **RECORDS SALES CONTRACTS**
by
verifying signatures; entering contract information in database; distributing copies; requesting referral fees; depositing money; reviewing change orders and color sheets.

____ 3. **MONITORS CLOSING SCHEDULES**
by
maintaining document processing schedule; reporting status to sales manager.

____ 4. **COMPLETES CLOSING REQUIREMENTS**
by
collecting and verifying loan information; entering loan information in database; providing lenders and attorneys with required documents and information.

____ 5. **COMPLETES SETTLEMENT STATEMENTS**
by
verifying information; recording settlement in database; notifying finance department; forwarding warranty check and application, buyer information sheet, home owners association check and information; depositing checks.

% of
time

____ 6. **SECURES INFORMATION**
by
backing up databases.

____ 7. **MAINTAINS CONTINUITY AMONG CORPORATE, DIVISION, AND LOCAL WORK TEAMS**
by
documenting and communicating actions, irregularities, and continuing needs.

____ 8. **MAINTAINS PROFESSIONAL AND TECHNICAL KNOWLEDGE**
by
attending educational workshops; reviewing professional publications.

____ 9. **CONTRIBUTES TO TEAM EFFORT**
by
accomplishing related results as needed.

JOB TITLE: REGULATORY ANALYST   R346_M

JOB PURPOSE: **IMPLEMENTS PUBLIC AFFAIRS STRATEGIES**
by
gathering and analyzing regulatory information; recommending actions;
lobbying interested parties.

ESSENTIAL JOB RESULTS:

% of
time

% of
time

____ 1. **PROMOTES COMPANY INTERESTS AND CONCERNS**
by
attending and appearing before legislative and regulatory agencies; developing proposals and amendments; performing lobbying efforts with state and federal agencies and national trade associations.

____ 2. **ACHIEVES REGULATORY OBJECTIVES**
by
gathering pertinent information; identifying and evaluating options; choosing a course of action.

____ 3. **MAINTAINS RAPPORT WITH STATE DEPARTMENT PERSONNEL**
by
researching and analyzing regulations and legislation; lobbying state department; maintaining rapport with state department personnel.

____ 4. **RECOMMENDS COMPANY POLICY**
by
analyzing proposed and adopted legislation and regulations; completing compliance-oriented projects.

____ 5. **RESPONDS TO COMPLAINTS AND MARKET CONDUCT EXAMINATIONS**
by
preparing research supporting company procedures.

____ 6. **DEVELOPS AUDITING PROCEDURES**
by
producing materials for compliance, including disclosures, advertising requirements, and forms.

____ 7. **INFORMS KEY EXECUTIVES**
by
determining governmental and public affairs needs; producing compliance bulletins on legislative and regulatory changes and new company procedures.

____ 8. **MAINTAINS PROFESSIONAL AND TECHNICAL KNOWLEDGE**
by
attending educational workshops; reviewing professional publications; establishing personal networks; benchmarking state-of-the-art practices; participating in professional societies.

____ 9. **CONTRIBUTES TO TEAM EFFORT**
by
accomplishing related results as needed.

JOB PURPOSE: **SUPPORTS MANUFACTURING OPERATIONS**
by
specifying ingredients; recommending process technologies.

ESSENTIAL JOB RESULTS:

% of
time

% of
time

____ 1. **DEVELOPS INGREDIENTS**
by
studying consumer requirements;
preparing formulations; conducting
sensory or chemical analyses;
conducting product shelf-life tests;
participating in off-site research.

____ 2. **RECOMMENDS SUPPLY
SPECIFICATIONS**
by
studying consumer requirements and
manufacturing capabilities; determining
cost/benefit relationships; conferring
with management, operations,
engineering, or technical staff.

____ 3. **RECOMMENDS FOOD
MANUFACTURING AND BLENDING
PROCESSES, SYSTEMS, AND
TECHNOLOGIES**
by
evaluating current, new, or improved
processes or process aids, systems,
and technologies; analyzing problems
resulting from existing approaches and
techniques; designing experiments;
collecting samples and preparing
products for testing; scheduling trial
runs; evaluating test results.

____ 4. **IMPLEMENTS MANUFACTURING
PROCESSES**
by
preparing specifications; monitoring
ingredient scale-up in manufacturing;
monitoring plant production.

____ 5. **DOCUMENTS ACTIONS**
by
maintaining scientific logs; compiling
technical journals.

____ 6. **PREPARES REPORTS**
by
collecting, analyzing, and summarizing
information and trends; writing technical
reports.

____ 7. **PROTECTS ASSETS**
by
maintaining confidentiality.

____ 8. **MAINTAINS KOSHER STATUS FOR
PRODUCTS**
by
maintaining liaison with kosher
overseers; coordinating operational
needs with overseers.

____ 9. **MAINTAINS QUALITY SERVICE**
by
establishing and enforcing organization
standards.

____ 10. **MAINTAINS SAFE AND CLEAN
WORK ENVIRONMENT**
by
complying with procedures, rules, and
regulations, and good manufacturing
practices.

____ 11. **MAINTAINS PROFESSIONAL AND
TECHNICAL KNOWLEDGE**
by
attending educational workshops;
reviewing professional publications;
establishing personal networks;
benchmarking state-of-the-art practices;
participating in professional societies.

____ 12. **CONTRIBUTES TO TEAM EFFORT**
by
accomplishing related results as
needed.

JOB TITLE: SALES ADMINISTRATOR S358_M

JOB PURPOSE: **SUPPORTS CUSTOMERS, BROKERS, AND SALES MANAGERS**
by
processing orders, invoices, sample requests, and trade promotions.

ESSENTIAL JOB RESULTS:

% of
time

_____ 1. **MAINTAINS CUSTOMER SATISFACTION**
by
establishing rapport with customers and others in a position to help meet customer needs.

_____ 2. **PREPARES ORDERS FOR SHIPPING**
by
answering phones; receiving facsimiles; editing, verifying, and coordinating information with production scheduling, plant shipping, and customer service departments; inputting data.

_____ 3. **PROCESSES CUSTOMER INVOICES**
by
matching bills of lading; adding additional charges; completing daily billing.

_____ 4. **PROCESSES INVOICING EDIT**
by
sorting and running balancing tapes; printing edit; reviewing for accuracy; forwarding totals to customer service department daily; distributing invoices.

_____ 5. **RESOLVES PRODUCT AND SERVICE PROBLEMS**
by
researching the situation; identifying alternate means of filling customer needs; recommending solutions.

_____ 6. **PROCESSES SAMPLE REQUESTS**
by
answering phones; receiving facsimiles; inputting information into database; printing, copying, and forwarding to sample department for filling and mailing to customers.

% of
time

_____ 7. **RESOLVES INVENTORY ALLOCATION PROBLEMS**
by
monitoring finished goods; anticipating needs; placing and expediting inventory replenishment; verifying receipt of inventory; reconciling transaction reports.

_____ 8. **PUBLISHES TRADE PROMOTIONS**
by
distributing trade promotion information to brokers and regional managers.

_____ 9. **PAYS BILLS**
by
verifying amounts; selecting account numbers; processing for payment.

_____10. **MAINTAINS QUALITY SERVICE**
by
following organization standards.

_____11. **MAINTAINS TECHNICAL KNOWLEDGE**
by
attending educational workshops; reviewing publications.

_____12. **CONTRIBUTES TO TEAM EFFORT**
by
accomplishing related results as needed.

JOB PURPOSE: **BUILDS BUSINESS**
by
identifying and selling prospects; maintaining relationships with clients.

ESSENTIAL JOB RESULTS:

% of
time

_____ 1. **IDENTIFIES BUSINESS OPPORTUNITIES**
by
identifying prospects and evaluating their position in the industry; researching and analyzing sales options.

_____ 2. **SELLS PRODUCTS**
by
establishing contact and developing relationships with prospects; recommending solutions.

_____ 3. **MAINTAINS RELATIONSHIPS WITH CLIENTS**
by
providing support, information, and guidance; researching and recommending new opportunities; recommending profit and service improvements.

_____ 4. **DEVELOPS PRODUCT IMPROVEMENTS OR NEW PRODUCTS**
by
remaining current on industry trends, market activities, and competitors.

% of
time

_____ 5. **PREPARES REPORTS**
by
collecting, analyzing, and summarizing information.

_____ 6. **MAINTAINS QUALITY SERVICE**
by
establishing and enforcing organization standards.

_____ 7. **MAINTAINS PROFESSIONAL AND TECHNICAL KNOWLEDGE**
by
attending educational workshops; reviewing professional publications; establishing personal networks; benchmarking state-of-the-art practices; participating in professional societies.

_____ 8. **CONTRIBUTES TO TEAM EFFORT**
by
accomplishing related results as needed.

JOB TITLE: SALES REPRESENTATIVE–NEW HOMES   S365_M

JOB PURPOSE: **SATISFIES HOMEOWNERS**
by
identifying and selling prospects; completing contracts.

ESSENTIAL JOB RESULTS:

% of
time

% of
time

____ 1. **ATTRACTS POTENTIAL HOMEOWNERS**
by
studying competition; building broker relations; obtaining referrals; preparing advertisements; contacting leads; organizing special marketing events; inspecting appearance of models; training model attendants; recommending pricing.

____ 2. **IDENTIFIES POTENTIAL HOMEOWNERS**
by
greeting visitors at models; entering registration information; identifying needs; assessing interests; explaining the product and options.

____ 3. **SELLS HOMES**
by
following up on prospects; pointing out product advantages; representing company's interests.

____ 4. **COMPLETES HOME CONTRACT**
by
writing specifications; pricing changes; obtaining earnest money; setting appointment with decorator; following up on loan application and required papers.

____ 5. **MEETS CONTRACT REQUIREMENTS**
by
following up on adjustments and corrections; coordinating information and requirements with construction manager; completing preconstruction, drywall, and preclosing inspections.

____ 6. **MAINTAINS RAPPORT WITH HOMEOWNER**
by
communicating progress; resolving homeowner concerns.

____ 7. **COMPLETES HOME CLOSING**
by
fulfilling requirements; reviewing loan documents; attending closing.

____ 8. **MAINTAINS PROFESSIONAL AND TECHNICAL KNOWLEDGE**
by
attending educational workshops; reviewing professional publications.

____ 9. **CONTRIBUTES TO TEAM EFFORT**
by
accomplishing related results as needed.

JOB PURPOSE: SUPPORTS INTERNAL AND EXTERNAL SALES MANAGERS AND
BROKERS
by
scheduling activities; processing information.

ESSENTIAL JOB RESULTS:

% of
time

_____ 1. **MAINTAINS SALES DEPARTMENT
WORK FLOW**
by
scheduling daily activities; planning and
scheduling meetings, conferences,
teleconferences, and travel.

_____ 2. **CONSERVES SALES STAFF AND
BROKER TIME**
by
reading and routing correspondence
and reports; inputting and/or formatting
letters and documents; collecting
information; sending and receiving
telecommunications; completing
expense reports.

_____ 3. **RESOLVES INVENTORY
ALLOCATION PROBLEMS**
by
checking on and monitoring promoted
and nonpromoted items and finished
goods to determine and adjust
inventory levels; anticipating needs;
placing and expediting inventory
replenishment and allocation; verifying
receipt of inventory.

_____ 4. **PREPARES REPORTS**
by
collecting, analyzing, and summarizing
information and trends.

_____ 5. **COMPLETES PROJECTS**
by
planning and organizing sales
information and analyses.

% of
time

_____ 6. **PUBLISHES TRADE PROMOTIONS**
by
distributing trade promotion information
to brokers, regional managers, vice
president–sales, and other internal and
external sources with a need to know.

_____ 7. **PRESERVES HISTORICAL
RECORDS**
by
maintaining a working knowledge of
information sources; verifying accuracy
of statistics; entering data; backing up
system.

_____ 8. **MAINTAINS QUALITY SERVICE**
by
following organization standards.

_____ 9. **MAINTAINS TECHNICAL
KNOWLEDGE**
by
attending educational workshops;
reviewing publications.

_____10. **CONTRIBUTES TO TEAM EFFORT**
by
accomplishing related results as
needed.

JOB TITLE:	SALES SUPPORT SPECIALIST	S367_M

JOB PURPOSE: **SOLVES SALES OPERATIONS SOFTWARE REQUIREMENTS**
by
identifying and resolving problems.

ESSENTIAL JOB RESULTS:

% of
time

____ **1. IDENTIFIES SALES REQUIREMENTS**
by
establishing personal rapport with
persons in the position to understand
service requirements.

____ **2. IMPLEMENTS SPECIAL PROGRAMS**
by
developing and implementing special
system programs for management and
accounts for personal computer and
mainframe processes.

____ **3. MAINTAINS EQUIPMENT AND
SYSTEMS**
by
designing, implementing, and
maintaining information and technical
equipment and system requests.

____ **4. PROVIDES TECHNICAL SUPPORT
TO CLIENTS**
by
maintaining remote account system
access for clients; developing training
tools; providing system restructures.

% of
time

____ **5. MAINTAINS QUALITY SERVICE**
by
following organization standards.

____ **6. PREPARES REPORTS**
by
collecting, analyzing, and summarizing
information.

____ **7. MAINTAINS TECHNICAL
KNOWLEDGE**
by
attending educational workshops;
reviewing publications.

____ **8. CONTRIBUTES TO TEAM EFFORT**
by
accomplishing related results as
needed.

JOB PURPOSE: **MEETS THE PHYSICAL, EMOTIONAL, AND SOCIAL NEEDS OF STUDENTS**
by
promoting and providing healthy practices.

ESSENTIAL JOB RESULTS:

% of
time

% of
time

_____ 1. **DEVELOPS STUDENT HEALTH PROGRAM**
by
identifying and coordinating requirements with administrators and physicians; adhering to and enforcing school board policy; conferring with community agencies.

_____ 2. **PROMOTES HEALTH CARE**
by
publicizing health issues and preventive measures; providing information and resources; counseling students; presenting seminars and training.

_____ 3. **EVALUATES HEALTH STATUS**
by
conducting individual examinations and assessments.

_____ 4. **TREATS MEDICAL PROBLEMS**
by
rendering first aid; stabilizing ill or injured persons; arranging for emergency treatment.

_____ 5. **KEEPS PARENTS/GUARDIANS INFORMED**
by
providing information and advice.

_____ 6. **COMPLETES REPORTS**
by
entering required information.

_____ 7. **MAINTAINS STUDENT CONFIDENCE**
by
keeping information confidential.

_____ 8. **PREPARES REPORTS**
by
collecting, analyzing, and summarizing information.

_____ 9. **MAINTAINS SUPPLIES INVENTORY**
by
checking stock; anticipating needs; placing and expediting orders; verifying receipt.

_____10. **MAINTAINS SAFE AND HEALTHY ENVIRONMENT**
by
enforcing organization standards and legal regulations.

_____11. **ACCOMPLISHES FINANCIAL OBJECTIVES**
by
forecasting requirements; scheduling expenditures; analyzing variances; initiating corrective action.

_____12. **MAINTAINS PROFESSIONAL AND TECHNICAL KNOWLEDGE**
by
attending educational workshops; reviewing professional publications; establishing personal networks; benchmarking state-of-the-art practices; participating in professional societies.

_____13. **CONTRIBUTES TO TEAM EFFORT**
by
accomplishing related results as needed.

| JOB TITLE: | SCOUT LEADER | S370_M |

JOB PURPOSE: DEVELOPS CHILDREN WITH SCOUTING VALUES
by
planning, organizing, and monitoring activities.

ESSENTIAL JOB RESULTS:

% of
time

_____ 1. **RECRUITS MEMBERS**
by
explaining the value of membership;
providing information; visiting potential
members; giving speeches.

_____ 2. **PLANS ANNUAL PROGRAM**
by
identifying required training; developing
special-interest training and activities.

_____ 3. **TRAINS MEMBERS**
by
explaining, fostering, and modeling
scouting ideals; providing specific rank
training.

_____ 4. **APPROVES RANK ADVANCEMENT**
by
verifying accomplishments.

_____ 5. **CONDUCTS MEETINGS**
by
planning and organizing activities;
managing ceremonies.

_____ 6. **PROVIDES CAMPING EXPERIENCE**
by
arranging accommodations, equipment,
supplies, transportation, and
supervision.

_____ 7. **COMPLETES REPORTS**
by
documenting required information.

_____ 8. **MAINTAINS CONTINUITY OF
EXPERIENCE**
by
coordinating policies, information, and
activities with the Scouting council;
training support adult leadership.

% of
time

_____ 9. **MAINTAINS SAFE AND HEALTHY
ENVIRONMENT**
by
enforcing troop standards and legal
regulations.

_____10. **INVOLVES PARENTS OR
GUARDIANS**
by
providing information regarding child's
participation and progress; answering
questions; explaining Scouting culture.

_____11. **ACCOMPLISHES FINANCIAL
OBJECTIVES**
by
forecasting requirements; preparing an
annual budget; scheduling
expenditures; analyzing variances;
initiating corrective action; raising
funds.

_____12. **MAINTAINS TECHNICAL
KNOWLEDGE**
by
attending educational workshops;
reviewing publications.

_____13. **CONTRIBUTES TO TEAM EFFORT**
by
accomplishing related results as
needed.

JOB TITLE:	SECURITY TECHNICIAN	S377_M

JOB PURPOSE: **SERVES CUSTOMERS**
by
establishing and monitoring computer access.

ESSENTIAL JOB RESULTS:

% of
time

% of
time

____ **1. ESTABLISHES COMPUTER ACCESS**
by
analyzing requests; generating
identifications across environments.

____ **2. MAINTAINS ACCESS**
by
providing information and technical
support; troubleshooting or researching
security and identification problems.

____ **3. DOCUMENTS SERVICE**
by
logging and tracking requests and
problems.

____ **4. PROVIDES INFORMATION**
by
answering questions and requests.

____ **5. COMPLETES REPORTS**
by
entering required information.

____ **6. MAINTAINS TECHNICAL
KNOWLEDGE**
by
attending educational workshops;
reviewing publications.

____ **7. CONTRIBUTES TO TEAM EFFORT**
by
accomplishing related results as
needed.

JOB PURPOSE: **SUPPORTS WORKSTATION AND NETWORK SOFTWARE ENVIRONMENT**
by
monitoring and enforcing licensed software use.

ESSENTIAL JOB RESULTS:

% of
time

% of
time

_____ 1. **ENFORCES CORPORATE POLICY**
by
granting user access only to valid
licensed software; tracking requests
and changes.

_____ 2. **ENFORCES SOFTWARE LICENSES**
by
preventing unauthorized use.

_____ 3. **MAINTAINS SOFTWARE INVENTORY**
by
tracking location of workstation and
area network server software.

_____ 4. **SERVES CUSTOMERS**
by
providing information; resolving
problems.

_____ 5. **MAINTAINS QUALITY SERVICE**
by
following organization standards.

_____ 6. **REDUCES SOFTWARE COSTS**
by
tracking, balancing, and assigning
software licenses; employing available
technology that shares existing
purchased licenses across the network.

_____ 7. **KEEPS MANAGEMENT INFORMED**
by
conducting usage audits and reporting
results.

_____ 8. **MAINTAINS TECHNICAL
KNOWLEDGE**
by
attending educational workshops;
reviewing publications.

_____ 9. **CONTRIBUTES TO TEAM EFFORT**
by
accomplishing related results as
needed.

JOB TITLE: SPECIAL INVESTIGATOR   S382_M

JOB PURPOSE: **PROTECTS ASSETS**
by
identifying potential fraud; investigating suspected fraud.

ESSENTIAL JOB RESULTS:

% of
time

_____ 1. **MAINTAINS INVESTIGATIVE STAFF RESULTS**
by
training personnel to recognize fraud and to refer to special investigation unit for investigation.

_____ 2. **ACHIEVES OBJECTIVES**
by
gathering pertinent information; identifying and evaluating options; choosing a course of action.

_____ 3. **EVALUATES FILES**
by
reviewing financial claims, group insurance, and ordinary insurance open files; evaluating for fraud; initiating investigations.

_____ 4. **REFERS CASES TO INVESTIGATIVE AGENCIES**
by
identifying persons or organizations that are involved in suspicious insurance-related activities; contacting state fraud bureaus, law enforcement agencies, and other investigative units; initiating referrals to state insurance department fraud bureaus.

% of
time

_____ 5. **PROTECTS OPERATIONS**
by
enforcing procedures; keeping information confidential.

_____ 6. **MAINTAINS STABILITY AND REPUTATION**
by
complying with legal requirements.

_____ 7. **PREPARES REPORTS**
by
collecting, analyzing, and summarizing information.

_____ 8. **MAINTAINS PROFESSIONAL AND TECHNICAL KNOWLEDGE**
by
attending educational workshops; reviewing professional publications; establishing personal networks; benchmarking state-of-the-art practices; participating in professional societies.

_____ 9. **CONTRIBUTES TO TEAM EFFORT**
by
accomplishing related results as needed.

JOB TITLE: SPECIALTY STORE ASSISTANT MANAGER

S383_M

JOB PURPOSE: **SERVES CUSTOMERS**
by
training staff; purchasing and displaying products.

ESSENTIAL JOB RESULTS:

% of
time

_____ 1. **TRAINS SPECIALTY STORE STAFF**
by
reviewing and revising orientation to
specialty products and sales training
materials; delivering training sessions;
reviewing staff job results and learning
needs with retail store manager;
developing and implementing new
product training.

_____ 2. **EVALUATES COMPETITION**
by
visiting competing stores; gathering
information such as style, quality,
and prices of competitive
merchandise.

_____ 3. **PURCHASES INVENTORY**
by
researching emerging specialty
products; anticipating buyer interest;
negotiating volume price breaks;
placing and expediting orders; verifying
receipt.

_____ 4. **ATTRACTS CUSTOMERS**
by
originating display ideas; following
display suggestions or schedules;
constructing or assembling
prefabricated display properties;
producing merchandise displays in
windows and showcases, and on sales
floor.

_____ 5. **PROMOTES SALES**
by
demonstrating merchandise and
products to customers.

% of
time

_____ 6. **HELPS CUSTOMERS**
by
providing information; answering
questions; obtaining merchandise
requested; completing payment
transactions; preparing merchandise for
delivery.

_____ 7. **PREPARES SALES AND CUSTOMER
RELATIONS REPORTS**
by
analyzing and categorizing sales
information; identifying and
investigating customer complaints and
service suggestions.

_____ 8. **MAINTAINS A SAFE AND CLEAN
STORE ENVIRONMENT**
by
developing and publishing evacuation
routes; determining and documenting
locations of potentially dangerous
materials and chemicals.

_____ 9. **MAINTAINS INVENTORY**
by
checking merchandise to determine
inventory levels; anticipating customer
demand.

_____10. **PREPARES REPORTS**
by
collecting, analyzing, and summarizing
information.

_____11. **MAINTAINS QUALITY SERVICE**
by
establishing and enforcing organization
standards.

ESSENTIAL JOB RESULTS:

% of
time

% of
time

____12. **MAINTAINS PROFESSIONAL AND TECHNICAL KNOWLEDGE**
by
attending educational workshops;
reviewing professional publications;
establishing personal networks;
benchmarking state-of-the-art practices;
participating in professional societies.

____13. **CONTRIBUTES TO TEAM EFFORT**
by
accomplishing related results as needed.

JOB TITLE: STAFF COUNSEL — S385_M

JOB PURPOSE: **PROTECTS COMPANY INTERESTS**
by
preparing legal positions; providing counsel.

ESSENTIAL JOB RESULTS:

% of
time

_____ 1. **ACHIEVES LEGAL OBJECTIVES**
by
gathering pertinent information;
identifying and evaluating options;
choosing a course of action.

_____ 2. **PREPARES LEGAL POSITIONS**
by
researching issues; reviewing
documents.

_____ 3. **PROVIDES LEGAL COUNSEL**
by
researching transactional matters
related to corporation and subsidiaries;
drafting contracts and advising senior
management.

_____ 4. **RESOLVES DISPUTES BETWEEN
COMPANY AND OTHER ENTITIES**
by
retaining external counsel; representing
corporation in negotiations with
accounts and regulators; managing
litigation.

% of
time

_____ 5. **DEVELOPS ASSIGNED STAFF**
by
providing information, direction, and
educational opportunities.

_____ 6. **MAINTAINS QUALITY SERVICE**
by
establishing and enforcing organization
standards.

_____ 7. **MAINTAINS PROFESSIONAL AND
TECHNICAL KNOWLEDGE**
by
attending educational workshops;
reviewing professional publications;
establishing personal networks;
benchmarking state-of-the-art practices;
participating in professional societies.

_____ 8. **CONTRIBUTES TO TEAM EFFORT**
by
accomplishing related results as
needed.

JOB TITLE:	SUPERVISOR (MODEL)	S389_M

JOB PURPOSE: **ACCOMPLISHES DEPARTMENT OBJECTIVES**
by
supervising staff; organizing and monitoring work process.

ESSENTIAL JOB RESULTS:

% of
time

% of
time

____ 1. **MAINTAINS STAFF**
by
recruiting, selecting, orienting, and training employees; developing personal growth opportunities.

____ 2. **ACCOMPLISHES STAFF JOB RESULTS**
by
coaching, counseling, and disciplining employees; planning, monitoring, and appraising job results; conducting training; implementing enforcing systems, policies, and procedures.

____ 3. **MAINTAINS SAFE AND HEALTHY WORK ENVIRONMENT**
by
establishing and enforcing organization standards; adhering to legal regulations.

____ 4. **COMPLETES OPERATIONS**
by
developing schedules; assigning and monitoring work; gathering resources; implementing productivity standards; resolving operations problems; maintaining reference manuals; implementing new procedures.

____ 5. **CONTROLS EXPENSES**
by
gathering and submitting budget information; scheduling expenditures; monitoring variances; implementing corrective actions.

____ 6. **(ENTER JOB-SPECIFIC RESULTS)**
by
(enter job-specific duties)

____ 7. **PROVIDES QUALITY SERVICE**
by
enforcing quality and customer service standards.

____ 8. **MAINTAINS PROFESSIONAL AND TECHNICAL KNOWLEDGE**
by
attending educational workshops; reviewing professional publications.

____ 9. **CONTRIBUTES TO TEAM EFFORT**
by
accomplishing related results as needed.

| JOB TITLE: | SUPPORT SERVICES MANAGER | S390_M |

JOB PURPOSE: **SUPPORTS OPERATIONS**
by
managing staff; delivering orders and mailings.

ESSENTIAL JOB RESULTS:

% of
time

_____ 1. **MAINTAINS SUPPORT SERVICES STAFF**
by
recruiting, selecting, orienting, and training employees; maintaining a safe and secure work environment; developing personal growth opportunities.

_____ 2. **ACCOMPLISHES STAFF RESULTS**
by
communicating job expectations; planning, monitoring, and appraising job results; coaching, counseling, and disciplining employees; initiating, coordinating, and enforcing systems, policies, and procedures.

_____ 3. **ACHIEVES FINANCIAL OBJECTIVES**
by
forecasting functional requirements; preparing an annual budget; scheduling expenditures; analyzing variances; initiating corrective actions; providing information for profit meetings.

_____ 4. **DELIVERS ORDERS**
by
warehousing and distributing corporate items.

_____ 5. **PROVIDES PRINTED MATERIALS**
by
designing forms; operating in-house print shop; purchasing special printing requirements.

% of
time

_____ 6. **DELIVERS MAILINGS**
by
assembling and forwarding requirements.

_____ 7. **PROVIDES CORPORATE REFERENCES AND HISTORY**
by
storing, maintaining, distributing, and destroying archival records.

_____ 8. **MAINTAINS EFFICIENT OPERATIONS**
by
establishing and enforcing corporate guidelines.

_____ 9. **MAINTAINS PROFESSIONAL AND TECHNICAL KNOWLEDGE**
by
attending educational workshops; reviewing professional publications; establishing personal networks; benchmarking state-of-the-art practices; participating in professional societies.

_____10. **CONTRIBUTES TO TEAM EFFORT**
by
accomplishing related results as needed.

JOB TITLE: TECHNICAL BUYER   T395_M

JOB PURPOSE: **MAINTAINS PERSONAL COMPUTER INVENTORY**
by
researching and completing orders.

ESSENTIAL JOB RESULTS:

% of
time

_____ 1. **RESEARCHES PERSONAL COMPUTER PURCHASES, BIDS, AND PROMOTIONS**
by
investigating vendors and terms of sale; sharing information with information systems personnel.

_____ 2. **COMPLETES PERSONAL COMPUTER CONTRACTS**
by
negotiating price, payment terms, shipments, and quality with vendors.

_____ 3. **COMPLETES PURCHASE REQUESTS**
by
anticipating needed equipment; approving or denying purchase requests.

_____ 4. **APPROVES PAYMENT**
by
verifying bills from vendors with purchase orders.

_____ 5. **MAINTAINS DATABASE**
by
entering, verifying, and backing up data.

% of
time

_____ 6. **MAINTAINS QUALITY SERVICE**
by
following organization standards.

_____ 7. **MAINTAINS HISTORICAL REFERENCE OF SUPPLIES AND EQUIPMENT**
by
keeping records of items and services purchased, prices, delivery and shipping costs, and product or service acceptability.

_____ 8. **MAINTAINS PROFESSIONAL AND TECHNICAL KNOWLEDGE**
by
attending educational workshops; reviewing professional publications; establishing personal networks; participating in professional societies.

_____ 9. **CONTRIBUTES TO TEAM EFFORT**
by
accomplishing related results as needed.

JOB TITLE: TECHNICAL PRODUCTS MANAGER   T397_M

JOB PURPOSE: **CREATES PRODUCTS AND PROCESSES**
by
planning and developing products.

ESSENTIAL JOB RESULTS:

% of
time

____ 1. **APPRAISES PRODUCT AND PROCESS FEASIBILITY**
by
identifying and forecasting costs and requirements.

____ 2. **PLANS PROJECTS**
by
coordinating project and corporate priorities; conferring with other managers.

____ 3. **COMPLETES PROJECTS**
by
coordinating development and modification actions; following up on work results; developing specifications; implementing in-plant operations; initiating, coordinating, and enforcing project and operational policies and procedures.

____ 4. **IDENTIFIES DEVELOPMENT OPPORTUNITIES**
by
studying competitors' products; identifying trends in technology; studying plant processes.

____ 5. **SATISFIES CUSTOMERS**
by
identifying customer requirements and performance standards; studying project design; determining product specifications; completing technical studies; conducting and evaluating performance tests.

% of
time

____ 6. **COMPLETES PROJECT DOCUMENTATION**
by
maintaining laboratory notebooks of work; preparing project reports; maintaining project information files; summarizing projects on completion.

____ 7. **PROTECTS ASSETS**
by
maintaining confidentiality.

____ 8. **MAINTAINS PROFESSIONAL AND TECHNICAL KNOWLEDGE**
by
attending educational workshops; reviewing professional publications; establishing personal networks; benchmarking state-of-the-art practices; participating in professional societies.

____ 9. **CONTRIBUTES TO TEAM EFFORT**
by
accomplishing related results as needed.

JOB TITLE:	TECHNICAL SUPPORT MANAGER	T398_M

JOB PURPOSE: **SUPPORTS COMPUTER PLATFORMS**
by
managing staff; researching, planning, and implementing hardware, software, network, and communications solutions.

ESSENTIAL JOB RESULTS:

% of
time

____ 1. **ACCOMPLISHES TECHNICAL SUPPORT STAFF RESULTS**
by
communicating job expectations; planning, monitoring, and appraising job results; coaching, counseling, and disciplining employees; initiating, coordinating, and enforcing systems, policies, and procedures.

____ 2. **MAINTAINS STAFF**
by
recruiting, selecting, orienting, and training employees; maintaining a safe and secure work environment; developing personal growth opportunities.

____ 3. **SUSTAINS PLATFORM CAPACITY**
by
planning computer resources.

____ 4. **SATISFIES PROJECTED ORGANIZATION REQUIREMENTS**
by
researching and recommending hardware, software, network, and communications solutions.

____ 5. **OPTIMIZES RESOURCE UTILIZATION AND PERFORMANCE**
by
calibrating software controls.

% of
time

____ 6. **MAINTAINS OPERATING SYSTEMS**
by
installing and enhancing hardware and software.

____ 7. **RECOMMENDS DATA CENTER POLICY**
by
developing standards; preparing long-range objectives and budgets.

____ 8. **PREPARES USERS**
by
conducting training programs.

____ 9. **PREPARES REPORTS**
by
identifying activities, status, and performance.

____10. **MAINTAINS PLATFORM SECURITY**
by
developing, implementing, enforcing, and maintaining disaster prevention and recovery procedures.

____11. **MEETS FINANCIAL OBJECTIVES**
by
controlling expenses and contracts.

____12. **MAINTAINS QUALITY SERVICE**
by
establishing and enforcing organization standards.

ESSENTIAL JOB RESULTS:

% of
time

% of
time

_____13. **MAINTAINS PROFESSIONAL AND TECHNICAL KNOWLEDGE**
by
attending educational workshops;
reviewing professional publications;
establishing personal networks;
benchmarking state-of-the-art practices;
participating in professional societies.

_____14. **CONTRIBUTES TO TEAM EFFORT**
by
accomplishing related results as
needed.

JOB TITLE:	TECHNICAL TRAINER	T400_M

JOB PURPOSE: **PREPARES EMPLOYEES TO ACCOMPLISH JOB RESULTS**
by
planning, conducting, and evaluating computer training.

ESSENTIAL JOB RESULTS:

% of
time

% of
time

____ 1. **CONDUCTS COMPUTER TRAINING NEEDS ASSESSMENT**
by
collecting information pertaining to work procedures, work flow, and reports; understanding job-specific functions and tasks.

____ 2. **DETERMINES SYSTEM UTILIZATION REQUIREMENTS**
by
researching and testing systems.

____ 3. **DESIGNS COMPUTER TRAINING MANUALS**
by
identifying and describing information needs; using desktop publishing; submitting initial versions for review; revising and editing final copy.

____ 4. **MAINTAINS SAFE AND HEALTHY TRAINING ENVIRONMENT**
by
following organization standards and legal regulations.

____ 5. **CONDUCTS TRAINING CLASSES**
by
presenting job-specific, company-specific, and generic software applications and personal computer classes.

____ 6. **ENSURES OPERATION OF EQUIPMENT**
by
completing preventive maintenance requirements; following manufacturer's instructions; troubleshooting malfunctions; calling for repairs; maintaining equipment inventories; evaluating new equipment and techniques.

____ 7. **MAINTAINS QUALITY SERVICE**
by
establishing and enforcing organization standards.

____ 8. **EVALUATES TRAINING**
by
evaluating effectiveness of training to specific job applications.

____ 9. **MAINTAINS TECHNICAL KNOWLEDGE**
by
attending educational workshops; reviewing publications.

____ 10. **CONTRIBUTES TO TEAM EFFORT**
by
accomplishing related results as needed.

JOB PURPOSE: **SUPPORTS BUSINESS OPERATIONS**
by
recommending, implementing, and maintaining hardware and software installations.

ESSENTIAL JOB RESULTS:

% of
time

____ 1. SERVES CUSTOMERS
by
advising in the definition of business and technology operations enhancements.

____ 2. MAINTAINS OPERATING EFFICIENCY
by
recommending, developing, implementing, and maintaining new and existing technology infrastructures.

____ 3. COMPLETES PROJECTS
by
upgrading current software for different operating systems, compilers, utilities, databases, and networks; establishing target dates; monitoring installation.

____ 4. MAINTAINS SYSTEM PERFORMANCE
by
acquiring new software and hardware.

____ 5. ENSURES OPERATION OF EQUIPMENT
by
completing preventive maintenance requirements; following manufacturer's instructions; troubleshooting malfunctions; calling for repairs; maintaining equipment inventories; evaluating new equipment and techniques.

% of
time

____ 6. MAINTAINS CONSISTENT APPLICATIONS
by
establishing company standards.

____ 7. HELPS USERS ACCOMPLISH JOB RESULTS
by
training and coaching personnel.

____ 8. MAINTAINS QUALITY SERVICE
by
establishing and enforcing organization standards.

____ 9. PREPARES ACTIVITY REPORTS
by
collecting, summarizing, analyzing, and quantifying information.

____10. MAINTAINS PROFESSIONAL AND TECHNICAL KNOWLEDGE
by
attending educational workshops; reviewing professional publications; establishing personal networks; benchmarking state-of-the-art practices; participating in professional societies.

____11. CONTRIBUTES TO TEAM EFFORT
by
accomplishing related results as needed.

JOB TITLE:	TELEMARKETING OUTBOUND ANALYST	T405_M

JOB PURPOSE: **SOLVES EXTERNAL TELEMARKETING PROBLEMS**
by
coordinating information; resolving complaints.

ESSENTIAL JOB RESULTS:

% of
time

% of
time

_____ 1. **IDENTIFIES EXTERNAL TELEMARKETING REQUIREMENTS**
by
establishing personal rapport with persons in a position to understand service requirements.

_____ 2. **MAINTAINS PROCESS FLOW AND PROBLEM SOLVING**
by
coordinating information between the sales force and businesses or clients; correcting program deficiencies; recommending process improvements; answering inquiries; troubleshooting.

_____ 3. **MAINTAINS EXTERNAL TELEMARKETING SERVICES PROGRAMS**
by
implementing, monitoring, and troubleshooting programs.

_____ 4. **RESOLVES COMPLAINTS**
by
answering customer requests for information, requests for proof of enrollments, and "do-not-solicit" requests.

_____ 5. **INFORMS PERSONNEL**
by
coordinating information with market and sales force; distributing post-surveys of campaigns to accounts.

_____ 6. **MAINTAINS EXTERNAL VENDOR PROGRAM**
by
monitoring and reporting on performance.

_____ 7. **PREPARES REPORTS**
by
producing management plans; distributing performance reports.

_____ 8. **MAINTAINS QUALITY SERVICE**
by
following organization standards.

_____ 9. **MAINTAINS TECHNICAL KNOWLEDGE**
by
attending educational workshops; reviewing publications.

_____10. **CONTRIBUTES TO TEAM EFFORT**
by
accomplishing related results as needed.

JOB TITLE: TELEMARKETING REPRESENTATIVE   T406_M

JOB PURPOSE: **CONVERTS INQUIRIES INTO SALES**
by
answering inbound telephone calls.

ESSENTIAL JOB RESULTS:

% of
time

_____ 1. **ADVISES PRESENT OR PROSPECTIVE CUSTOMERS**
by
answering incoming calls on a rotating basis; operating telephone equipment, automatic dialing systems, and other telecommunications technologies.

_____ 2. **INFLUENCES CUSTOMERS TO BUY OR RETAIN PRODUCT OR SERVICE**
by
following a prepared script to give product reference information.

_____ 3. **DOCUMENTS TRANSACTIONS**
by
completing forms and record logs.

_____ 4. **MAINTAINS DATABASE**
by
entering, verifying, and backing up data.

_____ 5. **KEEPS EQUIPMENT OPERATIONAL**
by
following manufacturer's instructions and established procedures; notifying team leader of needed repairs.

% of
time

_____ 6. **MAINTAINS OPERATIONS**
by
following policies and procedures; reporting needed changes.

_____ 7. **MAINTAINS QUALITY SERVICE**
by
following organization standards.

_____ 8. **MAINTAINS TECHNICAL KNOWLEDGE**
by
attending educational workshops; reviewing publications.

_____ 9. **CONTRIBUTES TO TEAM EFFORT**
by
accomplishing related results as needed.

278

JOB TITLE:	TELESALES SPECIALIST	T407_M

JOB PURPOSE: **SELLS PRODUCTS**
by
taking and upgrading orders.

ESSENTIAL JOB RESULTS:

% of
time

____ 1. **RECORDS CUSTOMER INFORMATION**
by
obtaining and entering required data.

____ 2. **CONFIRMS CUSTOMER INFORMATION**
by
restating and clarifying data.

____ 3. **PROMOTES PRODUCTS**
by
suggesting related products; offering quantity discounts or special promotions.

____ 4. **INITIATES ORDERS**
by
obtaining product information.

____ 5. **CONFIRMS ORDERS**
by
restating and clarifying customer requirements and product description.

____ 6. **RESOLVES CUSTOMER CONCERNS**
by
obtaining information from customer service representative; calling customer back with new information.

% of
time

____ 7. **PREVENTS FINANCIAL LOSSES**
by
reporting suspected fraudulent transactions.

____ 8. **PROVIDES SALES RESULTS INFORMATION**
by
preparing and submitting shift summary report of transactions.

____ 9. **MAINTAINS QUALITY SERVICE**
by
following organization standards.

____10. **MAINTAINS TECHNICAL KNOWLEDGE**
by
attending educational workshops; reviewing publications.

____11. **CONTRIBUTES TO TEAM EFFORT**
by
accomplishing related results as needed.

JOB TITLE: THEATER MANAGER T501_M

JOB PURPOSE: **SERVES PATRONS**
by
managing staff; planning and booking presentations.

ESSENTIAL JOB RESULTS:

% of
time

_____ 1. **MAINTAINS THEATER STAFF**
by
recruiting, selecting, orienting, and
training employees; maintaining a safe
and secure work environment;
developing personal growth
opportunities.

_____ 2. **ACCOMPLISHES STAFF
RESULTS**
by
communicating job expectations;
planning, monitoring, and appraising
job results; coaching, counseling,
and disciplining employees;
initiating, coordinating, and
enforcing systems, policies, and
procedures.

_____ 3. **PROMOTES PATRONAGE**
by
identifying patrons' interests;
booking and advertising
presentations.

_____ 4. **ESTABLISHES ADMISSION PRICE**
by
surveying competitive pricing; studying
overhead costs; determining special
promotional opportunities.

_____ 5. **ACCOMPLISHES FINANCIAL
OBJECTIVES**
by
collecting admissions; forecasting
requirements; preparing an annual
budget; scheduling expenditures;
analyzing variances; initiating
corrective action.

% of
time

_____ 6. **MAINTAINS PREMISES**
by
completing inspections; contracting with
and supervising maintenance and
cleaning services; ordering and
maintaining supplies; recommending
renovations; maintaining security
devices; responding to emergencies.

_____ 7. **ENSURES OPERATION OF
EQUIPMENT**
by
completing preventive maintenance
requirements; following manufacturer's
instructions; troubleshooting
malfunctions; calling for repairs;
maintaining equipment inventories;
evaluating new equipment and
techniques.

_____ 8. **HELPS PATRONS**
by
providing first-aid assistance; calling for
emergency care; maintaining order.

_____ 9. **COMPLETES REPORTS**
by
entering required information.

_____10. **MAINTAINS TECHNICAL
KNOWLEDGE**
by
attending educational workshops;
reviewing publications.

_____11. **CONTRIBUTES TO TEAM EFFORT**
by
accomplishing related results as
needed.

┌───┐
│ **JOB TITLE:**   **TOUR GUIDE**   **T503_M** │
└───┘

JOB PURPOSE: **SATISFIES TOUR CLIENTS**
by
making arrangements and completing itinerary.

ESSENTIAL JOB RESULTS:

% of
time

____ **1. PREPARES FOR TOUR**
by
studying itinerary, points of interest,
local history, and customs; arranging
contacts and emergency assistance.

____ **2. PREPARES ITINERARY**
by
confirming route, stops, transportation,
and accommodations; determining
optional points of interest and activities.

____ **3. WELCOMES TOUR CLIENTS**
by
greeting them; providing directions;
offering refreshments; providing
information; answering questions;
verifying required papers and personal
responsibilities.

____ **4. ESCORTS TOUR**
by
arranging and/or confirming
transportation; providing route
directions when necessary; explaining
points of interest, local history, and
customs; translating language.

____ **5. PROVIDES FOR CLIENTS'
COMFORT**
by
arranging meals, accommodations,
personal facilities, luggage, customs,
currency, and similar requirements.

% of
time

____ **6. PROVIDES FOR CLIENTS'
PLEASURE**
by
arranging recreation, special tours,
entertainment, and similar options.

____ **7. COMPLETES REPORTS**
by
entering required information.

____ **8. MAINTAINS QUALITY SERVICE**
by
following tour standards.

____ **9. MAINTAINS TECHNICAL
KNOWLEDGE**
by
attending educational workshops;
reviewing publications.

____**10. CONTRIBUTES TO TEAM EFFORT**
by
accomplishing related results as
needed.

JOB TITLE: TOURIST CAMP ATTENDANT   T504_M

JOB PURPOSE: **SERVES CAMPERS**
by
preparing and maintaining facilities and services.

ESSENTIAL JOB RESULTS:

% of
time

% of
time

_____ **1. SELLS SERVICES**
by
explaining facilities and
accommodations.

_____ **2. REGISTERS CAMPERS**
by
obtaining information; maintaining
records.

_____ **3. OBTAINS REVENUE**
by
collecting fees.

_____ **4. DIRECTS CAMPERS TO
ACCOMMODATIONS**
by
providing instructions; providing escort.

_____ **5. SELLS SUPPLIES**
by
checking stock; anticipating needs;
placing and expediting orders; verifying
receipt; collecting payment.

_____ **6. OFFERS RECREATION SERVICES**
by
renting equipment; arranging tours.

_____ **7. MAINTAINS FACILITIES**
by
identifying requirements; completing
preventive maintenance; arranging for
maintenance and repairs; mowing lawn;
cleaning buildings; completing minor
repairs.

_____ **8. PROVIDES INFORMATION**
by
answering questions and requests.

_____ **9. PROVIDES COMMUNICATIONS
SERVICES**
by
arranging for connections and repairs.

_____**10. MAINTAINS QUALITY SERVICE**
by
following organization standards.

_____**11. MAINTAINS SAFE AND HEALTHY
ENVIRONMENT**
by
following and enforcing camp standards
and legal regulations.

_____**12. MAINTAINS TECHNICAL
KNOWLEDGE**
by
attending educational workshops;
reviewing publications.

_____**13. CONTRIBUTES TO TEAM EFFORT**
by
accomplishing related results as
needed.

JOB PURPOSE: VERIFIES TRADE PROMOTION CLAIMS
by
analyzing and resolving claims.

ESSENTIAL JOB RESULTS:

% of
time

_____ 1. PREPARES WORK TO BE ACCOMPLISHED
by
gathering and sorting documents and related information.

_____ 2. VERIFIES CUSTOMER AND BROKER INVOICES
by
reviewing transaction information; determining statement of performance; tracking trade promotion expenditures.

_____ 3. RESOLVES CUSTOMER ACCOUNT DISCREPANCIES
by
investigating documentation; issuing transaction adjustments; reconciling and authorizing deductions in conjunction with brokers, regional managers, national sales managers, and director of trade marketing.

_____ 4. RESOLVES PRODUCT OR SERVICE CLAIMS
by
clarifying the customer's claim or deduction; researching to determine cause of claim; selecting and explaining solution to resolve claim; expediting correction or adjustment; following up to ensure resolution.

% of
time

_____ 5. PREPARES REPORTS
by
collecting, analyzing, and summarizing information and trends; producing the post-promotional analysis.

_____ 6. CREATES AND REVISES POLICIES AND PROCEDURES
by
analyzing operating practices, policies, and procedures; implementing changes.

_____ 7. MAINTAINS TRADE PROMOTION HISTORICAL RECORDS
by
filing trade promotion documentation; inputting data; backing up data.

_____ 8. MAINTAINS QUALITY SERVICE
by
following organization standards.

_____ 9. MAINTAINS TECHNICAL KNOWLEDGE
by
attending educational workshops; reviewing publications.

_____10. CONTRIBUTES TO TEAM EFFORT
by
accomplishing related results as needed.

JOB TITLE: TRAFFIC SPECIALIST   T508_M

JOB PURPOSE: **DELIVERS MERCHANDISE TO CUSTOMERS**
by
verifying orders; arranging method of shipment.

ESSENTIAL JOB RESULTS:

% of
time

% of
time

_____ 1. **MAINTAINS INVENTORIES OF OUTSIDE WAREHOUSES**
by
checking stock to determine inventory levels; anticipating needed product; placing and expediting orders for customers.

_____ 2. **DETERMINES METHOD OF SHIPMENT**
by
examining items to be shipped, destination, route, rate, and time of delivery; dispatching items to carriers.

_____ 3. **KEEPS CUSTOMERS INFORMED**
by
notifying customers of shipping and stock availability issues; answering questions and responding to requests.

_____ 4. **PROCESSES ORDERS**
by
editing for price, promotional problems, customer comment requirements, and weight compliance; sorting orders.

_____ 5. **VERIFIES ITEMS SHIPPED**
by
matching bills of lading; reconciling quantities; noting discrepancies.

_____ 6. **MAINTAINS TRAFFIC OPERATIONS AND ORGANIZES WORK**
by
reading and routing correspondence; collecting information; initiating telecommunications; following policies and procedures.

_____ 7. **REPLACES DAMAGED ITEMS, SHORTAGES, AND MIS-SHIPMENTS**
by
informing customer and transporter/shipper of damage, shortage, or mis-shipped items; returning refused product to stock; issuing credit for damage and/or shortages.

_____ 8. **MAINTAINS CARRIER AND CUSTOMER CONFIDENCE**
by
keeping rate, carrier, price, promotions, purchase orders, and credit limit information confidential.

_____ 9. **PREPARES REPORTS**
by
collecting and analyzing data; reporting information; initiating telecommunications.

_____10. **MAINTAINS TECHNICAL KNOWLEDGE**
by
attending educational workshops; reviewing publications.

_____11. **CONTRIBUTES TO TEAM EFFORT**
by
accomplishing related results as needed.

JOB PURPOSE: CONTROLS RISKS AND LOSSES
by
collecting and analyzing information; generating checks; verifying collateral.

ESSENTIAL JOB RESULTS:

% of
time

% of
time

_____ 1. **PROTECTS ASSETS**
by
establishing, monitoring, and enforcing
internal controls.

_____ 2. **DOCUMENTS FINANCIAL TRANSACTIONS**
by
entering account information.

_____ 3. **SUMMARIZES CURRENT FINANCIAL STATUS**
by
collecting information; preparing
statements and other reports.

_____ 4. **MAINTAINS CHECK PRINTING SYSTEM**
by
completing daily download of check
data files from source systems;
conducting daily generation of checks;
maintaining inventory of paper and
toner cartridges; serving as check
printing system backup for subsidiaries.

_____ 5. **MAINTAINS SPECIAL COLLATERAL ACCOUNTS**
by
complying with procedures for
safekeeping, maintenance, and control
of collateral; executing and maintaining
investment accounts; maintaining
records and control of investment
accounts; completing accounting
functions.

_____ 6. **MAINTAINS DATABASE**
by
entering, verifying, and backing up
data.

_____ 7. **PROTECTS OPERATIONS**
by
keeping financial information
confidential.

_____ 8. **MAINTAINS TECHNICAL KNOWLEDGE**
by
attending educational workshops;
reviewing publications.

_____ 9. **CONTRIBUTES TO TEAM EFFORT**
by
accomplishing related results as
needed.

JOB TITLE: TREASURY COORDINATOR   T513_M

JOB PURPOSE: **SUPPORTS TREASURY MANAGEMENT FUNCTION**
by
collecting, entering, and maintaining information; tracking transactions.

ESSENTIAL JOB RESULTS:

% of
time

____ 1. **ENSURES ACCURACY OF RECEIPTS**
by
identifying, researching, and correcting lockbox deposits and returned items.

____ 2. **PLACES STOP-PAYMENT ORDERS**
by
gathering and reviewing requests; inputting information into bank systems; preparing correspondence to banks; confirming orders with requesters.

____ 3. **EXECUTES OVERNIGHT INVESTMENT FUNDS TRADES**
by
collecting and inputting trade information; verifying interest received; preparing trading reports for all companies and special deposits; maintaining related reports.

____ 4. **MAINTAINS DATABASE**
by
entering, verifying, and backing up data.

____ 5. **FORWARDS INFORMATION**
by
distributing daily bank activity report and incoming wire transfer information.

% of
time

____ 6. **SECURES FUNDING OF SPECIAL ACCOUNTS**
by
funding accounts; drawing on letters of credit.

____ 7. **ACQUIRES SPECIAL BANK SERVICES**
by
processing requests for official bank checks and electronic transfers.

____ 8. **PROTECTS OPERATIONS**
by
keeping financial information confidential.

____ 9. **MAINTAINS TECHNICAL KNOWLEDGE**
by
attending educational workshops; reviewing publications.

____10. **CONTRIBUTES TO TEAM EFFORT**
by
accomplishing related results as needed.

JOB TITLE: TREASURY OPERATIONS ANALYST   T514_M

JOB PURPOSE: SUPPORTS TREASURY MANAGEMENT OBJECTIVES
by
preparing and documenting transactions.

ESSENTIAL JOB RESULTS:

% of
time

% of
time

____ **1. MINIMIZES IDLE FUNDS**
by
concentrating cash from depository
accounts.

____ **2. COMPLETES ELECTRONIC
PAYMENTS**
by
inputting clearinghouse transactions
and electronic funds transfers for
domestic and international wires into
bank personal computer system;
completing tax payments via tax
system.

____ **3. RECORDS INCOMING CASH
RECEIPTS**
by
researching, identifying, and distributing
incoming checks; preparing lockbox
and in-house deposits; preparing
documentation for daily shipping;
reconciling and balancing daily deposit
activity; distributing daily bank reports
to subsidiaries and financial accounting.

____ **4. RECOVERS FUNDS**
by
processing check forgeries.

____ **5. PREPARES ACCOUNTING ENTRIES
AND RECONCILIATION**
by
compiling and analyzing account
information for concentration of funds,
interest received, lockboxes, and
outstanding items.

____ **6. DOCUMENTS FINANCIAL
TRANSACTIONS**
by
maintaining account information
records.

____ **7. SUMMARIZES CURRENT FINANCIAL
STATUS**
by
collecting information; preparing and
reconciling monthly and quarterly
treasury reports to cash schedules and
general ledgers; preparing cash and
interest reports.

____ **8. MAINTAINS BANK ACCOUNTS**
by
establishing, maintaining, documenting,
and closing banking relationships for
corporate headquarters and
subsidiaries.

____ **9. PREPARES DOCUMENTS**
by
analyzing and preparing contracts,
corporate resolutions, powers of
attorney, and authorized signers lists.

____ **10. PROTECTS OPERATIONS**
by
keeping financial information
confidential.

ESSENTIAL JOB RESULTS:

% of
time

% of
time

____**11. MAINTAINS RECORDS**
by
updating bank records of treasury
management system and electronic
cash transfer system; updating records
of authorized signers.

____**12. MAINTAINS PROFESSIONAL AND
TECHNICAL KNOWLEDGE**
by
attending educational workshops;
reviewing professional publications;
establishing personal networks;
benchmarking state-of-the-art practices;
participating in professional societies.

____**13. CONTRIBUTES TO TEAM EFFORT**
by
accomplishing related results as
needed.

JOB TITLE: TREASURY SYSTEM COORDINATOR   T515_M

JOB PURPOSE: **MAINTAINS DEPARTMENTAL SYSTEM OPERATIONS**
by
securing inventories and deposits; maintaining work flow.

ESSENTIAL JOB RESULTS:

% of
time

% of
time

_____ 1. **PREPARES WORK TO BE ACCOMPLISHED**
by
gathering, sorting, and distributing daily bank activity reports.

_____ 2. **MAINTAINS EQUIPMENT**
by
completing preventive maintenance requirements; inventorying and ordering supplies; calling for repairs.

_____ 3. **SECURES VAULT**
by
maintaining physical securities inventory and quality logs.

_____ 4. **CONTROLS INVESTMENT LOCKBOXES**
by
reviewing and recording in-house deposits; reconciling and balancing deposit activity.

_____ 5. **MAINTAINS SYSTEM-RELATED INFORMATION**
by
setting up electronic funds transfer; supporting system with automation enhancements.

_____ 6. **CONTROLS PETTY CASH FUND**
by
balancing and reimbursing cash transactions.

_____ 7. **PREPARES CHECKS ON SYSTEM**
by
downloading and printing.

_____ 8. **MAINTAINS DATABASE**
by
entering, verifying, and backing up data.

_____ 9. **ENHANCES THE EFFICIENCY OF THE TREASURY MANAGEMENT STAFF**
by
identifying automation opportunities; formulating and implementing recommendations.

_____ 10. **PROTECTS OPERATIONS**
by
keeping financial information confidential.

_____ 11. **MAINTAINS PROFESSIONAL AND TECHNICAL KNOWLEDGE**
by
attending educational workshops; reviewing professional publications; establishing personal networks; benchmarking state-of-the-art practices; participating in professional societies.

_____ 12. **CONTRIBUTES TO TEAM EFFORT**
by
accomplishing related results as needed.

JOB PURPOSE: ACCOMPLISHES CORPORATE BUSINESS OBJECTIVES
by
directing staff; planning, implementing, and evaluating project results.

ESSENTIAL JOB RESULTS:

% of
time

_____ 1. PRODUCES VALUE-ADDED EMPLOYEE RESULTS
by
implementing recruitment, selection, orientation, training, coaching, counseling, and disciplinary programs; communicating values; assigning accountabilities; planning, monitoring, and appraising job results; compensating for results.

_____ 2. ACHIEVES FINANCIAL OBJECTIVES
by
forecasting functional requirements; preparing an annual budget; scheduling expenditures; analyzing variances; initiating corrective actions; analyzing and recommending information and trends for senior executive decision making.

_____ 3. INCREASES STAKEHOLDER VALUE
by
establishing functional objectives aligned with corporate mission; initiating, coordinating, and enforcing new strategic initiatives; enhancing organization's stability and reputation; measuring and ensuring profit- and service-driven outcomes.

% of
time

_____ 4. SERVES CUSTOMERS
by
establishing critical service factors; maintaining quality service and operations; analyzing, defining, developing, and providing systems and resources; assessing results; anticipating trends.

_____ 5. (ENTER JOB-SPECIFIC RESULTS)
by
(enter job-specific duties)

_____ 6. SHARES PROFESSIONAL AND TECHNICAL KNOWLEDGE
by
presenting cutting-edge concepts at professional society symposia; implementing state-of-the-art practices; publishing trend-setting concepts in professional publications.

_____ 7. BUILDS AND STRENGTHENS CORPORATE REPUTATION
by
accomplishing related results as needed.

<table>
<tr><td colspan="2">JOB TITLE: VICE PRESIDENT–CONSTRUCTION SERVICES</td><td>V520_M</td></tr>
</table>

JOB PURPOSE: **SUPPORTS MANAGEMENT OBJECTIVES AND OPERATIONS**
by
directing staff; acquiring and developing land; supporting construction projects.

ESSENTIAL JOB RESULTS:

% of
time

____ 1. **MAINTAINS CONSTRUCTION SERVICES STAFF**
by
recruiting, selecting, orienting, and training employees; maintaining a safe and secure work environment; developing personal growth opportunities; building productive sub-contractor relationships.

____ 2. **ACCOMPLISHES STAFF RESULTS**
by
communicating job expectations; planning, monitoring, and appraising job results; coaching, counseling, and disciplining employees; initiating, coordinating, and enforcing systems, policies, and procedures.

____ 3. **ACQUIRES LAND**
by
identifying new acreage; analyzing development profitability; obtaining bids; negotiating land purchase.

____ 4. **DEVELOPS LAND**
by
preparing best-possible lots; complying with, overcoming, or modifying state and municipal regulations; obtaining utilities; maintaining erosion control; coordinating product design.

____ 5. **BUILDS SUBCONTRACTOR RELATIONSHIPS**
by
negotiating contracts; maintaining productivity, quality, and costs.

% of
time

____ 6. **IMPROVES QUALITY RESULTS**
by
directing facilitation of process improvement teams; monitoring implementation of recommendations.

____ 7. **MAINTAINS SAFE WORK ENVIRONMENT**
by
establishing and enforcing safety policies and procedures; ensuring compliance with federal, state, and local requirements; directing the investigation of accidents and preventive improvements; providing safety and first-aid training.

____ 8. **MAINTAINS FLEET OPERATION**
by
establishing and enforcing fleet operating policies and practices; identifying fleet requirements; negotiating leases; ensuring fleet maintenance.

____ 9. **PROVIDES COMMUNICATION SUPPORT**
by
establishing and enforcing communication policies and procedures; identifying communication requirements; approving major expenditures.

ESSENTIAL JOB RESULTS:

% of
time

% of
time

____10. **MAINTAINS DISASTER PREPAREDNESS**
by
establishing and enforcing disaster preparedness policies and procedures; identifying business operating requirements; monitoring preparedness.

____11. **ACHIEVES FINANCIAL OBJECTIVES**
by
forecasting requirements; scheduling and monitoring expenditures; analyzing variances; initiating corrective action.

____12. **MAINTAINS CONTINUITY AMONG CORPORATE, DIVISION, AND LOCAL WORK TEAMS**
by
documenting and communicating actions, irregularities, and continuing needs.

____13. **MAINTAINS PROFESSIONAL AND TECHNICAL KNOWLEDGE**
by
attending educational workshops; reviewing professional publications; establishing personal networks; benchmarking state-of-the-art practices; participating in professional societies.

____14. **CONTRIBUTES TO TEAM EFFORT**
by
accomplishing related results as needed.

<table>
<tr><td colspan="2">JOB TITLE:</td><td>VICE PRESIDENT–CORPORATE BRAND MARKETING</td><td>V521_M</td></tr>
</table>

JOB PURPOSE: OPTIMIZES MARKETING ACTIONS AMONG CORPORATE DIVISIONS by integrating brand name usage and advertising.

ESSENTIAL JOB RESULTS:

% of
time

% of
time

_____ 1. **ACCOMPLISHES BRAND INTEGRATION**
by
participating in key divisional brand development projects.

_____ 2. **STRATEGICALLY POSITIONS INTERDIVISIONAL BRAND NAME USAGE**
by
directing an interrelated multidivisional marketing campaign; identifying and sharing best practices among divisions.

_____ 3. **CREATES CORPORATE BRAND "OWNERSHIP"**
by
ensuring multidivisional representation in the campaign; focusing division personnel on corporate program.

_____ 4. **ENSURES VALUE-ADDED ADVERTISING EFFORTS**
by
securing, managing, and evaluating agency resources; gaining division management support for selection.

_____ 5. **ACHIEVES CAMPAIGN OBJECTIVES**
by
gathering pertinent information; identifying and evaluating options; choosing a course of action; directing the steering process.

_____ 6. **OBTAINS EMERGING RETAIL CHANNELS**
by
establishing marketing and selling strategies; maintaining long-term, helping relationships with retailers; creating financial schemes attractive to growing businesses.

_____ 7. **DEVELOPS MAJOR RETAIL BUSINESS**
by
developing marketing, selling, and business development strategies; identifying optimal internal brand name candidates for leveraging across product categories; identifying external brand names as acquisition opportunities; recommending long-term organizational structure for expanding business.

_____ 8. **LEVERAGES DIRECT CHANNELS**
by
developing marketing and selling strategies.

_____ 9. **MAINTAINS PROFESSIONAL AND TECHNICAL KNOWLEDGE**
by
attending educational workshops; reviewing professional publications; establishing personal networks; benchmarking state-of-the-art practices; participating in professional societies.

_____10. **CONTRIBUTES TO TEAM EFFORT**
by
accomplishing related results as needed.

JOB TITLE: VICE PRESIDENT–CORPORATE COUNSEL

V522_M

JOB PURPOSE: **ACCOMPLISHES CORPORATE BUSINESS OBJECTIVES**
by
directing staff; identifying and resolving legal issues.

ESSENTIAL JOB RESULTS:

% of
time

% of
time

_____ 1. **PRODUCES VALUE-ADDED EMPLOYEE RESULTS**
by
implementing recruitment, selection, orientation, training, coaching, counseling, and disciplinary programs; communicating corporate values; assigning accountabilities; planning, monitoring, and appraising job results.

_____ 2. **ACHIEVES FINANCIAL OBJECTIVES**
by
forecasting department requirements; preparing an annual budget; scheduling expenditures; analyzing variances; initiating corrective actions; reducing legal fees and costs.

_____ 3. **SERVES CUSTOMERS**
by
establishing legal objectives aligned with corporate objectives; initiating, coordinating, and enforcing legal policies and procedures; measuring and ensuring results; developing legal interpretations and options; completing legal responses; negotiating contracts.

_____ 4. **MAINTAINS QUALITY LEGAL SERVICE AND OPERATIONS**
by
establishing critical service factors; establishing productivity, quality, and service standards; developing and providing systems and resources; auditing results and identifying trends.

_____ 5. **COMPLIES WITH FEDERAL, STATE, AND LOCAL LEGAL REQUIREMENTS**
by
studying and reviewing existing and new laws; auditing and enforcing adherence to requirements; rendering opinions; advising management on needed actions.

_____ 6. **MAINTAINS PROFESSIONAL AND TECHNICAL KNOWLEDGE**
by
attending educational workshops; reviewing professional publications; establishing personal networks; benchmarking state-of-the-art practices; participating in professional societies.

_____ 7. **CONTRIBUTES TO TEAM EFFORT**
by
accomplishing related results as needed.

JOB TITLE:	VICE PRESIDENT–ENGINEERING	V523_M

JOB PURPOSE: **DEVELOPS QUALITY MANUFACTURING SYSTEMS**
by
directing staff; developing and maximizing manufacturing and quality systems.

ESSENTIAL JOB RESULTS:

% of
time

% of
time

____ 1. **ACCOMPLISHES ENGINEERING STAFF RESULTS**
by
communicating job expectations; planning, monitoring, and appraising job results; coaching, counseling, and disciplining employees; initiating, coordinating, and enforcing systems, policies, and procedures.

____ 2. **MAINTAINS STAFF**
by
recruiting, selecting, orienting, and training employees; maintaining a safe and secure work environment; developing personal growth opportunities.

____ 3. **ACHIEVES ENGINEERING STRATEGIC OBJECTIVES**
by
gathering pertinent information; identifying and evaluating options; choosing a course of action.

____ 4. **MAXIMIZES PRODUCTION**
by
developing processing technology; identifying additional applications of raw product.

____ 5. **MAINTAINS PRODUCT QUALITY**
by
establishing specifications, policies, and inspection practices for raw materials, work-in-process, and finished products.

____ 6. **RESEARCHES NEW AND IMPROVED PRODUCTS, PACKAGES, AND PROCESSES**
by
identifying development opportunities; conducting and evaluating experiments.

____ 7. **PROTECTS ASSETS**
by
registering patents.

____ 8. **MAINTAINS DISASTER PREPAREDNESS**
by
identifying potential problems; developing response plans; managing crises.

____ 9. **ACHIEVES ENGINEERING FINANCIAL OBJECTIVES**
by
preparing the engineering budget; scheduling expenditures; analyzing variances; initiating corrective action.

____10. **COMPLIES WITH LEGAL REQUIREMENTS**
by
studying existing and new legislation; enforcing adherence to requirements.

____11. **MAINTAINS ENGINEERING DATABASE**
by
developing information requirements; designing and maintaining an information system; providing backup mechanisms.

____12. **MAINTAINS QUALITY SERVICE**
by
establishing and enforcing organization standards.

____13. **PROTECTS OPERATIONS**
by
keeping engineering information confidential.

ESSENTIAL JOB RESULTS:

% of
time

% of
time

____14. **MAINTAINS PROFESSIONAL AND
TECHNICAL KNOWLEDGE**
by
attending educational workshops;
reviewing professional publications;
establishing personal networks;
benchmarking state-of-the-art practices;
participating in professional societies.

____15. **CONTRIBUTES TO TEAM EFFORT**
by
accomplishing related results as
needed.

JOB PURPOSE: ACCOMPLISHES ORGANIZATION'S STRATEGIC FINANCIAL OBJECTIVES
by
developing, monitoring, and evaluating plans and results; enforcing controls.

ESSENTIAL JOB RESULTS:

% of
time

1. DEVELOPS PLANS, BUDGETS, FORECASTS, AND FINANCIAL RESULTS TO GUIDE MANAGEMENT DECISIONS
by
forecasting requirements; preparing budgets; scheduling expenditures; analyzing variances; initiating corrective actions; preparing economic studies and forecasts; developing and providing background information; developing and enforcing planning schedules; preparing planning narratives.

2. SECURES FINANCING
by
tracking, measuring, evaluating, and forecasting financial results; identifying needs and trends; analyzing capital needs; managing deposits; negotiating credit with banks, brokers, and insurance companies.

3. CONDUCTS FINANCIAL ANALYSES TO IDENTIFY PROFIT IMPROVEMENT OPPORTUNITIES
by
studying business opportunities; determining expansion or purchase of plant facilities or product lines; evaluating options; recommending courses of action.

% of
time

4. PROTECTS ASSETS
by
establishing credit policies; developing and managing credit procedures; providing physical asset insurance coverage; establishing, auditing, and enforcing internal controls; arranging for and participating in external audits; managing legal counsel.

5. COMPLIES WITH REGULATORY REQUIREMENTS
by
approving and filing statements and reports; filing returns; paying taxes.

6. GUIDES INTERNAL ACTIONS
by
developing and enforcing policies and procedures.

7. OBTAINS REVENUE AND PAYS OBLIGATIONS
by
establishing accounts receivable and payable systems.

8. REPRESENTS THE ORGANIZATION
by
communicating and interacting with governmental agencies.

ESSENTIAL JOB RESULTS:

% of
time

% of
time

____ 9. **AUTHORIZES AGREEMENTS**
by
representing the organization with
financial institutions.

____10. **MAINTAINS OFFICE AND
INFORMATION SERVICES**
by
studying organization requirements;
approving policies, procedures,
programs, and expenditures.

____11. **PROTECTS OPERATIONS**
by
keeping financial information
confidential.

____12. **MAINTAINS PROFESSIONAL AND
TECHNICAL KNOWLEDGE**
by
attending educational workshops;
reviewing professional publications;
establishing personal networks;
benchmarking state-of-the-art practices;
participating in professional societies.

____13. **CONTRIBUTES TO TEAM EFFORT**
by
accomplishing related results as
needed.

JOB TITLE: VICE PRESIDENT–FINANCE, PLANNING, AND SYSTEMS   V525_M

JOB PURPOSE: PROVIDES MANAGEMENT DECISION-MAKING INFORMATION
by
directing staff; developing financial information; planning and enforcing administrative systems.

ESSENTIAL JOB RESULTS:

% of
time

% of
time

_____ 1. **MAINTAINS FINANCE, PLANNING, AND SYSTEMS STAFF**
by
recruiting, selecting, orienting, and training employees; maintaining a safe and secure work environment; developing personal growth opportunities.

_____ 2. **ACCOMPLISHES STAFF RESULTS**
by
communicating job expectations; planning, monitoring, and appraising job results; coaching, counseling, and disciplining employees; initiating, coordinating, and enforcing systems, policies, and procedures.

_____ 3. **MAINTAINS FINANCIAL CONTROLS**
by
developing and enforcing financial system, policies, and procedures; recommending and approving financial actions; managing cash requirements; preparing financial reports; auditing financial systems; monitoring budgets; identifying and obtaining insurance requirements.

_____ 4. **MANAGES STRATEGIC AND FINANCIAL PLANNING**
by
organizing the planning process; assembling and analyzing critical information; updating projections; recommending financial actions; monitoring outcomes.

_____ 5. **PROVIDES INFORMATION MANAGEMENT SUPPORT**
by
approving hardware and software concepts and technology; directing programming, operations, and support services.

_____ 6. **MAINTAINS QUALITY OPERATIONS**
by
analyzing, designing, and enforcing administrative systems; conducting audits.

_____ 7. **MAINTAINS LEGAL PROTECTIONS**
by
building rapport with legal counsel; investigating potentially litigious situations; recommending legal actions; reviewing contracts.

_____ 8. **MAINTAINS CONTINUITY AMONG CORPORATE, DIVISION, AND LOCAL WORK TEAMS**
by
documenting and communicating actions, irregularities, and continuing needs.

_____ 9. **PROTECTS OPERATIONS**
by
keeping financial information confidential.

ESSENTIAL JOB RESULTS:

% of
time

% of
time

____10. MAINTAINS PROFESSIONAL AND TECHNICAL KNOWLEDGE
by
attending educational workshops;
reviewing professional publications;
establishing personal networks;
benchmarking state-of-the-art practices;
participating in professional societies.

____11. CONTRIBUTES TO TEAM EFFORT
by
accomplishing related results as needed.

JOB TITLE:	VICE PRESIDENT–GOVERNMENT AFFAIRS	V526_M

JOB PURPOSE: **PROTECTS COMPANY INTERESTS**
by
directing staff; maintaining rapport with regulatory and other interested groups.

ESSENTIAL JOB RESULTS:

% of
time

% of
time

____ 1. **MAINTAINS GOVERNMENT AFFAIRS STAFF**
by
recruiting, selecting, orienting, and training employees; maintaining a safe and secure work environment; developing personal growth opportunities.

____ 2. **ACCOMPLISHES STAFF RESULTS**
by
communicating job expectations; planning, monitoring, and appraising job results; coaching, counseling, and disciplining employees; initiating, coordinating, and enforcing systems, policies, and procedures.

____ 3. **ACCOMPLISHES FINANCIAL OBJECTIVES**
by
developing a budget; controlling expenses.

____ 4. **DETERMINES GOVERNMENT AFFAIRS REQUIREMENTS**
by
surveying current public policy influences, political issues, and trends; evaluating proposed organization actions; proposing alternatives.

____ 5. **MAINTAINS QUALITY SERVICE**
by
establishing and enforcing organization standards.

____ 6. **KEEPS MANAGEMENT INFORMED**
by
tracking announcements and actions of legislative proposals and public interest organizations; summarizing impact on the organization; recommending action.

____ 7. **REPRESENTS THE ORGANIZATION**
by
presenting information, observations, opinions, and arguments to federal, state, and local legislative and regulatory agencies, other organizations and individual legislators, whose actions might affect company interests; initiating legislative proposals.

____ 8. **SUPPORTS TRADE ORGANIZATIONS**
by
volunteering for committee assignments and offices.

____ 9. **DEVELOPS MEDIA PRESENTATIONS**
by
preparing a communication and distribution strategy; contracting with developers.

ESSENTIAL JOB RESULTS:

% of
time

% of
time

_____**10. MAINTAINS PROFESSIONAL AND TECHNICAL KNOWLEDGE**
by
attending educational workshops;
reviewing professional publications;
establishing personal networks;
benchmarking state-of-the-art practices;
participating in professional societies.

_____**11. CONTRIBUTES TO TEAM EFFORT**
by
accomplishing related results as
needed.

JOB TITLE: VICE PRESIDENT–HUMAN RESOURCES   V527_M

JOB PURPOSE: **PROVIDES AND MAINTAINS A COMPETENT, MOTIVATED WORKFORCE**
by
directing staff; developing, evaluating, and enforcing human resources systems.

ESSENTIAL JOB RESULTS:

% of
time

% of
time

_____ 1. **MAINTAINS HUMAN RESOURCES STAFF**
by
recruiting, selecting, orienting, and training employees; developing personal growth opportunities.

_____ 2. **ACCOMPLISHES HUMAN RESOURCES STAFF RESULTS**
by
communicating job expectations; planning, monitoring, and appraising job results; coaching, counseling, and disciplining employees; initiating, coordinating, and enforcing systems, policies, and procedures.

_____ 3. **ENHANCES ORGANIZATIONAL EFFECTIVENESS**
by
identifying and analyzing current circumstances; implementing organization development interventions; providing training programs; developing and maintaining succession plans; recommending new organization structures.

_____ 4. **IMPROVES EMPLOYEE SATISFACTION**
by
identifying and responding to concerns; developing morale-building programs.

_____ 5. **MAINTAINS WORKING RELATIONSHIP WITH THE UNION**
by
preparing for and representing the organization during negotiations; administering the collective bargaining agreement; resolving grievances.

_____ 6. **MAINTAINS CONSISTENT ACTIONS ACROSS THE ORGANIZATION**
by
initiating, coordinating, and enforcing human resources policies and procedures; obtaining senior management buy-in on new programs; developing managers' leadership skills.

_____ 7. **MAINTAINS ORGANIZATION COMPLIANCE**
by
identifying and enforcing legal requirements; providing training for completing requirements; submitting reports.

_____ 8. **SECURES QUALIFIED EMPLOYEES FOR ORGANIZATION**
by
developing and managing recruiting, orientation, and placement programs.

_____ 9. **SUSTAINS EQUITABLE COMPENSATION**
by
designing and administering pay, benefits, incentive, and bonus programs; managing the payroll function.

_____10. **SUPPORTS FOCUS ON JOB RESULTS IN ALL DIVISIONS**
by
designing and maintaining a job-results planning, monitoring, and appraising program; training managers to focus on results.

ESSENTIAL JOB RESULTS:

% of
time

% of
time

____11. **KEEPS EMPLOYEES INFORMED**
by
publishing an employee newsletter;
preparing and disseminating
communications; responding to and
analyzing requests.

____12. **SAFEGUARDS PERSONNEL
RECORDS**
by
establishing, controlling, and storing
records management systems;
maintaining employee confidentiality.

____13. **PROTECTS EMPLOYEES AND
ORGANIZATION ASSETS**
by
establishing and enforcing safety
practices; providing safety
communication and training.

____14. **ACHIEVES FINANCIAL OBJECTIVES**
by
forecasting requirements; preparing a
budget; managing expenditures.

____15. **CONTRIBUTES TO THE
ORGANIZATION'S EFFECTIVENESS**
by
offering information and opinions as a
member of senior management team;
integrating objectives with other
functions.

____16. **MAINTAINS PROFESSIONAL AND
TECHNICAL KNOWLEDGE**
by
attending educational workshops;
reviewing professional publications;
establishing personal networks;
benchmarking state-of-the-art practices;
participating in professional societies.

____17. **CONTRIBUTES TO TEAM EFFORT**
by
accomplishing related results as
needed.

JOB PURPOSE: **MEETS CUSTOMER REQUIREMENTS**
by
directing staff; developing and implementing purchasing, logistical, and production systems.

ESSENTIAL JOB RESULTS:

% of
time

____ 1. **MAINTAINS MANUFACTURING STAFF**
by
recruiting, selecting, orienting, and training employees; maintaining a safe and secure work environment; developing personal growth opportunities.

____ 2. **ACCOMPLISHES STAFF RESULTS**
by
communicating job expectations; planning, monitoring, and appraising job results; coaching, counseling, and disciplining employees; initiating, coordinating, and enforcing systems, policies, and procedures.

____ 3. **PRODUCES PRODUCTS**
by
establishing production planning systems; maintaining good manufacturing practices; enforcing quality standards; improving products and processes.

____ 4. **PROVIDES MATERIALS**
by
developing purchasing and logistical systems; controlling inventory.

____ 5. **RECORDS CUSTOMER ORDERS**
by
maintaining order-receipt process.

____ 6. **ACHIEVES FINANCIAL OBJECTIVES**
by
establishing objectives; developing budgets; controlling costs; maximizing use of assets.

% of
time

____ 7. **DELIVERS PRODUCTS**
by
developing storage and transportation systems; negotiating contracts.

____ 8. **COMPLIES WITH LEGAL REQUIREMENTS**
by
enforcing company policies and procedures, and regulatory requirements.

____ 9. **DEVELOPS NEW PLANT LOCATIONS**
by
studying expansion of facilities, new plants, and co-producer arrangements; recommending best option.

____10. **MAINTAINS PROFESSIONAL AND TECHNICAL KNOWLEDGE**
by
attending educational workshops; reviewing professional publications; establishing personal networks; benchmarking state-of-the-art practices; participating in professional societies.

____11. **CONTRIBUTES TO TEAM EFFORT**
by
accomplishing related results as needed.

JOB TITLE: VICE PRESIDENT–PROFITS   V529_M

JOB PURPOSE: **CONTROLS PROFIT OBJECTIVES**
by
studying, controlling, and improving product results.

ESSENTIAL JOB RESULTS:

% of
time

____ 1. **ENSURES PROFITABILITY AND VIABILITY STANDARDS**
by
administering the corporate profit control process; conducting profit control meetings; counseling product managers.

____ 2. **INCREASES PRODUCT PROFITABILITY**
by
studying product results; recommending marketing and product changes.

____ 3. **INCREASES BUSINESS LINE PROFITABILITY**
by
studying business line results; recommending changes; targeting alliances.

____ 4. **OBTAINS MARGIN OBJECTIVES**
by
establishing pricing guidelines; approving pricing sheets.

% of
time

____ 5. **DEVELOPS NEW PRODUCTS**
by
coordinating information and requirements with research and development.

____ 6. **PROTECTS OPERATIONS**
by
keeping financial information confidential.

____ 7. **MAINTAINS PROFESSIONAL AND TECHNICAL KNOWLEDGE**
by
attending educational workshops; reviewing professional publications; establishing personal networks; benchmarking state-of-the-art practices; participating in professional societies.

____ 8. **CONTRIBUTES TO TEAM EFFORT**
by
accomplishing related results as needed.

JOB TITLE: VICE PRESIDENT–REENGINEERING V530_M

JOB PURPOSE: OPTIMIZES CORPORATE PRODUCTIVITY
by
reengineering work processes; building improvement teams.

ESSENTIAL JOB RESULTS:

% of
time

% of
time

____ 1. **ESTABLISHES REENGINEERING PLANS**
by
studying corporate objectives; analyzing work systems; identifying improvement opportunities; setting priorities.

____ 2. **INTEGRATES SYSTEMS DEVELOPMENT EFFORTS**
by
identifying merging points; coordinating developmental actions and information.

____ 3. **ACCOMPLISHES REENGINEERING PROJECTS**
by
setting project objectives and priorities; assembling project teams; managing project work; providing support services.

____ 4. **BUILDS SUPPORT FOR PROJECTS**
by
communicating expectations and rationales; meeting with managers and employees; explaining requirements; implementing reward and recognition programs.

____ 5. **EVALUATES PROJECT RESULTS**
by
establishing standards; measuring outcomes.

____ 6. **MAINTAINS ORGANIZATION EFFICIENCY**
by
coordinating changes and requirements across functional lines.

____ 7. **ACCOMPLISHES FINANCIAL OBJECTIVES**
by
monitoring budget; controlling variances.

____ 8. **MAINTAINS QUALITY SERVICE**
by
establishing and enforcing organization standards.

____ 9. **MAINTAINS PROFESSIONAL AND TECHNICAL KNOWLEDGE**
by
attending educational workshops; reviewing professional publications; establishing personal networks; benchmarking state-of-the-art practices; participating in professional societies.

____10. **CONTRIBUTES TO TEAM EFFORT**
by
accomplishing related results as needed.

JOB PURPOSE: **INCREASES REVENUE**
by
directing staff; developing and exploiting markets.

ESSENTIAL JOB RESULTS:

% of
time

____ 1. **MAINTAINS SALES STAFF**
by
recruiting, selecting, orienting, and
training employees; maintaining a safe
and secure work environment;
developing personal growth
opportunities.

____ 2. **ACCOMPLISHES STAFF RESULTS**
by
communicating job expectations;
planning, monitoring, and appraising
job results; coaching, counseling, and
disciplining employees; initiating,
coordinating, and enforcing systems,
policies, and procedures.

____ 3. **DEFINES MARKET POTENTIAL**
by
analyzing market surveys and sales
statistics; estimating volume and profit
potential; preparing forecasts.

____ 4. **IMPROVES MARKET POSITION**
by
improving current products;
researching, testing, and introducing
new products.

____ 5. **DEVELOPS DOMESTIC AND
INTERNATIONAL SALES VOLUME**
by
establishing sales policy, objectives,
pricing, and discounts; establishing
territories; assigning quotas;
maintaining broker network; negotiating
key contracts.

% of
time

____ 6. **ACHIEVES MARKET SHARE**
by
developing and establishing
promotional strategies; implementing
advertising campaigns.

____ 7. **MAINTAINS RAPPORT WITH KEY
CUSTOMERS**
by
making periodic visits; exploring
specific needs; resolving problems.

____ 8. **MAINTAINS ASSETS AND
ORGANIZATION REPUTATION**
by
protecting brand and image in export
advertising.

____ 9. **MAINTAINS QUALITY SERVICE**
by
establishing and enforcing organization
standards.

____ 10. **MAINTAINS PROFESSIONAL AND
TECHNICAL KNOWLEDGE**
by
attending educational workshops;
reviewing professional publications;
establishing personal networks;
benchmarking state-of-the-art practices;
participating in professional societies.

____ 11. **CONTRIBUTES TO TEAM EFFORT**
by
accomplishing related results as
needed.

JOB TITLE: WAREHOUSE ASSOCIATE W534_M

JOB PURPOSE: **COMPLETES SHIPMENTS**
by
processing and loading orders.

ESSENTIAL JOB RESULTS:

% of
time

% of
time

_____ 1. **PREPARES ORDERS**
by
processing requests and supply orders;
pulling materials; packing boxes;
placing orders in delivery area.

_____ 2. **COMPLETES DELIVERIES**
by
driving truck or van to and from
vendors.

_____ 3. **MAINTAINS TRUCK OR VAN**
by
completing preventive maintenance
requirements; arranging for repairs.

_____ 4. **MAINTAINS INVENTORY CONTROLS**
by
collecting stock location orders and
printing requests.

_____ 5. **MAINTAINS QUALITY SERVICE**
by
following organization standards.

_____ 6. **MAINTAINS SAFE AND CLEAN WORK ENVIRONMENT**
by
keeping shelves, pallet area, and
workstations neat; maintaining clean
shipping supply area; complying with
procedures, rules, and regulations.

_____ 7. **COMPLETES REPORTS**
by
entering required information.

_____ 8. **MAINTAINS TECHNICAL KNOWLEDGE**
by
attending educational workshops;
reviewing publications.

_____ 9. **CONTRIBUTES TO TEAM EFFORT**
by
accomplishing related results as
needed.

JOB TITLE: WASTE PLANT OPERATOR

W536_M

JOB PURPOSE: **MAINTAINS WASTEWATER FACILITIES**
by
operating and maintaining equipment.

ESSENTIAL JOB RESULTS:

% of
time

____ 1. **SECURES INFORMATION**
by
collecting and analyzing water samples.

____ 2. **MAINTAINS AND OPERATES WASTEWATER TREATMENT FACILITIES**
by
completing preventive maintenance requirements; following manufacturer's instructions; troubleshooting; calling for repairs; adhering to good manufacturing practices; making operator adjustments.

____ 3. **MAINTAINS QUALITY SERVICE**
by
establishing and enforcing organization standards.

____ 4. **PROTECTS OPERATIONS**
by
complying with legal requirements.

____ 5. **MAINTAINS DATABASE**
by
entering and updating wastewater information.

% of
time

____ 6. **MAINTAINS HISTORICAL RECORDS**
by
completing database backups; maintaining hard copy files of specified original data.

____ 7. **PREPARES REPORTS**
by
printing and assembling analysis results.

____ 8. **MAINTAINS ANALYSIS LAB**
by
cleaning facility; maintaining records and files; maintaining test equipment in certifiable condition.

____ 9. **MAINTAINS TECHNICAL KNOWLEDGE**
by
attending educational workshops; reviewing publications.

____ 10. **CONTRIBUTES TO TEAM EFFORT**
by
accomplishing related results as needed.

JOB PURPOSE: **TREATS AND DISCHARGES PROCESS WASTEWATER**
by
monitoring and analyzing samples.

ESSENTIAL JOB RESULTS:

% of
time

% of
time

_____ 1. **MONITORS SOLIDS**
by
operating belt press and drying bed.

_____ 2. **DETERMINES WASTEWATER CHARACTERISTICS**
by
conducting laboratory analysis of wastewater.

_____ 3. **DOCUMENTS WASTEWATER CHARACTERISTICS**
by
recording test results on spreadsheets.

_____ 4. **MAINTAINS SAFE AND CLEAN WORK ENVIRONMENT**
by
complying with procedures, rules, and regulations.

_____ 5. **MAINTAINS QUALITY SERVICE**
by
following organization standards.

_____ 6. **PREPARES CHARTS AND GRAPHS**
by
processing statistical information.

_____ 7. **MAINTAINS DATABASE**
by
entering, verifying, and backing up data.

_____ 8. **MAINTAINS PLANT AND EQUIPMENT**
by
completing routine maintenance and troubleshooting.

_____ 9. **MAINTAINS TECHNICAL KNOWLEDGE**
by
attending educational workshops; reviewing publications.

_____10. **CONTRIBUTES TO TEAM EFFORT**
by
accomplishing related results as needed.

JOB PURPOSE: MAINTAINS WASTEWATER TREATMENT OPERATIONS
by
managing staff; completing analyses and treatments; complying with
regulations.

ESSENTIAL JOB RESULTS:

% of
time

% of
time

_____ 1. **MAINTAINS WASTEWATER TREATMENT STAFF**
by
recruiting, selecting, orienting, and training employees; developing personal growth opportunities.

_____ 2. **ACCOMPLISHES STAFF RESULTS**
by
communicating job expectations; planning, monitoring, and appraising job results; coaching, counseling, and disciplining employees; initiating, coordinating, and enforcing systems, policies, and procedures.

_____ 3. **COMPLETES TREATMENT OPERATIONAL REQUIREMENTS**
by
scheduling and coordinating daily discharge of effluent within prescribed Department of Energy limits; operating equipment.

_____ 4. **DOCUMENTS OPERATING CONDITIONS**
by
completing daily records and periodic reports to comply with Department of Energy requirements.

_____ 5. **MAINTAINS EQUIPMENT**
by
completing preventive maintenance requirements; troubleshooting malfunctions; calling for repairs; evaluating new equipment and techniques.

_____ 6. **MAINTAINS LAND LEASE AGREEMENT**
by
supplying irrigation water, under pressure, to the land application system; coordinating placement of sprinklers and monitoring application of residuals.

_____ 7. **MAINTAINS SAFE AND CLEAN ENVIRONMENT**
by
complying with procedures, rules, and regulations.

_____ 8. **MAINTAINS PROFESSIONAL AND TECHNICAL KNOWLEDGE**
by
attending educational workshops; reviewing professional publications; establishing personal networks; benchmarking state-of-the-art practices; participating in professional societies.

_____ 9. **CONTRIBUTES TO TEAM EFFORT**
by
accomplishing related results as needed.

```
┌─────────────────────────────────────────────────────────────────────┐
│                                                                       │
│  JOB TITLE:    WINEMAKER                               W540_M         │
│                                                                       │
└─────────────────────────────────────────────────────────────────────┘
```

JOB PURPOSE: **PRODUCES WINE**
by
analyzing and processing fruit; storing wine.

ESSENTIAL JOB RESULTS:

% of
time

% of
time

_____ **1. OBTAINS FRUIT**
by
establishing specifications; contracting
with growers; coordinating
requirements with growers.

_____ **2. ENSURES QUALITY FRUIT**
by
monitoring growing conditions.

_____ **3. DETERMINES FRUIT TO BE PICKED**
by
conducting analyses.

_____ **4. PROCESSES FRUIT**
by
following established procedures;
making adjustments due to condition of
fruit.

_____ **5. FERMENTS JUICE**
by
controlling conditions; testing quality;
determining appropriate procedures.

_____ **6. BOTTLES WINE**
by
supervising use of bottling equipment;
determining blends.

_____ **7. STORES WINE**
by
controlling conditions.

_____ **8. IMPROVES WINE**
by
developing new processes and
standards.

_____ **9. MAINTAINS SAFE AND HEALTHY
WORK ENVIRONMENT**
by
establishing and enforcing organization
standards and legal regulations.

_____ **10. ACCOMPLISHES FINANCIAL
OBJECTIVES**
by
forecasting requirements; controlling
costs.

_____ **11. MAINTAINS PROFESSIONAL AND
TECHNICAL KNOWLEDGE**
by
attending educational workshops;
reviewing professional publications;
establishing personal networks;
benchmarking state-of-the-art practices;
participating in professional societies.

_____ **12. CONTRIBUTES TO TEAM EFFORT**
by
accomplishing related results as
needed.

JOB TITLE:	WORKERS' COMPENSATION ADMINISTRATOR	W543_M

JOB PURPOSE: CONTROLS WORKERS' COMPENSATION COSTS
by
managing medical cases.

ESSENTIAL JOB RESULTS:

% of
time

_____ 1. **INVESTIGATES ACCIDENTS**
by
interviewing victim and witnesses;
evaluating incident and medical reports.

_____ 2. **PREVENTS AND REDUCES ACCIDENTS**
by
studying accident reports; establishing
causes of accidents; recognizing trends
in types of accidents; coaching
supervisors and employees; publishing
accident-prevention information.

_____ 3. **PAYS MEDICAL BILLS**
by
verifying required documents.

_____ 4. **PAYS EMPLOYEES**
by
verifying and processing claims and
benefits.

_____ 5. **SECURES REIMBURSEMENT**
by
submitting subrogation claims and
criminal cases.

% of
time

_____ 6. **MAINTAINS RECORDS**
by
updating records management system.

_____ 7. **PREPARES REPORTS**
by
collecting, analyzing, and summarizing
information.

_____ 8. **MAINTAINS TECHNICAL KNOWLEDGE**
by
attending educational workshops and
conventions; benchmarking state-of-
the-art practices; reviewing
publications.

_____ 9. **CONTRIBUTES TO TEAM EFFORT**
by
accomplishing related results as
needed.

JOB TITLE:	ZOO CARETAKER	Z544_M

JOB PURPOSE: **MAINTAINS EXHIBITS**
by
caring for animals; maintaining quarters.

ESSENTIAL JOB RESULTS:

% of
time

____ 1. **PREPARES WORK TO BE ACCOMPLISHED**
by
determining requirements; setting priorities; organizing schedule.

____ 2. **FEEDS ANIMALS**
by
preparing foods and formulas; adding vitamins or medications; placing food in cages.

____ 3. **MAINTAINS ANIMALS' QUARTERS**
by
cleaning and disinfecting area; maintaining temperature and humidity; completing repairs.

____ 4. **MAINTAINS ANIMALS**
by
completing bathing and grooming; transferring animals; assisting veterinarian with procedures.

____ 5. **PROTECTS ANIMALS**
by
detecting disease and injury; reporting problems; rescuing animals from potentially dangerous situations; adhering to and enforcing regulations.

% of
time

____ 6. **EDUCATES VISITORS**
by
explaining species, care, native habitats, and breeding habits.

____ 7. **COMPLETES REPORTS**
by
entering required information.

____ 8. **MAINTAINS TECHNICAL KNOWLEDGE**
by
attending educational workshops; reviewing publications.

____ 9. **CONTRIBUTES TO TEAM EFFORT**
by
accomplishing related results as needed.

Appendix
Combined Lists of Job Descriptions
From *Results-Oriented JOB Descriptions* and *More Results-Oriented JOB Descriptions*

Alphabetical, Including Software File Names

Job Title	File Name	Job Title	File Name
Account executive	A001_R	Assembler, wire harness	A020_R
Accountant	A002_R	Association executive	A021_R
Accountant in-charge	**A003_M**	**Attorney**	**A022_M**
Accountant supervisor	**A004_M**	Audio-visual technician	A023_R
Accounts receivable/payable clerk	A005_R	Auditor	A024_R
		Automatic screw-machine operator	A025_R
Actuary associate	**A006_M**		
Administrative assistant	A007_R	Automatic teller-machine clerk	A026_R
Administrative manager	**A008_M**		
Advertising manager	A009_R	Automobile fleet maintenance manager	A027_R
Aircraft mechanic	A010_R		
Airline pilot	**A011_M**	Benefits manager	B028_R
Airport director	**A012_M**	Benefits specialist	B029_R
Air-traffic controller	A013_R	Billing clerk	B030_R
Analyst/programmer	A014_R	Blood bank manager	B031_R
Animal control officer	**A015_M**	Bookkeeper	B032_R
Apartment house manager	**A016_M**	Branch manager	B033_R
Aquarist	**A017_M**	**Broadcast engineer**	**B034_M**
Artist	**A018_M**	**Budget accounting clerk**	**B035_M**
Assembler	A019_R	**Budget analyst**	**B036_M**

Job Title	File Name
Budget officer	B037_R
Building custodian	B038_R
Building maintenance supervisor	B039_R
Building maintenance technician	B040_R
Bus driver	**B041_M**
Business process analyst	**B042_M**
Business systems analyst	**B043_M**
Buyer (manufacturing)	B044_R
Buyer (merchandising)	B045_R
Cable supervisor	**C046_M**
Cable/television program director	**C047_M**
Cafeteria line attendant	C048_R
Carpenter	C049_R
Caseworker	C050_R
Cash clerk	C051_R
Cash manager	**C052_M**
Cashier/checker	C053_R
Ceramic engineer	C054_R
Chaplain	**C055_M**
Chef	C056_R
Chemist	C057_R
Chief executive officer	**C058_M**
Child care aide	**C059_M**
Child care teacher	**C060_M**
Child life specialist	**C061_M**
City/county trustee	**C062_M**
City engineer	**C063_M**
City manager	C064_R
Civil engineer	C065_R
Claims adjuster	C066_R
Claims examiner	**C067_M**
Claims investigator	**C068_M**
Claims manager	**C069_M**
Claims specialist	**C070_M**
Claims support specialist	**C071_M**
Clerk/typist	C072_R
Client service manager	**C073_M**
Clinical engineer	C074_R
Clinical psychologist	C075_R
Clinical social work therapist	C076_R
Club host/hostess	**C077_M**
Collection manager	C078_R

Job Title	File Name
Commercial loan account specialist	C079_R
Commercial loan administration manager	C080_R
Communications specialist	C081_R
Community services agency board member (volunteer)	C082_R
Community services agency president	C083_R
Compensation manager	C084_R
Compensation specialist	C085_R
Compliance analyst	**C086_M**
Computer operator	C087_R
Computer programmer	C088_R
Computer systems hardware analyst	C089_R
Computer-aided design assistant	**C090_M**
Conference planner	C091_R
Construction manager	**C092_M**
Construction secretary	**C093_M**
Consumer affairs administrator	**C094-M**
Consumer loan operations supervisor	C095_R
Contract administrator	C096_R
Contract development analyst	**C097_M**
Contract specialist	C098_R
Control desk coordinator	**C099_M**
Controller	C100_R
Copywriter–direct mail	**C101_M**
Corporate intelligence director	**C102_M**
Corporate planner	**C103_M**
Corporate secretary	**C104_M**
Cost accountant	C105_R
Cost analyst–construction	**C106_M**
Cost analyst–land development	**C107_M**
Courier	**C108_M**
Court clerk	C109_R
Craft center manager	**C110_M**
Craft demonstrator	**C111_M**
Credit analyst	C112_R
Credit manager	C113_R

Job Title	File Name	Job Title	File Name
Cruise ship captain	**C114_M**	Employee relations representative	E150_R
Customer service engineer	**C115_M**	**Employment clerk**	**E151_M**
Customer service manager	C116_R	Employment interviewer	E152_R
Customer service representative	C117_R	Employment manager	E153_R
Cutter operator	C118_R	Engineering manager	E154_R
Data center analyst	**D119_M**	Engineering technician	E155_R
Data center operator	**D120_M**	Environmental analyst	E156_R
Data entry clerk	D121_R	Environmental technician	E157_R
Data processing manager	D122_R	**Equal employment opportunity manager**	**E158_M**
Database administrator	**D123_M**	Equipment design and maintenance technician	E159_R
Database analyst	D124_R	Estimator	E160_R
Dental assistant	D125_R	**Estimator–construction**	**E161_M**
Dental hygienist	D126_R	**Facilities and transportation assistant**	**F162_M**
Design services supervisor–construction	**D127_M**	Facilities planner	F163_R
Design technician–construction	**D128_M**	**Farm crew supervisor**	**F164_M**
Desktop technical analyst	**D129_M**	**Farm manager**	**F165_M**
Die maker	D130_R	**Fast-food server**	**F166_M**
Dietitian	D131_R	**Field claims adjuster**	**F167_M**
Dining room manager	D132_R	**Field services manager**	**F168_M**
Direct response analyst	**D133_M**	File clerk	F169_R
Director of investments	**D134_M**	**Finance accounting clerk**	**F170_M**
Director of quality improvement	**D135_M**	**Financial analyst**	**F171_M**
Disaster relief services director	**D136_M**	**Financial coordinator–information services**	**F172_M**
Distribution manager	**D137_M**	Financial economist	F173_R
District sales manager	**D138_M**	**Financial planning analyst**	**F174_M**
Diversity consultant	**D139_M**	Fire fighter	F175_R
Division president–home construction	**D140_M**	**Fishing laborer**	**F176_M**
Document control processor	**D141_M**	**Fixed asset accountant**	**F177_M**
Drafter	D142_R	**Flight attendant**	**F178_M**
Electrical engineer	E143_R	**Food sampling specialist**	**F179_M**
Electrical maintenance supervisor	E144_R	**Food technologist–production**	**F180_M**
Electrical-electronic specialist	E145_R	**Food technologist–quality**	**F181_M**
Electronics technician	E146_R	**Forest technician**	**F182_M**
Elementary school principal	E147_R	**Forest worker**	**F183_M**
Elementary school teacher	E148_R	**Forester**	**F184_M**
Emergency medical technician	**E149_M**	**Form designer**	**F185_M**
		Fund development director	F186_R
		Funds transfer coordinator	F187_R
		Funeral home director	**F188_M**
		General manager	**G189_M**

Job Title	File Name		Job Title	File Name
Golf club manager	**G190_M**		**Investment analyst**	**I222_M**
Government affairs analyst	**G191_M**		**Investment operations**	
Graphic designer	G192_R		assistant	**I223_M**
Hair stylist	**H193_M**		**Investor relations manager**	**I224_M**
Health and wellness			Job analyst	J225_R
instructor	**H194_M**		**Judge**	**J226_M**
Health care administrator	H195_R		Laboratory manager	L227_R
Heating-ventilating-air			**Land development manager**	**L228_M**
conditioning maintenance			**Landscape architect**	**L229_M**
supervisor	H196_R		**Landscape contractor**	**L230_M**
Help-desk representative	H197_R		Laser technician	L231_R
Home decorator	**H198_M**		**Law firm administrator**	**L232_M**
Horticulture supervisor	**H199_M**		**Law office manager**	**L233_M**
Hostperson	H200_R		**Letter carrier**	**L234_M**
Hotel clerk	H201_R		**Librarian**	**L235_M**
House supervisor	**H202_M**		Loan review manager	L236_R
Human resources assistant	**H203_M**		Machine cleaner	M237_R
Human resources clerk	H204_R		Machine operator	M238_R
Human resources manager	H205_R		Mail clerk	M239_R
Human resources records			**Mainframe technical**	
clerk	**H206_M**		specialist	**M240_M**
Inbound marketing operations			Maintenance electrician	M241_R
manager	**I207_M**		Maintenance manager	M242_R
Industrial engineer	I208_R		Maintenance mechanic	M243_R
Information security			**Maintenance supply leader**	**M244_M**
specialist	**I209_M**		**Manager (model)**	**M245_M**
Information specialist	I210_R		Manufacturing engineer	M246_R
Information systems manager–			Manufacturing manager	M247_R
manufacturing	**I211_M**		**Marina manager**	**M248_M**
Information technology			Marketing director	M249_R
manager	**I212_M**		**Marketing director–**	
International business			construction	**M250_M**
operations coordinator	**I213_M**		**Marketing manager**	**M251_M**
International development			Marketing research analyst	M252_R
manager	**I214_M**		**Marketing research specialist**	**M253_M**
International development			**Marketing support**	
managing director	**I215_M**		representative	**M254_M**
International human			**Masseur/masseuse**	**M255_M**
resources administrator	**I216_M**		Material handler	M256_R
International marketing			Mechanical engineer	M257_R
director	**I217_M**		Media center manager	M258_R
Inventory and invoice clerk	**I218_M**		**Media library specialist**	**M259_M**
Inventory clerk	I219_R		Medical director	M260_R
Inventory specialist	**I220_M**		Medical records technician	M261_R
Investment accountant	**I221_M**		Medical technologist	M262_R

Job Title	File Name	Job Title	File Name
Medical transcriptionist	M263_R	Pharmacy technician	P300_R
Meeting and promotion services director	**M264_M**	Physical therapist	P301_R
Meeting planner	**M265_M**	Physician assistant	P302_R
Methods and procedures analyst	M266_R	**Pilot plant technician**	**P303_M**
Microcomputer services manager	**M267_M**	**Pipeline manager**	**P304_M**
		Plumber	P305_R
Microcomputer systems analyst	**M268_M**	Police officer	P306_R
		Power line operator	**P307_M**
Microfilm processor	**M269_M**	**Pricing analyst**	**P308_M**
Mine manager	**M270_M**	Printer	P309_R
Mixer	M271_R	**Procurement manager**	**P310_M**
Museum education director	**M272_M**	Product manager	P311_R
Nail technician	**N273_M**	**Production accounting clerk**	**P312_M**
National account representative	**N274_M**	**Production clerk**	**P313_M**
		Production control clerk	P314_R
Network analyst	**N275_M**	**Production coordinator–direct mail**	**P315_M**
Network technician	**N276_M**	Production equipment technician	P316_R
Nurse manager	N277_R		
Nurse, registered	N278_R	Production inventory clerk	P317_R
Nursery manager	**N279_M**	Production operator	P318_R
Nursing services director	**N280_M**	Production scheduler	P319_R
Occupational physician	**O281_M**	**Production supervisor**	**P320_M**
Occupational therapist	O282_R	Project director	P321_R
Office manager	O283_R	Project engineer	P322_R
Operations analyst	**O284_M**	Public health educator	P323_R
Operations manager	O285_R	Public relations and communications manager	P324_R
Operations manager– distribution	**O286_M**	Purchasing director	P325_R
Order clerk	O287_R	Purchasing specialist	P326_R
Order processing representative	**O288_M**	**Quality assurance analyst– information systems**	**Q327_M**
Organization development consultant	O289_R	**Quality assurance coordinator– home construction**	**Q328_M**
Packaging engineer	P290_R	Quality assurance director	Q329_R
Paralegal	**P291_M**	**Quality assurance specialist– telemarketing**	**Q330_M**
Parcel post clerk	P292_R	Quality assurance technician	Q331_R
Patient care coordinator	**P293_M**	**Quality engineer**	**Q332_M**
Patient care unit clerk	P294_R	**Quality improvement facilitator**	**Q333_M**
Pattern maker	P295_R		
Payroll clerk	P296_R	**Quality manager–home construction**	**Q334_M**
Payroll manager	P297_R		
Performance technologist	**P298_M**	**Quality processing laboratory technician**	**Q335_M**
Pharmacist	P299_R		

Job Title	File Name
Quality research analyst–food	**Q336_M**
Radiologic technologist	R337_R
Real estate closing coordinator	**R338_M**
Receptionist	R339_R
Receptionist, medical office	R340_R
Records clerk	R341_R
Records management analyst	R342_R
Recreation supervisor	R343_R
Recreation therapist	R344_R
Refinery operator	R345_R
Regulatory analyst	**R346_M**
Research scientist–food manufacturing	**R347_M**
Reservation clerk	R348_R
Respiratory therapist	R349_R
Retail store manager	R350_R
Returned-goods clerk	R351_R
Returned-items clerk	R352_R
Right-of-way engineer	R353_R
Risk and insurance manager	R354_R
Safe deposit box custodian	S355_R
Safety director	S356_R
Safety engineer	S357_R
Sales administrator	**S358_M**
Sales clerk	S359_R
Sales engineer	S360_R
Sales executive	**S361_M**
Sales manager	S362_R
Sales promotion manager	S363_R
Sales representative	S364_R
Sales representative–new homes	**S365_M**
Sales secretary	**S366_M**
Sales support specialist	**S367_M**
Salesperson, apparel	S368_R
School nurse	**S369_M**
Scout leader	**S370_M**
Secretary	S371_R
Secretary, executive	S372_R
Securities broker	S373_R
Security director	S374_R
Security guard	S375_R
Security supervisor	S376_R
Security technician	**S377_M**

Job Title	File Name
Sewing machine operator	S378_R
Shipping/receiving technician	S379_R
Social worker	S380_R
Software compliance analyst	**S381_M**
Special investigator	**S382_M**
Specialty store assistant manager	**S383_M**
Speech therapist	S384_R
Staff counsel	**S385_M**
Statistical analyst	S386_R
Stock clerk	S387_R
Student loan officer	S388_R
Supervisor (model)	**S389_M**
Support services manager	**S390_M**
Systems analyst	S391_R
Systems programmer	S392_R
Tax accountant	T393_R
Tax examiner	T394_R
Technical buyer	**T395_M**
Technical illustrator	T396_R
Technical products manager	**T397_M**
Technical support manager	**T398_M**
Technical support specialist	T399_R
Technical trainer	**T400_M**
Technical writer	T401_R
Technology manager	**T402_M**
Telecommunications specialist	T403_R
Telemarketer	T404_R
Telemarketing outbound analyst	**T405_M**
Telemarketing representative	**T406_M**
Telesales specialist	**T407_M**
Teller	T408_R
Test engineer	T409_R
Test technician	T500_R
Theater manager	**T501_M**
Tool maker	T502_R
Tour guide	**T503_M**
Tourist camp attendant	**T504_M**
Tractor-trailer truck driver	T505_R
Trade promotion assistant	**T506_M**
Traffic manager	T507_R
Traffic specialist	**T508_M**

Job Title	File Name	Job Title	File Name
Trainer	T509_R	Vice president–human resources	V527_M
Training manager	T510_R	Vice president–operations	V528_M
Travel counselor	T511_R	Vice president–profits	V529_M
Treasury analyst	**T512_M**	Vice president–reengineering	V530_M
Treasury coordinator	**T513_M**	Vice president–sales	V531_M
Treasury operations analyst	**T514_M**	Videographer	V532_R
Treasury system coordinator	**T515_M**	Waitperson	W533_R
Trust administrator	T516_R	**Warehouse associate**	**W534_M**
Underwriter	U517_R	Warehouse manager	W535_R
Vending machine attendant	V518_R	**Waste plant operator**	**W536_M**
Vice president (model)	**V519_M**	**Wastewater specialist**	**W537_M**
Vice president–construction services	**V520_M**	**Wastewater treatment manager**	**W538_M**
Vice president–corporate brand marketing	**V521_M**	Weight reduction specialist	W539_R
Vice president–corporate counsel	**V522_M**	**Winemaker**	**W540_M**
Vice president–engineering	**V523_M**	Wooden-frame builder	W541_R
Vice president–finance and administration	**V524_M**	Word-processing operator	W542_R
Vice president–finance, planning, and systems	**V525_M**	**Workers' compensation administrator**	**W543_M**
Vice president–government affairs	**V526_M**	**Zoo caretaker**	**W544_M**

By Occupation

Roman letters = first volume, *Results-Oriented Job Descriptions*
Boldface = second volume, *More Results-Oriented Job Descriptions*

ACCOUNTING AND FINANCE

Accountant	A002_R
Accountant in-charge	**A003_M**
Accountant supervisor	**A004_M**
Accounts receivable/payable clerk	A005_R
Auditor	A024_R
Bookkeeper	B032_R
Budget accounting clerk	**B035_M**
Budget analyst	**B036_M**
Budget officer	B037_R
Cash manager	**C052_M**
Control desk coordinator	**C099_M**
Controller	C100_R
Cost accountant	C105_R
Cost analyst–construction	**C106_M**
Cost analyst–land development	**C107_M**
Director of investments	**D134_M**
Finance accounting clerk	**F170_M**
Financial analyst	**F171_M**
Financial economist	F173_R
Financial planning analyst	**F174_M**
Fixed asset accountant	**F177_M**
Investment accountant	**I221_M**
Investment analyst	**I222_M**
Investment operations assistant	**I223_M**
Payroll clerk	P296_R
Payroll manager	P297_R
Production accounting clerk	**P312_M**
Tax accountant	T393_R
Treasury analyst	**T512_M**
Treasury coordinator	**T513_M**
Treasury operations analyst	**T514_M**
Treasury system coordinator	**T515_M**
Vice president–finance and administration	**V524_M**
Vice president–finance, planning, and systems	**V525_M**
Vice president–profits	**V529_M**

ANIMAL CARE

Animal control officer	**A015_M**
Aquarist	**A017_M**
Zoo caretaker	**Z544_M**

CREDIT AND COLLECTION

Billing clerk	B030_R
Collection manager	C078_R
Credit analyst	C112_R
Credit manager	C113_R

EDUCATION

Aquarist	**A017_M**
Child care aide	**C059_M**

Child care teacher	**C060_M**
Craft center manager	**C110_M**
Craft demonstrator	**C111_M**
Elementary school principal	E147_R
Elementary school teacher	E148_R
Librarian	**L235_M**
Museum education director	**M272_M**
Zoo caretaker	**Z544_M**

ENGINEERING, METHODS, AND RESEARCH

Broadcast engineer	**B034_M**
Ceramic engineer	C054_R
Civil engineer	C065_R
Computer-aided design assistant	**C090_M**
Design services supervisor– construction	**D127_M**
Design technician– construction	**D128_M**
Drafter	D142_R
Electrical engineer	E143_R
Electrical-electronic specialist	E145_R
Electronics technician	E146_R
Engineering manager	E154_R
Engineering technician	E155_R
Estimator	E160_R
Estimator–construction	**E161_M**
Industrial engineer	I208_R
Laser technician	L231_R
Manufacturing engineer	M246_R
Mechanical engineer	M257_R
Methods and procedures analyst	M266_R
Packaging engineer	P290_R
Pilot plant technician	**P303_M**
Project director	P321_R
Project engineer	P322_R
Research scientist–food manufacturing	**R347_M**
Right-of-way engineer	R353_R
Technical products manager	**T397_M**
Test engineer	T409_R
Test technician	T500_R
Vice president–engineering	**V523_M**
Vice president–reengineering	**V530_M**

FARMING, FISHING, AND FORESTRY

Farm crew supervisor	**F164_M**
Farm manager	**F165_M**
Fishing laborer	**F176_M**
Forest worker	**F183_M**
Forester	**F184_M**
Forest technician	**F182_M**
Horticulture supervisor	**H199_M**
Nursery manager	**N279_M**

FINANCIAL SERVICES

Automatic teller-machine clerk	A026_R
Branch manager	B033_R
Commercial loan account specialist	C079_R
Commercial loan administration manager	C080_R
Consumer loan operations supervisor	C095_R
Funds transfer coordinator	F187_R
Loan review manager	L236_R
Operations manager	O285_R
Returned-items clerk	R352_R
Safe deposit box custodian	S355_R
Student loan officer	S388_R
Teller	T408_R
Trust administrator	T516_R

FOOD SERVICES

Cafeteria line attendant	C048_R
Chef	C056_R
Dining room manager	D132_R
Fast-food server	**F166_M**
Hostperson	H200_R
Vending machine attendant	V518_R
Waitperson	W533_R
Weight reduction specialist	W539_R

GENERAL MANAGEMENT

Chief executive officer	**C058_M**
Corporate intelligence director	**C102_M**
Corporate planner	**C103_M**

General manager	**G189_M**	Health care administrator	H195_R
Investor relations manager	**I224_M**	Laboratory manager	L227_R
Manager (model)	**M245_M**	Medical records technician	M261_R
Supervisor (model)	**S389_M**	Medical technologist	M262_R
Vice president (model)	**V519_M**	Medical transcriptionist	M263_R
		Nurse manager	N277_R
GOVERNMENT		Nurse, registered	N278_R
		Nursing services director	**N280_M**
Airport director	**A012_M**	Occupational therapist	O282_R
Animal control officer	**A015_M**	**Occupational physician**	**O281_M**
Air-traffic controller	A013_R	**Patient care coordinator**	**P293_M**
City/county trustee	**C062_M**	Patient care unit clerk	P294_R
City engineer	**C063_M**	Pharmacist	P299_R
City manager	C064_R	Pharmacy technician	P300_R
Court clerk	C109_R	Physical therapist	P301_R
Disaster relief services		Physician assistant	P302_R
director	**D136_M**	Public health educator	P323_R
Fire fighter	F175_R	Radiologic technologist	R337_R
Judge	**J226_M**	Receptionist, medical office	R340_R
Letter carrier	**L234_M**	Recreation therapist	R344_R
Police officer	P306_R	Respiratory therapist	R349_R
Recreation supervisor	R343_R	**School nurse**	**S369_M**
Tax examiner	T394_R	Speech therapist	S384_R
GRAPHIC AND VISUAL ARTS		**HUMAN RESOURCES**	
Artist	**A018_M**	Benefits manager	B028_R
Audio-visual technician	A023_R	Benefits specialist	B029_R
Cable/television program		Compensation manager	C084_R
director	**C047_M**	Compensation specialist	C085_R
Form designer	**F185_M**	Employee relations	
Graphic designer	G192_R	representative	E150_R
Media center manager	M258_R	**Employment clerk**	**E151_M**
Printer	P309_R	Employment interviewer	E152_R
Technical illustrator	T396_R	Employment manager	E153_R
Technical writer	T401_R	**Equal employment**	
Videographer	V532_R	**opportunity manager**	**E158_M**
		Health and wellness	
HEALTH CARE		**instructor**	**H194_M**
		Human resources assistant	**H203_M**
Blood bank manager	B031_R	Human resources clerk	H204_R
Child life specialist	**C061_M**	Human resources manager	H205_R
Clinical engineer	C074_R	**Human resources records**	
Dental assistant	D125_R	**clerk**	**H206_M**
Dental hygienist	D126_R	**International human**	
Dietitian	D131_R	**resources administrator**	**I216_M**
Emergency medical		Job analyst	J225_R
technician	**E149_M**	Medical director	M260_R

Organization development
  consultant   O289_R
Performance technologist   **R298_M**
Technical trainer   **T400_M**
Trainer   T509_R
Training manager   T510_R
**Vice president–human
  resources**   **V527_M**
**Workers' compensation
  administrator**   **W543_M**

INFORMATION SYSTEMS

Analyst/programmer   A014_R
Business systems analyst   **B043_M**
Computer operator   C087_R
Computer programmer   C088_R
Computer systems hardware
  analyst   C089_R
Data center analyst   **D119_M**
Data center operator   **D120_M**
Data entry clerk   D121_R
Data processing manager   D122_R
Database administrator   **D123_M**
Database analyst   D124_R
Desktop technical analyst   **D129_M**
**Financial coordinator–
  information services**   **F172_M**
Help-desk representative   H197_R
**Information security
  specialist**   **I209_M**
Information specialist   I210_R
**Information systems manager–
  manufacturing**   **I211_M**
**Information technology
  manager**   **I212_M**
**Mainframe technical
  specialist**   **M240_M**
Media library specialist   **M259_M**
**Microcomputer services
  manager**   **M267_M**
**Microcomputer systems
  analyst**   **M268_M**
Network analyst   **N275_M**
Network technician   **N276_M**
Operations analyst   **O284_M**
**Quality assurance analyst–
  information systems**   **Q327_M**

Security technician   **S377_M**
Software compliance analyst   **S381_M**
Systems analyst   S391_R
Systems programmer   S392_R
Technical support manager   **T398_M**
Technical support specialist   T399_R
Technology manager   **T402_M**

INSURANCE, RISK, AND SECURITIES

Actuary associate   **A006_M**
Claims adjuster   C066_R
Claims examiner   **C067_M**
Claims investigator   **C068_M**
Claims manager   **C069-M**
Claims specialist   **C070_M**
Claims support specialist   **C071_M**
Compliance analyst   **C086_M**
Contract development analyst   **C097_M**
Field claims adjuster   **F167_M**
Risk and insurance manager   R354_R
Securities broker   S373_R
Special investigator   **S382_M**
Underwriter   U517_R

LEGAL

Attorney   **A022_M**
Law firm administrator   **L232_M**
Law office manager   **L233_M**
Paralegal   **P291_M**
Staff counsel   **S385_M**
**Vice president–corporate
  counsel**   **V522_M**

MAINTENANCE AND FACILITIES

Aircraft mechanic   A010_R
Automobile fleet
  maintenance manager   A027_R
Building custodian   B038_R
Building maintenance
  supervisor   B039_R
Building maintenance
  technician   B040_R
Carpenter   C049_R
Electrical maintenance
  supervisor   E144_R

Environmental analyst — E156_R
Environmental technician — E157_R
Facilities planner — F163_R
Heating-ventilating-air conditioning maintenance supervisor — H196_R
Landscape architect — **L229_M**
Landscape contractor — **L230_M**
Maintenance electrician — M241_R
Maintenance manager — M242_R
Maintenance mechanic — M243_R
Plumber — P305_R

MARKETING, SALES, SALES PROMOTION, AND RETAIL

Account executive — A001_R
Advertising manager — A009_R
Business process analyst — **B042_M**
Cash clerk — C051_R
Cashier/checker — C053_R
Client service manager — **C073_M**
Consumer affairs administrator — **C094_M**
Copywriter–direct mail — **C101_M**
Customer service engineer — **C115_M**
Customer service manager — C116_R
Customer service representative — C117_R
Direct response analyst — **D133_M**
District sales manager — **D138_M**
Field services manager — **F168_M**
Home decorator — **H198_M**
Inbound marketing operations manager — **I207_M**
International development manager — **I214_M**
International development managing director — **I215_M**
International marketing director — **I217_M**
Marketing director — M249_R
Marketing director–construction — **M250_M**
Marketing manager — **M251_M**
Marketing research analyst — M252_R
Marketing research specialist — **M253_M**

Marketing support representative — **M254_M**
Meeting and promotion services director — **M264_M**
National account representative — **N274_M**
Pricing analyst — **P308_M**
Product manager — P311_R
Production coordinator–direct mail — **P315_M**
Retail store manager — R350_R
Sales administrator — **S358_M**
Sales clerk — S359_R
Sales engineer — S360_R
Sales executive — **S361_M**
Sales manager — S362_R
Sales promotion manager — S363_R
Sales representative — S364_R
Sales representative–new homes — **S365_M**
Sales support specialist — **S367_M**
Salesperson, apparel — S368_R
Specialty store assistant manager — **S383_M**
Telemarketing outbound analyst — **T405_M**
Telemarketing representative — **T406_M**
Telesales specialist — **T407_M**
Trade promotion assistant — **T506_M**
Vice president–corporate brand marketing — **V521_M**
Vice president–sales — **V531_M**

NON-PROFIT ORGANIZATIONS

Association executive — A021_R
Community services agency board member (volunteer) — C082_R
Community services agency president — C083_R
Fund development director — F186_R
Scout leader — **S370_M**

PERSONAL SERVICES

Funeral home director — **F188_M**
Hair stylist — **H193_M**
Masseur/masseuse — **M255_M**
Nail technician — **N273_M**

PRODUCTION, MANUFACTURING, OPERATIONS

Assembler	A019_R
Assembler, wire harness	A020_R
Automatic screw-machine operator	A025_R
Cable supervisor	**C046_M**
Construction manager	**C092_M**
Cutter operator	C118_R
Die maker	D130_R
Division president–home construction	**D140_M**
Equipment design and maintenance technician	E159_R
Food sampling specialist	**F179_M**
Food technologist–production	**F180_M**
International business operations coordinator	**I213_M**
Land development manager	**L228_M**
Machine cleaner	M237_R
Machine operator	M238_R
Manufacturing manager	M247_R
Maintenance supply leader	**M244_M**
Mine manager	**M270_M**
Mixer	M271_R
Pattern maker	P295_R
Pipeline manager	**P304_M**
Power line operator	**P307_M**
Production clerk	**P313_M**
Production control clerk	P314_R
Production equipment technician	P316_R
Production inventory clerk	P317_R
Production operator	P318_R
Production scheduler	P319_R
Production supervisor	**P320_M**
Refinery operator	R345_R
Sewing machine operator	S378_R
Tool maker	T502_R
Vice president–construction services	**V520_M**
Vice president–operations	**V528_M**
Waste plant operator	**W536_M**
Wastewater specialist	**W537_M**
Wastewater treatment manager	**W538_M**

Winemaker	**W540_M**
Wooden-frame builder	W541_R

PUBLIC/GOVERNMENT RELATIONS

Communications specialist	C081_R
Government affairs analyst	**G191_M**
Public relations and communications manager	P324_R
Regulatory analyst	**R346_M**
Vice president–government affairs	**V526_M**

PURCHASING

Buyer (manufacturing)	B044_R
Buyer (merchandising)	B045_R
Contract administrator	C096_R
Contract specialist	C098_R
Inventory specialist	**I220_M**
Order clerk	O287_R
Order processing representative	**O288_M**
Procurement manager	**P310_M**
Purchasing director	P325_R
Purchasing specialist	P326_R
Technical buyer	**T395_M**

QUALITY AND ENVIRONMENT

Chemist	C057_R
Director of quality improvement	**D135_M**
Environmental analyst	E156_R
Food technologist–quality	**F181_M**
Quality assurance analyst–information systems	**Q327_M**
Quality assurance coordinator–home construction	**Q328_M**
Quality assurance director	Q329_R
Quality assurance specialist–telemarketing	**Q330_M**
Quality assurance technician	Q331_R
Quality engineer	**Q332_M**
Quality improvement facilitator	**Q333_M**
Quality manager–home construction	**Q334_M**

Quality processing laboratory technician	**Q335_M**
Quality research analyst–food	**Q336_M**

SAFETY AND SECURITY

Safety director	S356_R
Safety engineer	S357_R
Security director	S374_R
Security guard	S375_R
Security supervisor	S376_R

SECRETARIAL/CLERICAL/ ADMINISTRATIVE

Administrative assistant	A007_R
Administrative manager	**A008_M**
Clerk/typist	C072_R
Construction secretary	**C093_M**
Corporate secretary	**C104_M**
Courier	**C108_M**
Document control processor	**D141_M**
Facilities and transportation assistant	**F162_M**
File clerk	F169_R
Mail clerk	M239_R
Microfilm processor	**M269_M**
Office manager	O283_R
Real estate closing coordinator	**R338_M**
Receptionist	R339_R
Records clerk	R341_R
Records management analyst	R342_R
Sales secretary	**S366_M**
Secretary	S371_R
Secretary, executive	S372_R
Statistical analyst	S386_R
Support services manager	**S390_M**
Telecommunications specialist	T403_R
Word-processing operator	W542_R

SOCIAL AND SPIRITUAL SERVICES

Caseworker	C050_R
Chaplain	**C055_M**

Clinical psychologist	C075_R
Clinical social work therapist	C076_R
Social worker	S380_R

TRAVEL, LODGING, CONFERENCES, AND ENTERTAINMENT

Apartment house manager	**A016_M**
Club host/hostess	**C077_M**
Conference planner	C091_R
Golf club manager	**G190_M**
Hotel clerk	H201_R
House supervisor	**H202_M**
Marina manager	**M248_M**
Meeting planner	**M265_M**
Reservation clerk	R348_R
Theater manager	**T501_M**
Tour guide	**T503_M**
Tourist camp attendant	**T504_M**
Travel counselor	T511_R

WAREHOUSING, DISTRIBUTION, AND TRANSPORTATION

Airline pilot	**A011_M**
Bus driver	**B041_M**
Cruise ship captain	**C114_M**
Distribution manager	**D137_M**
Flight attendant	**F178_M**
Inventory and invoice clerk	**I218_M**
Inventory clerk	I219_R
Material handler	M256_R
Operations manager– distribution	**O286_M**
Parcel post clerk	P292_R
Returned-goods clerk	R351_R
Shipping/receiving technician	S379_R
Stock clerk	S387_R
Tractor-trailer truck driver	T505_R
Traffic manager	T507_R
Traffic specialist	**T508_M**
Warehouse associate	**W534_M**
Warehouse manager	W535_R